OXBRIDGE ENTRANCE

THE REAL RULES

Elfi Pallis

Tell Books
London

TELL BOOKS
41 Canfield Gardens
London NW6 3 JL
www.tellbooks.com

This edition published by Tell Books 2007

First published by
Tell Books 2003

ISBN 0 9545944 28

Designed by www.anu-design.ie
Typeset by Academic + Technical, Bristol www.acadtech.co.uk
Printed and bound by Gutenberg Press Ltd.

Contents

Acknowledgements

This book would not have been possible without generous help from a large number of people. First credit belongs to the dozens of students, past and present, who mapped out their varied routes towards Oxford or Cambridge for me. They also shared what were often deeply moving tales and offered valuable insights. Similar credit must go to the many state school teachers who found the time to proffer technical advice, success stories and educational frustrations. It is a measure of the awe in which the two universities are still held that most people in either group did not want to be named. This necessitated the use of pseudonyms, though the stories told are unchanged.

Further thanks go to the members of ArRum, a London club for young Muslim professionals seeking to reflect the cultural diversity of Islam. Despite busy lives and responsible positions, these graduates managed to convey to me an ethnic minority experience of the Oxbridge entrance process.

For academic guidance I am indebted to Deborah Eyre, Joan Freeman, Ruth Heilbronn and Diane Montgomery. A number of current and former Oxbridge dons kindly talked me through their subject's general entry requirements. Among those were Peter Carey, Gabriel Dover, Françoise Friedman, Steve Hunt, Catherine Hood, William James, Avi Shlaim, Claudio Scazzoccio and Richard Stone.

Iain Chalmers, Elizabeth Laird, David McDowall, Anne Rodford, Karl Sabbagh, David Wolton and Roger van Zwanenberg added further advice.

Special appreciation must go to my editor, Liz Friend-Smith, whose tactful suggestions and love of precision were crucial in shaping this book. Lastly, Robert Smith provided moral support, literary help and the professional dramatist's sense of how to tell a story.

Naturally, none of the above is in any way responsible for the contents of this book.

London,
July 2003

The author and publisher are grateful to the following:

1. HarperCollins Publishers Ltd. for permission to reproduce an extract from *From the Land of Green Ghosts* by Pascal Khoo Thwe (HarperCollins, 2003)
2. Oxford University Press for permission to reproduce an extract from *A Jerseyman at Oxford* by Robert Randolph Marett (OUP, 1941)
3. Johnson & Alcock Ltd. for permission to reproduce an extract from *All Souls in My Time* by A.L. Rowse (Duckworth, 1993).

About the author

Elfi Pallis is a sociologist by training, but has worked as a print journalist, researcher and TV producer. She also produced a number of radio programmes on educational issues. Saturday workshops she used to run for exceptionally talented pupils led to her editing the London quarterly of the National Association for Gifted Children. When she discovered that workshop children from state schools failed to progress to Oxford or Cambridge, she set out to write this book.

The author lives in a traditional immigrant area of inner London and is the mother of an Oxford student.

1

Is there a road into Oxbridge?

There is no such place as Oxbridge, but it features in many families' dreams. The word, a blend of two town names, is a crucial part of its mystique. So are the turreted buildings, black-gowned students and bewilderingly complex entrance procedures.

There is, of course, far more to Britain's oldest universities. Your teachers may have mentioned their academic record, the great discoveries made and the Nobel Prizes won. If you are raising a bright, high-achieving teenager, Oxford and Cambridge can sound like a wonderful place for her, but also unreal or unwelcoming. And with so many richer, privately schooled pupils going there, how can you tell whether your state school educated daughter stands any chance at all?

The answer, on first sight, seems both positive and obvious. In recent years, Oxford and Cambridge have gone to great lengths to publicise that they invite applications from all sorts of talented young people. A Government-supported campaign run under a variety of names, but mainly known as Access, has resulted in every state school being contacted by at least one of the two universities. Millions of pounds, much of it taxpayer's money, have gone into promoting Oxbridge to a wider public. As a result, you might already be considering this slightly awesome university choice. Or perhaps you have been told by your daughter's teacher that the promising girl ought to apply.

In order to ease the initial decision-making process, this book explains what sets the two universities apart and why it is worth studying there. Their most attractive features, I believe, are far too little known.

Deciding to apply, though, is not at all the same as getting in. To guide your teenager towards this aim, the book carefully lays out the long, fiddly and not all that straightforward Oxbridge entrance process. Giving you the information absent from the official literature,

1

this book shows you how to do things right from the very start, well before you fill in the application form.

Rather than just sending off the girl and hoping for the best, this enables you to maximise her chances of acceptance. To that end, the book unpacks the kitbag of qualifications and qualities that candidates must bring with them to succeed. There are chapters about A-level choice and grades, colleges, academic activities, personal statements and Access initiatives. Readers are taken through the key interview skills and the rigid entry rules of the Oxbridge medical schools. Minor mysteries too, like what to wear to your Oxbridge interview, are resolved.

Before embarking on this road, though, it is best to know more about Oxford and Cambridge, two universities some 80 miles apart yet so similar and so coordinated in their approach that they are usually referred to as one. It is also crucial to address all those fears and myths that surround them.

Chances are, you will have heard discouraging stories. Some will be about the old- fashioned subjects studied there, which can worry a parent keen to ensure their offspring a good career. Others are about the strange way in which these subjects are taught.

Then there is the cost of sending a teenager to such a famous place. Isn't Oxbridge awfully expensive? Would another, less famous, university near home not do the same job of teaching you Maths, History or Economics?

Most discouraging can be the doubts about whether Oxbridge really wants candidates like your son or daughter at all. You may have read about Oxford's Millenium rejection of Laura Spence, a Whitley Bay schoolgirl with five top A-levels and a strong working class accent. So, is all that publicity bumph a genuine invitation or just a professor's equivalent of "you really must come to dinner sometime?"

It is only when these questions are resolved in your mind that you and your teenager can hope to successfully negotiate Oxbridge Entrance.

WHAT MAKES OXBRIDGE SPECIAL?

Oxford and Cambridge are intellectual powerhouses, but what makes them that is a quite intangible factor. The two universities do not contain "all the best academics," as many of their graduates like to claim. Mental ability, a gift for teaching and the research skills which can lead an academic towards exciting new discoveries are also found elsewhere. At lots of British universities brilliant young academics inspiringly pass on cutting-edge knowledge to their students; professors, whose research has won them international reputations, share their wisdom in seminars, lectures and laboratories.

What Oxbridge dons (as its academics are called) have, though, is time. Thanks to Government funding, which tops up the two universities' own inherited wealth and that of individual colleges, their student-teacher ratio is far lower than anywhere else. This allows their dons to employ a leisurely, personalised teaching system, the tutorial. It was affectionately described by Robert Ranulph Marett, a Jersey lad who went up to Oxford in the autumn of 1894 and later became its Professor of the new science he had invented, Anthropology:

> Oxford bases her method strictly on the Socratic use of the dialectic, that is conversation, as a means whereby an older man engages with a younger man in a friendly interchange of views, with truth as their common object... a companion of maturer experience can greatly help him to think critically... though he must do so, not by laying down the law, but by showing the inquirer how to put to himself the right questions.
> *(A Jerseyman at Oxford, OUP 1941)*

Little has changed in this method since, although both conversation partners might be female these days and the subject under discussion Computer Science.

The tutorial is not, strictly speaking, unique to Oxford and Cambridge. Although most other universities allocate their students a tutor, their system is far less intensive. Half a dozen students might share one tutor, or a personal tutor might see the student only once a term. Most learning outside Oxbridge takes place though large hall lectures and smaller groups called seminars.

Oxbridge tutorials do more than guide the student "towards the truth". They make it possible for her to critically absorb a huge amount of information. Staff may also show great flexibility. Even a first year can satisfy her curiosity about a course-related subject by raiding the college library, writing an essay on what she found and discussing it with her tutor. If the student's tutor has not read a specific book mentioned by her, he may well do so for the purpose of discussion. He is not burdened by the needs of hundreds of other students, long teaching hours or piles of paperwork, as are even the most brilliant, committed academics elsewhere.

Although Oxbridge students have a huge range of lecture options, this group-based learning is often optional. Much of their progress is expected to come from the conversations held with and work done for their individual tutor. It is a privileged learning system, but also one that puts great responsibility on the student. If she is keen, she will plough through mountains of written material, write long weekly essays and debate aspects of her course with her tutor and other students.

A student expecting to be jollied along is in for a shock. His tutor may not admonish him if he fails to pull his weight and although there are intermediate exams the lad must pass, they don't really count towards his degree; this is based on how he performs at his final exams, not on continuous assessment. Being told that "we are not here to teach you, you are here to learn" can be a liberating experience for a fast, inquisitive teenager.

The method works best for students who are quite independent-minded and willing to work hard. A student seeking firm guidance towards narrowly defined goals, on the other hand, might find it scary or confusing. It means mixing with adults and being treated like an adult while still allowing you to sleep until lunch – at least if you are an arts student.

The staff meanwhile still have time left to attend to their own research. Thanks to this, and to fabulously equipped research facilities in all fields, even the youngest don can expect to quickly make his mark in a competitive academic world. And his fame, in turn, will reflect back on Oxbridge.

THE NETWORK

Oxford and Cambridge, though, are not just is not just two high intensity learning and research centres. They also play another, equally important role in British life as discreet power brokers. When making his first speech as Chancellor of Oxford in June 2003, former Conservative Minister Chris Patten expressed this by asking rhetorically: "What should Oxford University aim to be and to do? As yesterday so tomorrow, our task is to shape and create the future. It is as simple and audacious as that."

This is not an empty boast. Britain has 114 universities, yet almost all its modern Prime Ministers studied at just two of them. So did most of those who determine what we see on TV or read in the newspapers. Mark Thompson, the director-general of the BBC, is an Oxford graduate, as is Rupert Murdoch, the owner of a media empire that includes Sky TV, The Sun and Times Newspapers. The BBC's chief interrogator, Jeremy Paxman, and the editor of The Guardian, Alan Rusbridger, who snap at the establishment's heels from the centre left, gained their degrees at Cambridge. So did the editor of the rightwing Sunday Telegraph, Dominic Lawson.

Oxbridge mass-produces judges, senior civil servants, politicians and most of the committee chairs appointed to pick the next great young artist or city boss. It also supplies much of the top level staff of other universities. Oxbridge dons pride themselves on their easy access to successful ex-students and the corridors of power.

As a result, the universities are, to many of their traditional students (not all!) a place for networking, for making useful, prestigious links that will last them a lifetime. "You might not remember me, but we were at Jesus in '99" is a meaningful phrase to any of its graduates. It is also a good way of asking for a job.

Meanwhile, successful ex-students drop in for college dinner and everybody who is anybody turns up as a speaker. An undergraduate who has impressed his tutor may meet famous scientists and authors, ennobled industrialists and enraged public campaigners. And because an Oxbridge qualification counts everywhere, a high proportion of graduates quickly emigrate to higher wage economies, which probably makes their expensive education a net loss for the taxpayer.

But it is an ever-renewing circle. Junior politicians are launched onto an unsuspecting public from medieval quads and eventually return, in old age, as college wardens or university chancellors. History students become famous British novelists and teenagers studying lower life forms turn into property tycoons thanks to the contacts they made over a college drink. Most Oxbridge graduates eventually become parents who regard a place at Oxbridge as their kids' birthright and go ballistic when anybody suggests letting more outsiders in.

FUN CITY

The best reason for going to Oxbridge remains its lively academic atmosphere. This does not mean everybody is terribly academic, or even above-average bright. A handful of students, most of them male, will have been admitted to keep up the glorious reputation their college has enjoyed for a few hundred years in rugby or rowing and might leave with a poor degree but muscles that would be the envy of the Incredible Hulk.

The rest of the student body, though, can be pretty brainy. At Oxbridge it is OK to show off just how clever you are, to pepper

5

your conversation with long, fancy words; to have frantic all-night arguments about crazy, complex ideas; and to develop the most obscure artistic tastes. Alternatively, it is fine to walk around with your nose permanently buried in a physics book.

Thanks to the superb leisure facilities, Oxbridge students need not even sacrifice other interests for the sake of nurturing their brains. Instead, they are encouraged to pursue them, often to a semi-professional level. Generous funding for student society means that an undergraduate is able to combine the most diverse activities: History with directing a musical, Geography with ballroom dancing, or Physics with water polo. To a smart all-rounder who used to be very careful "not to show off" in a mixed ability set, this can feel like paradise.

It can also, so potential candidates should be warned, feel like hell. The workload, if you want to get at least a middling degree, is quite shocking. Students learn to prioritise or collapse in a heap after too many sleepless, deadline-cursed nights. Courses can be too abstract for some tastes, tutor and tutee don't always hit it off and a student from an ethnic minority or working class background may pass several uncertain months before she considers herself at home. Still, the tears shed at graduation parties are real enough, and not just due to the champagne donated by parents whose money pit is about to become self-supporting.

CAN YOU AFFORD IT?
Having glimpsed those immaculate lawns and high maintenance ancient buildings on TV behind Inspector Morse, you may well assume that sending your daughter to Oxbridge is far too expensive for someone like you. Unlike with most things in life, such pessimism is unjustified – for the moment at least. Many parents, alas, remain unaware of this.

When asked why there are not more students from ordinary families applying to Oxbridge, nearly all the dons I spoke to attributed this to shyness or, as they put it, low self esteem. Parents, on the other hand, often mentioned quite a different factor: money. They could not possibly afford, they said, to educate their child at a famous university like that. In fact, many regarded the mere idea of sending a son away to study when he could do so right in their own home town as wasteful.

However, this can be short term thinking. Generally, living out is likely to broaden your son's outlook. He may hear about careers he never considered before, talk to and visit students whose parents do interesting, unfamiliar things. If your own family and friends all work in similar fields, and so do the parents of his classmates, university can catapult him into a world of more varied options.

Also, the more desirable jobs are often obtained through personal contacts. Graduates tip off one another and academics make recommendations, but this only works for those who have established close links in the university years. Students who live at home and go to college simply to attend lectures tend to keep their old friends, rather than make new ones. They don't hang around after a lecture to chat. As a result, the young man who is still out of work months after graduating will probably be the one his financially careful parents kept at home.

What is yet more useful to know is that Oxford and Cambridge charge the same tuition fees as nearly all other UK universities, namely £3,000 a year. Even better, up-front fees were abolished in 2005. This means parents no longer need to dip into their pockets at all. Instead, young people who have completed their degree, found work and are earning more than £15,000 a year are expected to pay back the fees like a bank loan. They can do so in small amounts and over several decades.

LIVING IT UP

As most potential university students come to realise, tuition fees are not the only item of expenditure you need to budget for. So, what about rental costs at Oxbridge?

Well, college room generally cost between £65 and £90 a week, depending on the facilities. Oxbridge rents tend to be lower than those charged by other top universities. Thanks to generous university subsidies, most students live in during their entire course and pay no more weekly rent for a room in an historic building with a view "to kill for" than they would for a bedsit in some concrete maze. Their college covers the cost of internet connection and other maintenance bills. Also, since Oxbridge terms are much shorter than those at other educational institutions, there is less rent.

Food too need not cost you an arm and leg at Oxbridge. Each college tries to ensure that a student eating in its dining room or cafeteria will pay no more for this than he would at most other universities. A good meal can be had for the cost of a ready supermarket dish. Outside the college gates, popular student haunts like Pizza Hut and McDonalds charge the same wherever you go.

Unlike in other university towns, students incur no travel costs, and there is a built-in night life. Every college has a bar, as well as a club room, the Junior Common Room (JCR), and most have their own theatre or a cinema society that shows recent films on a big, proper screen. Pints can cost very slightly more than in most redbricks, but university club nights, called Bops or Entz, cost less. Being smallish towns, neither Oxford nor Cambridge can sustain any really flash clubs, so there is no need for dressing up (although your daughter might disagree). Students are also entitled to cheap tickets for gigs or shows in town.

Even those annual newspaper shots of students attending the college May Ball in full evening dress can be misleading. Dinner jackets and ball gowns are often hired or bought at the excellent local Oxfam shop, which circulates them among the student generations. And while May Ball tickets may cost a hefty £90, they include dinner and all you can drink. There are also several ways of not paying: anyone willing to promote the event, clean up afterwards or do a couple of hours waiting at tables gets in for free. This is a popular option, since by that stage of the university year funds are often tight, and all the students I spoke to insisted that there was no stigma attached. Members of the May Ball organising committee, a post open to all comers, also get in free the subsequent year.

One female Cambridge don has run a protracted campaign to get the May Ball abolished, as she feels it gives outsiders quite the wrong impression of College life, but she is annually defeated by the student body. "We girls really like it, because it's a bit like being a princess for the day, and the men quite like what they see," Jess, who is the daughter of a train driver and the president of her college May Ball committee, told me with a giggle.

BARE ESSENTIALS
Text books, an essential of student life, cost the same at Oxbridge as anywhere else. However, only here can a student get by without ever buying a single one. Reading lists may be terrifyingly long, but no student has to make do without. The main university libraries of Oxford and Cambridge contain copies of every book ever published in the UK. Books are also available from other sources, so that any work mentioned in any course is normally available to all. An English student at Oxford, for instance, can find anything on his reading list or just mentioned by staff either at his college library or at the library of the university's English faculty or, if it is fairly obscure, at the university's reference library, the Bodleian. And, by the way, most of these lovely libraries are open 24 hours a day.

Of course, some people prefer owning books to borrowing, and there is no shortage of wealthy Oxbridge students who buy. Some do it because they to want underline, scribble in the margins and generally vandalise the printed page; but others just like to own everything mentioned in class. This has a very useful side effect. On the first day of each new year, these students sell off their books (or at least the ones still in tolerable condition) for a fraction of the original price to people in the year below.

The expensive photocopying of key chapters, which is so common in other universities with a limited book supply, is almost unknown at Oxbridge.

What about the peculiar black outfits that you always see students wear on TV? Well, most students at Oxbridge, like elsewhere, live in sweatshirts and jeans. Formal occasions, such as exams or special dinners (which are a bit like wedding meals, including the long speeches), call for a dark suit or two-piece, plus a cap and gown, bought from a local shop, a graduate or, again, Oxfam. Only very few colleges nowadays insist that students must wear formal dress for ordinary dinners, so gowns tend to last forever. The only unavoidable expense is the £13.99 white tie which male students have to wear with the suit. Apparently, whenever you try to borrow one, it always has tomato ketchup on it.

For those seeking to recover from the wine flowing at these events, there is a choice of sports facilities which are truly amazing and totally free. In fact, there are few experiences for which you actually need to pay; one is membership of your university debating society, the Oxford or Cambridge Union. Joining these historic launch pads of government ministers and government critics for life costs £99 at Oxford, but only £85 at Cambridge. Alternatively, a student can pay £5 a night to attend a debate on an issue of the day. Only the Drinking Societies charge higher fees.

But what about student social life? Well, "Brideshead" it ain't, not any more. A student can go out every night of the week (though they'd better not, if they want to pass) without paying for anything at all. This is not say there is no high spending Hooray Henry set, dressed head to sun-bronzed toe in designer labels. If your daughter wants to keep up with them, she'll have to get a part-time job. There are quite a few of those in local shops or at the college bar. The universities, although not keen on such distractions, also offer students work in the library, which is reas-suring for non-drinkers.

OXBRIDGE GRANTS

The most important fact is the one I have left to the end: Oxbridge offers a substantial grant (not loan) to poorer students. If your family income is no more than £17,500 a year, Cambridge will pay you £3,100 a year from 2008, while Oxford will pay £10,000 over three years or £13,000 over four. Students whose parents earn up to £37,425 a year will still qualify for part of this grant. None of it needs to be paid back and it comes in addition to the new government grant covering most of their tuition fees. Few other universities can afford to be that generous.

On top of this, Oxbridge is rich enough to have very substantial hardship funds. A student who has genuinely fallen on tough times will be directed towards the right application forms, especially in the crucial third year. Once in, no student has to leave Oxbridge because of genuine poverty.

In addition, are quite a few minor bursaries, each worth around £100. Designed to reward achievement, these are open to anyone. Some are bestowed for an outstanding bit of course work, while others require the student to complete a specially defined task. Information about all bursaries can be found in the student handbook.

Still unsure how you will pay for your designer cycling shorts? There is one further source of money you can access. The Student Loans Company (SLC), a government-regulated scheme, will lend you several thousand pounds a year (how much depends on your individual circumstances) at a very low rate. Its loans are meant to help with living costs, whether you are at Oxbridge or elsewhere.

The important thing to realize is that once a student has been accepted, most of his basic financial worries can be resolved. Oxford and Cambridge today are pretty flexible societies. Students have similar, but not identical living standards. If your son is on a tight budget, he will not be shunned. There are always other students whose parents cannot pay them to keep up with the Chelsea set. Should your son wonder how he'll manage, I pass on some advice from a recent graduate: if you want your term money to last, don't smoke and drink only at weekends.

THINKING AHEAD

So, while an Oxbridge education is no longer as freely available as it was until the introduction of tuition fees in 2005, it is unlikely to be out of your reach. Disadvantaged families will, in fact, benefit from the new fee structure and the new, very generous Oxbridge grants.

On the other hand, the vast majority of couples with a child set on Oxbridge probably earn just a little too much to qualify for financial help. Given that the current Labour Government is dominated by Oxbridge graduates, pulling up the ladder by making young people pay for higher education was a pretty rotten thing to do.

Having said this, it's worth repeating that an Oxbridge education constitutes a great investment in a career. Employers, many of them products of the system themselves, love an Oxbridge degree, and many don't care which subject the applicant took. A degree in Classics was for some two hundred years seen as the ideal qualification for the post of Prime Minister. We have moved on only a little since: Margaret Thatcher's Oxford degree was in Chemistry; Tony Blair's, in Law.

Which is not to say that all Oxbridge graduates go into "sensible" careers. A few always drop out, or embark on wildly eccentric and quite unprofitable schemes, something perceived as a legitimate choice. This is, however, far less common than most people think. Anyway, should that solitary desert traveller ever feel like touching base and introducing his tribal friends to someone in Britain, his tutor will probably be delighted to oblige. He'll almost certainly know a chap who understands the visitors' dialect, has done research into their culture or might wish to discuss their national aspirations with them.

And should the traveller want to return to society or his studies in some way, the door is always open. Oxbridge graduates retain their opportunities whatever they do (even, it seems, if they commit treason). There is no excuse for any of them to say that he could not develop a career.

MIX AND MATCH

If it is the other students you are worried about, don't be. Oxbridge undergraduates these days come from a wide range of backgrounds. Not that the mixing process always goes smoothly, especially at the start. Discovering that someone with a Scouse accent may have read more of James Joyce comes as a shock to many a public school boy. Nor do enough teachers tell their pupils that it is possible to have a deep love of British medieval history and yet not be white. Luckily, the brainier Oxbridge students tend to cotton on to these facts reasonably fast.

By the end of the first year, certainly, friendships have usually been formed that will cut across income, class or colour lines. Many of these will last a lifetime. Oxbridge graduates keep in touch and tend to employ, gossip about, and marry one another.

Telling your daughter this may still not be enough to remove her doubts about Oxbridge, especially if she attends a school that does not usually sends students there. Rather than give up, you might find it helpful to remember that at seventeen all adult suggestions sound bad. So does university in general. The girl is being asked to consider a long-term project, for a start, and at a moment at which the question whether she will have somewhere to go next Saturday night is far more urgent.

A more forward-thinking student may have her own ideas. Even if you're a bright, well-read young woman determined to become a TV chef, though, it is wise to research career paths. Did you know that Nigella Lawson did modern languages at Oxford?

Parents may also need to address the most immutable of teenage emotions: fear of loneliness. Having looked though the prospectus and admitted that the course and facilities look pretty good, your teenager will turn to you and say firmly: "I can't possibly. None of my friends are going. It'll be horrible. All the other students will be from somewhere else. I'll be totally on my own."

Don't laugh. And don't bother pointing out that, as an adult, you know that one's best friends are quite rarely the people one has smoked one's first fag behind the bike sheds with. Or that it is possible, maybe even exciting, to make friends with people different from yourself.

Instead, just deal with the basics. Make it clear that you agree that your daughter's current friends are great, and may well remain friends for life. After all, she will see them in the extra-long Oxbridge holidays. Then remind her that she actually wanted to go out into the world and meet some new people. If you are bright, interested in ideas and/or academic subjects, Oxbridge is a great place to do just that.

And, of course, there will be ways she can hang out and meet people she is not already attending seminars or lectures with: at the student common room or the bar, at her college sports club or the university drama society. Moreover, Oxford and Cambridge are small towns and she will be bumping into fellow students at the local Boots, River Island and Tesco Metro.

BUT WILL I BE SNUBBED?

This is the real fear, the subtext behind many teenage hesitations. Your son may well be flattered by the idea of being thought academically bright enough to apply for Oxbridge, but worried that, once there, other students will make him feel he does not belong.

You shouldn't sneer at such fears because they reflect an historic reality. When Roger Dataller, a South Yorkshire collier, went up to Oxford on a miners' scholarship in 1928, after years of preparation at night school, he encountered a world of petty snobbishness chronicled in his book *A Pitman looks at Oxford*. In this world, students from private schools treated all others with total contempt. Even sport did nothing to bridge the gap. "In my first term at Oxford I played soccer," a fellow working class student confided in Dataller soon after he arrived at the university. "Everything went swimmingly the first game. I played back. The other back was Lord – son of –, He wasn't bad at first. He'd chat a little when play went up the field. Then he discovered who I was. Never spoke to me again. Never tried . . ."

Until well into the 1970s, Oxbridge churned out embittered young men (and occasionally women) whose much longed-for Oxbridge education was won at the price of social agony and isolation. Their degree, they knew, would impress others enough to land them good jobs, but they would forever feel that they themselves had failed to impress. Oxbridge was a public school club, dominated by richer, more confident young people who all seemed to know one another and whose vocabulary, accent and manners made everybody else feel a clod.

But this was generations ago. Now Oxbridge is eager to emphasize its varied student body. At Oxford, I was encouraged to meet Gail, a current student from the same region and social background as Roger Dataller. A quick, bubbly girl with a distinct Yorkshire drawl, she is writing a history of her local football club, Barnsley, as part of her course and describes going to Oxbridge as "the best thing I ever did."

Which is not to say that Oxbridge is a totally modern, homogeneous place. It still has quite a few male, upper middle class customs, made more obscure by their incomprehensible Latin names, but they are not designed to trip up ordinary students. The university guides sent to all those accepted explain what students are expected to wear and do. Also, every newcomer is contacted in advance by a "college parent", a student from the year above. Not only will this student try to answer any worrying questions, but she will be at hand in the first week to guide the newcomer.

13

So, tell your daughter not be scared by popular misconceptions. Despite what you may have seen on TV (*Brideshead Revisited, The Glittering Prizes, Inspector Morse* and all those dramas about the Cambridge spies all have a lot to answer for), Oxbridge is no longer the homeland of the toff who specialises in put-downs. Not everyone is poor, but whenever I was there everyone was watching Big Brother.

THE NUMBERS GAME

Oxbridge admissions staff have not come quite as far as their students in terms of adapting to a changing world. If your daughter is now thinking of applying, it may reassure her to know that the two universities, between them, admit over 3,000 state school students a year. This equals 55 per cent of their British student intake. It can be less reassuring to know that these are mostly middle class kids and that students from private schools, who teach eight per cent of British children, constitute most of the other 45 per cent. This makes Oxbridge a possible destination for a bright student from a state school, but not exactly a certain one.

Given these facts, and given that the Chancellor, Gordon Brown, described the rejection of Laura Spence in January 2001 as "an absolute scandal", you might like to know what the Government, keen on improving opportunities for all, is doing about this. Well, in January 2003 it announced plans to appoint, in three years' time, a so-called Access Regulator, who would tie a university's Government funding to its success in admitting more students from disadvantaged backgrounds.

Much of this was aimed at the country's oldest universities, and when Education Minister Margaret Hodge visited Cambridge in February 2003 she explained the need for such a regulator by spelling out the current situation: "Let's not pretend that Cambridge is wonderful by letting people in on low incomes," declared Hodge.

"Cambridge does not. Only 9 per cent come from the three lowest socio-economic groups."

That remark went down like a lead balloon, and senior Oxbridge academics rushed to lobby the Minister's Oxbridge-educated superiors. Within days, Prime Minister Tony Blair told the Commons that pupils ought to gain places "based on merit, not on their class background." By April 2003, the new Education Secretary, Charles Clarke, had promised that the regulator would not set external targets or quotas for university intakes.

In October 2004, Sir Martin Harris, like Charles Clarke a graduate of Cambridge, was finally appointed as Britain's first Access Regulator, or rather as Director of Fair Access. The change from the original job title proved to be significant. When journalists enquired what his organisation would do about the latest Oxbridge admissions figures, they were put right. Admissions, so staff at the Office of Fair Access (OFFA) explained, were altogether outside its remit. It only concerned itself with increasing applications.

SO, CAN PEOPLE LIKE US REALLY GET IN?

The answer is yes, absolutely, but you would be unwise to rely on Oxbridge automatically recognising your daughter's ability, or on any imminent Government intervention in favour of state school pupils. Those candidates who do get in tend to be not just bright, but also very clear about just how the Oxbridge entrance process works.

On the other hand, a lack of focused preparation harms many promising applicants. Even pupils formally identified as "gifted or talented" by their state schools and offered academic enrichment activities every year fail to gain an interview, never mind a place, at Oxbridge.

As a result, state school pupils remain underrepresented and underappreciated at both universities. Still, this is not to say that you cannot improve the odds considerably for your bright son. All you need to do is follow the advice in this book.

The best way to start is by treating an Oxbridge education not as a dream, but as a perfectly reasonable aspiration, no matter what you are earning and where your teenager goes to school. This does not mean it automatically goes to those who would most benefit from it. Oxbridge entrance is not actually an ability test, as the universities like to think, but nor is it a lottery. It is a snakes and ladders game based on a set of unwritten rules, known to all the parents who went there and to all public school teachers.

This book, based on dozens of interviews with Oxbridge academics, sixth form teachers, Oxbridge students and Oxbridge rejects, as well as on a study of the available literature, spells out those rules. Taking you through them step by step, it reveals the true road to the only two British towns known as one, Oxford and Cambridge. Most importantly, though, the book does not stop there: having taken you right up to the Oxbridge gates, it identifies the hidden forces which keep them as narrow as they are and suggests opening strategies.

MEASURING OXBRIDGE

Universities differ in lots of ways, some of which are particularly important when deciding where to apply. The quality of a university's teaching and research, the learning facilities available, the degrees obtained and the level of employment after graduation are generally regarded as key factors. Most broadsheets, notably The Times and The Guardian, therefore publish annual university league tables based on them. The Higher Education Funding Council of England (HEFCE) also publishes comparative records of university performance.

On all these tables, both Oxford and Cambridge tend to occupy positions at or near the top.

There is another way of grading a university, which is by the company it keeps. Most universities are affiliated to one of three groups, *The 1994 Group, The Coalition of Modern Universities* and *The Russell Group*. Of these, the Russell Group of twelve long established universities is the most eminent one. Its members employ staff with top qualifications, seek to maintain the highest academic standards and are internationally renowned for their work. Oxford and Cambridge form part of this group, but also hold a special position due to their great age, reputation and financial resources.

Having said this, it is important to realise that it is crucial to look out for variations by subject when it comes to university choice. Even an excellent university may not be at the top in, for example, physics, or may not specialise in a subject area which a student might be interested in, for example nuclear physics.

Moreover, the excellence of individual academics may not show up in a university's general rating. Outstanding researchers, university teachers, theoreticians and writers can be found in a great variety of places. While Oxbridge offers a great education, it should therefore never be regarded as a bright student's only suitable choice.

2

The brightest and best

Having decided that Oxbridge might appeal to your teenager, the next stage is to work out whether the girl or boy might appeal to one of the two most picky universities in Britain. You cannot apply for both places, but their tastes are so similar that you do not, at this stage, need to make a choice.

So, what kind of students does Oxbridge want? The simple answer is in all their publicity bumph: they want "the brightest and the best." This is excellent news for today's generation, because things were rather different in the past. In his autobiography, *All Souls in My Time*, the historian A.L. Rowse recalls that when he applied for his first lecturing job at Christ Church College, Oxford, in the 1920s, the question put to him by the appointment panel was: "Would you be more interested in teaching the more intelligent pupils, or the less intelligent?" Rowse replied "the more intelligent" – and was promptly rejected.

When an Oxbridge working party in the late 1950s proposed to restrict entry to academic students in response to Government pressure, the master of Pembroke College, Cambridge, R.B. McCallum, implored his fellow dons to maintain "a rational suspicion of over-intellectualisation... there are young men and woman who by their heredity and upbringing in more leisured and cultivated homes have some special contribution to make."

Even a 1965 Commission of Inquiry could not persuade all Oxbridge dons to select by brightness alone. The eminent Classics don Sir Maurice Bowra warned that "young men (and perhaps young women) who are chosen for not strictly academic reasons may not feel entirely at home in a society of which the members are for the most part chosen for their academic promise, and this may be bad for their self-respect."

This was a tragic prospect indeed, but it too could not stop the onwards march of brightness, driven by an influx of new, often state-educated dons, as well as by Government threats to cut university subsidies. In 1996, Professor John Stein, admissions tutor at

Magdalen College, Oxford, declared that "all our students are admitted on their individual academic achievements alone." Stein would briefly come to national prominence four years later, when justifying the university's rejection of Laura Spence, but the principle stood. Laura's place, said Stein, had gone to "another talented candidate from a similarly modest background."

QUALITY STREET

When reminded of the old ways, today's Oxbridge dons respond with the embarrassment which a young man visiting home with his first girlfriend might feel as his mother affectionately brings out a framed picture of him sitting on his potty. Oxbridge, like the young man, has long outgrown that childish stage. One Oxford admissions tutor I met proudly told me that he had just rejected the son of a university professor.

"The brightest and best" is an extremely vague term. It does not tell you what qualities or personal record Oxbridge candidates need if they are going to stand a chance in the highly intensive selection process. There is no measuring rod that is marked with the words "Brightest and Best" at the top and, presumably, "Daftest and Worst" at the bottom. So, how can you possibly know whether the hunched figure gripping his mobile with one hand, a tattered copy of Beowulf in the other and a bag of crisps with his teeth fits the Oxbridge bill?

An IQ test is certainly not the answer. Oxbridge does not administer the standard test and is not interested in the results if it was taken elsewhere. The SATs tests used by American universities are seen as too easy for potential Oxbridge students.

There has been some cautious experimenting with universities' own "aptitude tests", which trawl for sound background knowledge and a quick, sharp mind. Cambridge was the first of the two universities to devise such a test for all applicants to its science courses. However, several years after its introduction, some of its dons worry that students are now being professionally coached for it, thereby distorting the outcome. Therefore, not all Cambridge colleges are using the test.

Oxford has taken a more optimistic view. From 2008, it will be using new, universal tests for History, English and Math (in addition to the Medicine and Law tests used by both Oxford and Cambridge). Further pre-interview tests may follow, perhaps in a refined form. Most Oxbridge places, though, still go to students who have not sat any professionally designed entrance exam.

So, what does count? In search of some details about "the brightest and best" whose application Oxbridge awaits, I interviewed numerous dons involved in the admissions process and others who had spent some of their working life at Oxbridge before moving on to other top universities. Although my interviewees taught in widely different fields, from History to Physics and from Mathematics to Medicine, the lists they produced were almost identical.

There was a kitbag of very specific qualities which, all of them felt sure, marked out the potential Oxbridge student. At the top was intellectual curiosity, meaning a desire to learn more about a familiar subject and find new subjects to learn about. The right candidate was interested in exploring problems, not just in rattling off solutions. A highly motivated young person, she had a flexible mind and, ideally, a creative bent. The dons also invariably mentioned more general qualities like independence, resourcefulness and determination.

These are very impressive qualities indeed, and if your teenager does not have them all, don't panic. Almost nobody else's does either, certainly not at the tender age of seventeen. Any expert on teenage development will tell you that pupils gearing up for university entrance are only at the start of their intellectual growth curve. They have not yet developed definite character traits, a permanent learning style or a clear sense of their own abilities. They will acquire these later, as a result of time, experience, trial and error.

BRIGHT SPARKS

This is not to say that brightness never manifests itself early on. The boy who gets obsessed with a different grown-up subject each month, which can be anything from architecture to zoology, and then reads every scrap of paper he can find about it, could well be Oxbridge material. So could the girl who is almost exclusively interested in IT, but does not merely use it to play: instead, she is forever trying to create new games and will also use the computer for Maths or Physics related problem solving.

Talent in the humanities (or arts, as Oxbridge calls them) can take longer to show up. A future English student writes well, ploughs through the library shelves and may wonder how his favourite tales are constructed years before he starts shaving. Future philosophers and theologians, on the other hand, are more difficult to spot. Although avid readers, they can be dreamy, unfocused and helpless, rather than independent, determined or resourceful. And that little pest who keeps asking difficult questions when she should be finishing her homework may just be the candidate Oxbridge is looking for. Brightness, as experts will tell you, can show up in a variety of guises and in combination with all sorts of character traits.

So, the dons' list merely describes a pretty unattainable ideal. Like the teenage girl who dreams of a relationship with Leonardo di Caprio but ends up dating the gawky lad next door, Oxbridge has to make do with the talent available in the real world. Still, it would be nice if at least two items on its wish list, intellectual curiosity and a real interest in exploring problems, were there, even in embryonic form.

Cynics may argue (and more than one cynical state school teacher has done) that it is the job of a university to inculcate these very qualities in their students. Many universities indeed do so every day of the week. In fact, Oxford and Cambridge can be brilliant at turning a bright and dreamy teenager into a deep and focused young thinker, but both seem strangely unconfident about this.

All this means that your teenager's Oxbridge ambitions may well be realistic and therefore worth pursuing. As long as the girl or boy is blessed with some of the above traits and perceived by most teachers as intelligent or academic – two terms which suggest a university-oriented type of brightness – the road is open.

HOW TO BE ACADEMIC

To be on the road is not the same as having reached one's destination, of course. Given that most Oxbridge applicants have at least some academically desirable traits, this leaves a student with the question of how to develop his own enough to stand out. Is there anything you can feed that teenage brain with, apart from smelly capsules of fish oil?

Fortunately, you can find suitable, brain-enhancing activities in many places, often independently of any school. A bit of online or library research, along the lines suggested below, will unearth a huge range of options. Most are publicly funded too, which means that they will be free or at least cheap, and all are good at creating the academically "interesting young people" admissions tutors like. So don't worry if your son's comprehensive has no science society, or if he is nervous about joining it, in case he is persecuted as a swot.

But how should you choose? The answer, if you are a parent, is that you can only suggest. The rest is up to your son. You want him to feel that he is an explorer, not burdened with more pesky chores. So, merely explain that the best activities expand academic learning, but also show that a student is capable of initiative and hard work. They may even send strong, positive messages about him to teachers and universities.

Identifying activities which will perform this multiple task may take a bit of thought and forward planning by the lad, but this quickly pays off. School subjects become more comprehensible and university choices increase. The right activities may also provide a student with interests or hobbies he will enjoy throughout life.

STARTING THEM YOUNG

Where you start on this quest depends largely on your son's age. If the boy is still young and you live in a larger town, just take him along to the odd children's event at your nearest library, museum or cultural centre. It does not matter if it is a talk, a workshop or an exhibition. If he shows any interest, check whether the notice board offers relevant leaflets or further events. Or is there, perhaps, a junior science club?

And once you've both gone to the event and it has not been a disaster (most events are amazing, but occasionally a lecture can be dull, workshops under-staffed or geared to the wrong age) let your son take charge. Ask whether he might like a book that will explain more. Accept that interests will change and suggest that understanding can be enriched by looking at quite unrelated issues. The subject of light, for instance, can be explored through the disciplines of physics or art.

An older pre-teen can probably be persuaded to attend a workshop only by explaining that it will help her with a particular school project, but it is worth suggesting. Once there, your daughter will not only pick up educational tips but meet other young people interested in a field which may have marked her out as peculiar at school. She will also get used to differed styles of adult academic language, to different accents and vocabularies.

Such a visit gives the girl a chance to experience what could, if encountered for the first time, be intimidating physical environments. The premises of the Royal Geographical Society or of Somerset House in London, where many junior academic events are held, are not a bad preparation for the imposing architectural splendour of Oxbridge. (Don't point out the old building's features in awe, just move comfortably amongst them.)

Of course, outings like this will only work if your daughter cares to find out more. There has to be some flexibility on your part, too. If the girl is into art, but only wants to see contemporary installations, don't try to make her pour over Russian icons. Do encourage her to explore all aspects of her field via exhibitions, books and internet sites. Ideally, not all her pursuit of the subject should be via the net; while it can help explore things at great depth, there is no real substitute for personal contact with adult experts and other young fans when it comes to sustaining an interest. If you can get a word in edgeways, try to get across (ideally by questions, not by statements) that every subject has its rules, history and protagonists.

IN AT THE DEEP END

While starting academic life young is a good thing, the reality is that Oxbridge appears on many family horizons only once a pupil reaches her teens. This is also the stage when being among one's peers matters most, so keep an eye out for group events and workshops.

The best, by all accounts, are run by *The National Academy for Gifted and Talented Youth* (NAGTY). Despite its dull name, the organisation is great at presenting intellectual pursuits as fun stuff. Founded to help young people of strong academic ability to convert their potential into achievement, it offers them a social, as well as academic framework. A student defined as gifted can join anytime between the ages of 11 and 19. This allows her to explore a variety of intellectual fields, from forensics to creative writing, for little or no charge.

NAGTY runs online study groups led by academic specialists, as well as young people's discussion forums on a range of topics. Its weekend courses, taught by experts all over the country, also bring together budding thinkers. Most popular are the academy's lively, university based summer schools, which combine an in-depth focus on some intellectual subject with great leisure activities. NAGTY membership is even something you are asked about on your university application form.

A student who already has a clear focus of interest has further options, especially in the scientific field. Most scientific societies in England, Scotland and Wales run their own junior branches. Designed to encourage interest and spread expert knowledge, they are either free or charge as little as £8 per annum. For this money you usually get a magazine, invitations to scientific outings or field trips and a chance to meet other members.

How though do you become a society figure? The best route is via the internet. Reptile lovers, for instance, will find that they can join a junior herpetologists club (www.thebhs.org), which offers local talks, wildlife walks and involvement in conservation projects. To find a society to your taste, go to the BBC website (www.bbc.co.uk) and type in, say, "Astronomy Society". Alternatively, there is the Royal Society's virtual science club (www.royalsoc.ac.uk), which runs online debates on big issues like the use of GM and gives you entry to its lectures.

And if your son knows what he'd like to study at Oxbridge, but is worried he has joined the wrong science society or club, tell him not to worry. Science has general principles and rules, so an interest in reptiles can prove helpful, even if you later decide to study physics.

Math lovers can aim for the British Mathematical Olympiad (www.bmoc.maths.org). If you sign up with BMO, its staff will provide you with a steady supply of interesting problems. If you're really good, they will send you on one of its summer camps at Oxford or Cambridge for a week of Math lectures, problem-solving sessions, competitions and social events. For those who get into the finals, the next stage is a free trip to the International Mathematical Olympiad. Coming up is the Vietnam one in 2007, to be followed by Spain in 2008 and Germany in 2009.

English candidates can keep their noses in a book longer, but a regular burst of creativity develops literary skills. Writing for (a however modest) publication also teaches you not to miss deadlines and double-check every word. If your daughter's school won't publish her stories, reports or poems, of if there is no school magazine at all, she could always try to get them into one of an infinity of online magazines. Some of these offer prizes for the best work.

Those even vaguely considering a university course involving history may have to start out on their own. Once your daughter is clear what she wants to know more about, which can be a place or a period, even a family holiday with her cousins in Ireland can, with a bit of forethought, become an opportunity for research. Suggest the girl makes contact with one of the many local history societies, again via the BBC's website (www.bbc.co.uk).

READ ALL AROUND IT

A sixth former who already has a specific Oxbridge course in mind needs to focus more sharply. The rather vague advice you are often given at this point is to "read all around it". Just in case you are wondering, this does not mean that you are expected to slowly girdle the nearest tree while holding open a copy of *Plant Pathology*.

Instead, what to do depends on the subject you have picked. An aspiring biologist simply needs to add to his stack of knowledge. A specialist magazine such as *New Scientist* or *Scientific American*, found in every public library, will tell him about new discoveries in the field and the problems raised by older ones.

A good science book, aimed at adult readers, will help him see the point behind his own experiments. Instead of just getting the powder in his lab dish to turn green, as predicted in his school text book, an A-level chemistry student will learn to perceive what the scientist Richard Feynman has called "the beauty of the inner structure". He'll discover how scientists think and how they arrive at their understanding of the natural world.

For a pupil hoping to study something not taught at school, "read all around it" means grasping her way towards a quite mysterious subject. A budding architecture student, for instance, may dream about the cool new buildings she will design, but first she needs to look at (and perhaps sketch) some existing ones. This might be followed by a book on architectural history or styles. Next, she'll want to explore the physics of engineering, which prevent that brick ceiling above from falling on your head. Specialist magazines, although they exist, may not make sense until the university stage.

Equally, "reading around" a subject can mean exploring it through various other media. The BBC offers interested students great radio programmes on science (most of which are broadcast on Radio 4) and great TV ones on art, history and architecture. Many academically useful radio series are now archived, which means that you can listen to them not just online but long after they were first aired. The BBC site also contains detailed, lively fact sheets on lots of subjects.

To a potential literature student, on the other hand, "Reading around it" means keeping your eyes firmly on the printed page. As a sixth form mentor, I did not know whether to laugh or cry after hearing from one bright boy planning to read English Lit. I had recommended a favourite novel to him and when he did not contact me after the summer holidays, I sent a slightly worried email. The answer was clearly meant to reassure me: "Haven't had a chance to look at *Brighton Rock*, but I've done some internet research on it."

That student, sadly, had lost the plot altogether. No amount of research would make any sense unless he read the novel itself first. Only then was it time to explore what the net, or rather a few, carefully selected sites, had to offer him. In his case, this probably meant going to Converse (http://aspirations.english.cam.ac.uk/ converse/home.acds), a site run by Cambridge.

CAUGHT IN THE WEB

Quite a few other websites can be a boon to the aspiring Oxbridge student. What matters, though, is finding a reliable source. Those run by universities, academic societies, specialist magazines and quality newspapers offer full-length, expert-written features on almost anything you might like to research.

Just reading what comes up first on *Google*, as a staggering number of sixth formers still do, can mean that you end up being not just under-informed but wrong. Anyone can set up a website and, if carefully linked to others, it might come up on page one. Corporations are highly skilled at promoting their goods online under the guise of offering information.

Even much respected sites are not always problem-free. *Wikipedia* recently had to admit that a 24 year old Kansas student, pretending to be a professor, had altered over 20,000 of its entries as a joke. The BBC's excellent, compact fact pages are almost too tempting. Skimming a couple of reports, summaries or extracts, which are easily found there, can make you feel smart within minutes. Unfortunately, this may be an illusion. If you plan to impress a major university, you need to draw at least some of your knowledge from a primary source, which usually means a book. Only this will provide you with sufficient details.

There is only one exception to this rule: even the most ambitious Maths A-level student can probably get by without ever moving from the screen. Thanks to sites like http://www.nrich.maths.org/ public/index.php or http://plus.maths.org/index.html it is the net, rather than the library, which can offer her the endless supply of problems, debates and explanations on which born mathematicians thrive.

OXBRIDGE CANDIDATES

Having a sound knowledge base is the basis of Oxbridge success, but many pupils who have worked hard to build it still won't apply because they feel unsure what kind of person the two universities seek. To help you decide, here are short profiles of four imaginary Oxbridge candidates, based on the dozens of young people I interviewed for this book.

Kate goes to a comprehensive which used to be a grammar school in a small Midlands town. She is extremely hard-working and when she gained eleven top GCSE's the headmaster suggested she should try for Oxbridge. Although the idea had not occurred to anyone in her family, they were delighted. Her father is a van driver and her mother looks after three younger children. The family is evangelical and Kate is active in Church work: she helps to run a youth club for girls, plays netball and sings in the choir. An avid follower of events in Africa, she is also the head girl of her school.

Sam moved to an urban sixth form college after attending an inner city comprehensive. He has been interested in science all his life and had read his way through several Oxbridge texts already in his AS year. His father is a welder and his mother works as a part-time machinist. When he gained what were exceptional GCSE results for his poorly rated comprehensive, they were unsure what this meant. It was Sam's physics teacher who put him on the college's "gifted and talented" list, so he could be offered academic enrichment work. He also encouraged Sam to apply to Oxbridge. Sam spends his free evenings either with his girlfriend, playing online chess or listening to Hip Hop in his room. He also has a Saturday job as a warehouse porter.

Jill attends a selective state grammar school in an affluent southern suburb. The smallish school regularly sends around four pupils a year to Oxbridge and when Jill proved to be an excellent language student, she was put into its Oxbridge group, even though her GCSE's were good, rather than brilliant. Jill's parents run a thriving specialist shop and encouraged her to follow a range of interests. She cycles, plays the viola to concert level, won a prize for her sculpting and is active in the School Assembly, which led to her being sent as its delegate to a national schools conference. During her language exchange, she ran a musical movement class.

John goes to a small rural public school near his father's farm, which takes pupils of all abilities and sends about eight students a year to Oxbridge. John gained twelve, mainly good GCSEs, taken over two years and including four re-takes. He is not a great reader, but is the chairman of the school's physics society and the treasurer of a recycling scheme it runs for the local village. He also plays squash and is on the school's rowing team. John commands his school's cadet force, has completed the Duke of Edinburgh award scheme and plays the tuba in his spare time.

Well, who got in? If you instantly blurt out "only John!" you are still living in the 1960s. If you think everyone of these remarkable people did, you are an incurable optimist. The real answer is everybody but Sam.

But why is that? To the careful reader, it will be obvious that each student except Sam could point to not just academic ability but also a wide range of interest and activities. These created the kind of personal profile which, according to experienced headmasters, Oxbridge dons liked. Brains mattered most, but there had to be evidence of independent use, usually provided by an academic interest beyond the school syllabus. In addition, "good candidates" had done a spot of voluntary work, practiced some form of sport and were often involved with music. Many had also held some leadership position, however minor. Students who fitted the bill were most likely to get in.

Most of the candidates admitted certainly were busy young people. As one Physics student put it to me, "You want to come across as quite driven." The Cambridge educated author Philip Hensher, writing in *The Independent* of 15th April 2002 under the title "Sorry, but Oxbridge graduates are the best", took this point rather further by claiming, "The sort of people who at 18 have the drive to get into these universities are the sort of people who are going to rise to eminence in later life."

Although he has what psychologists might regard as the clearest indicators of academic ability, Sam did not fit that bill. This is not his fault. His comprehensive long ago sold off its playing fields and laid off its music teacher. He lives in an area with little public transport and his parents do not have a car. Nor do they have the money to supplement the activities his sixth form college offers. Also, Oxbridge does not accept a school's definition of a pupil as "gifted and talented".

This way of picking pupils has traditionally worked against state school and especially poorer applicants. They could seem dull and unmotivated in comparison with young people from private schools. There, teachers run regular school competitions whose prizes can add distinction to a pupil's record. Many provide their teenagers with carefully manufactured adult CVs: cultural, scientific and sporting activities are laid on and can even be mandatory. Besides, pupils are often boarders and cannot go to the movies instead.

As a result, teenagers leading sheltered and tightly structured lives would sometimes come across as more determined, resourceful and academically curious than bright young people who were handling the complexities of inner city life. Proving that you have "the drive", which Philip Hensher identified as a key feature of the best, can be harder if you are poor.

CHANGING TIMES

Perhaps not being poor yourself, you may wonder why you should care. The answer is because of one last and vitally important thing about Sam: he is a thoroughly modern teenager and so is most likely to resemble your son. Listening to CDs or playing computer games (or going to gigs, or shopping) are favourite leisure pursuits among the brightest of today's teenagers. With every generation physically maturing a little earlier, today's Oxbridge candidates often have an active sex life, or at least actively seek to acquire one by clubbing, etc.

Fortunately a new generation of dons blessed with CD racks, store cards and torrid love lives of their own feel that modern life-styles are compatible with academic thought. They have no trouble grasping the abilities of non-traditional Oxbridge candidates or doubts about admitting them. More than one told me with feeling that he never wanted to hear about the Duke of Edinburgh Award again. Unfortunately, it was not safe until recently for candidates to generalize from this.

In his review of this book's first edition (2003), Geoff Parks, the Cambridge director of admissions, described it as "doing an excellent job of identifying and describing what is good and distinctive about the two universities and why it is worth going to them", before dismissing the importance of extra-curricular activities. "Selection", he pointed out, "is based overwhelmingly on academic potential". This is undoubtedly true, but given the presence of so many students with a wide range of cultural achievements, it was hard to believe that extra-curricular activities were, as he claimed, "entirely incidental."

Nevertheless, a couple of Oxbridge dons promptly went on student websites to indignantly declare that they, personally, had never asked candidates about such a thing as sport or music. Consequently, academic ability was all that counted at their university. Students, they said, would be wise to disregard any references to extra-curricular activities.

This was not always good advice, as other dons, sometimes working from the college rooms next door, merrily went on grilling students at length about these same irrelevant activities at the

Oxbridge interview. Questions like 'What could you contribute to college life?' or 'If you could only pursue three extra-curricular activities here, which ones would you pick?' remained fairly common. More importantly, applicants who could handle them were more successful than others, sometimes at the same school, who could not.

So, were extra-curricular activities important or not, and what was the point of them? After all, doing very well in your school subjects is a pretty good indication of academic interest and ability. Why should future historians hit the race track or concert hall? Which benefit, exactly, do future scientists gain from rattling a collection box? And what is the point of an post that a teenager can hold?

No general answer was ever forthcoming, but it is clear that entrance criteria often just reflected individual preference. A friend teaching at a private school during the late 1990s recalls the guidance offered to him by a visiting Oxbridge don, who was also one of the school's governors (a not uncommon situation). "Not much point sending us a linguist this year," proclaimed the distinguished figure. "Too many good ones coming up already. But let's think: there's a new college fellow. What he might go for is an interest in microscopic sea urchins and a taste for Chopin."

Dons' own explanations were far from revealing. During my book research, one leftish, public-school educated admissions tutor described extra-curricular activities as merely something you could dip into in order to break the ice at the interview. A very conservative one, educated at a state grammar school, suggested they proved that the candidate was good at time management. A young female don from a top comprehensive argued that such activities "show that you've got a bit of a life."

When it came to sport, there was more of a consensus. The ancient Greek belief that there is "a healthy mind in a healthy body", today associated with totalitarian rulers who like to see their name spelt out by the bodies of massed gymnasts, featured in several replies.

VICTORIAN VALUES

In fairness, the emphasis on music and sport has its roots in something slightly more spiritual, the ideal of Muscular Christianity embraced by the Victorians. Originally coined by the author E. Cobham Brewer to describe the qualities of the perfect Christian knight, the concept was developed by Charles Kingsley, a professor of Modern History at Cambridge and in later life the author of *The Water Babies*. In the 1860s Kingsley, who supported universal voting rights, put forward the argument that physical prowess could and should co-exist with moral and mental activity. This meant that there was nobility also in the working man.

The idea of a Christian manliness that combined quite aggressive action with mental pursuits was next taken up by Matthew Arnold, a professor of Poetry at Oxford. Arnold, though, had a different agenda. To him, the male student's sporting values could prevent the same working man from taking over. Strength and piety were the qualities needed by a Victorian gentleman, in addition to learning. They were also handy for defending British civilisation in its Imperial outposts. Arnold advised educators to strive for "harmonious perfection, only to be won by unreservedly cultivating many sides in us."

It is this salad of somewhat contradictory Greco-Victorian values that for generations helped to determine who would be a successful Oxbridge applicant. Academic ability was a must, but when it came to choosing between different candidates, "the best" were often those who spent their leisure time like a Muscular Christian. While girls of a similar background were sometimes willing to play along, even the brightest, most ambitious modern working class boy was likely to reject the Victorian ideal with horror. This worked in favour of wealthier pupils from traditional schools.

A mix of generation shift, government concerns and Oxbridge soul searching has gradually altered the picture. Also, the changes have become explicit and thus binding on all dons. For a start, they can no longer grill students about their sporting prowess. Such questions, Geoff Parks told the public in 2006, "are now in the past". By 2007, Oxford was stating that there were no credits for extra-curricular activities and Cambridge that "all admissions decisions are based on academic criteria, and excellence in an extra-curricular activity will never 'compensate' for lower academic potential".

Oxbridge, this suggests, does now accept that widening participation is incompatible with vague, old-fashioned entrance criteria, a fact first pointed out by this book in 2003. Students, teachers and parents should rejoice at the news.

SHOULD YOU SHAKE A LEG ANYWAY?

If you are a potential Oxbridge candidate happily hunched in front of your screen, the announcement that you don't need to ever think about Scottish country dancing or cricket may go down rather well. This does not necessarily mean that you should load up the next computer game.

Why? Primarily because reading, writing and researching beyond curriculum requirements do not come under extra-curricular activities but under academic interests. Also, many of the qualities and skills Oxbridge does seek are most easily acquired in this way.

Drama is a case in point. While directly relevant only to an English Literature or Modern Languages course, learning how to hold the stage can benefit students targeting other subjects. An Oxbridge interviewee who thinks before she speaks and nicely articulates her words may be judged more intelligent than one mumbling rush answers. Students who have been involved in dance often come across as thoughtful and calm.

Or take politics, as leadership is now known. Campaigning for change teaches you to argue your points clearly and convincingly, as well as to counter other people's. By becoming a member or chair of an organisation, however small, you'll develop self-discipline and teamwork skills. Don't worry that strong views might alienate Oxbridge. Dons tends to look equally benignly upon a candidate writing for the Conservative Party's Heartland magazine and for Socialist Worker, upon a canvasser for the Green Party and a contributor to Young Labour eZine. What matters is that a student can rationally defend her views, but also grasps that these are not immutable facts. The two universities have been in the business of producing leaders, as well as thinkers, for hundreds of years and are not easily shocked.

An applicant keen to hone his arguing skills without going out into the world might want to join a debating society. Once common, such societies are now quite rare in state schools, but there is little to stop you from starting up your own. There is almost invariably one teacher keen on verbal battles who will help you find topics, time-table space and unbroken chairs.

While the concept of a debating society may be too far removed from some pupils' lives, concerns about human rights are not. Groups like Amnesty International, which has branches in many schools, offer members a chance to talk. So do school conferences, set up to discuss burning issues from the European Union to Militant Islam. Students will research and prepare the event, organise and publicise it and often invite outside speakers. It's a great way of learning how to clarify your ideas, phone up total strangers and cope with last minute disasters.

Volunteering for a local charity has benefits too. Unlike those charity sponsorship projects which charge you a fortune to do unskilled work in a far-away, sunny country full of poor people who'd love to be paid, local ones really help local people. Placements can be hard to find because the under-18s legally now need to be chaperoned, but keep looking. One project, Millennium Volunteers (www.millenniumvolunteers.gov.uk), set up by the Department for Education and Skills, offers 16 to 24 year olds a chance to pass on their own skills, from sports coaching to creating websites.

Do especially consider volunteering, at least for a brief period, if you are planning to take a year off. Oxbridge Maths tutors especially are not wild about gap years because students forget so much. Teachers, though, often encourage the idea. It may seem especially harsh to suggest disadvantaged young people should play Lady Bountiful, but charities claim that volunteering benefits both sides: it fosters maturity, increases confidence, develops skills and helps you to meet fascinating people at both ends of the social spectrum.

Activities like those, or the fact that you've been appointed your school's head girl or break-time librarian, also tell others something positive about you. The Oxford head of admissions, Mike Nicholson, has praised candidates for "exhibiting significant responsibility in roles that they have within their school, colleges and/or local community."

Playing an instrument has a variety of potential spin-offs, apart from conceivably getting you into one of the prestigious Oxbridge Music courses. Being in an orchestra or a band teaches you about group dynamics; playing on your own encourages you to concentrate or, if it is a leisure activity, to relax. Singing can even benefit you financially. Colleges at both Oxford and Cambridge offer choral scholarships worth several hundred pounds a year.

But what about sport? If you love it, the answer is obvious. Even if you remember those ghastly, sweat-soaked gym shorts with dread, try to admit that physical exercise can come in handy at times. A bit of running or aerobics will stop you from getting fat while you comfort-eat before exams. Winning a kick-boxing match will make you feel great and just kicking a ball at the dog can unstress you after a bad day's revision.

It's even worth checking what will be on offer at the Oxbridge college you are aiming for and limbering up for it. Sport has come a long way since an Oxbridge candidate was asked to make clear whether he was "a dry bod or a wet bod", which meant whether he played the "dry" university sports of cricket or rugby, or preferred "wet" rowing. Now badminton, mountain biking, water polo, netball, snooker and table tennis all have their fans. Football, played by both sexes, is today more popular than rugby at both universities. It's also great for meeting new people.

Other activities can improve personal confidence. Writing poetry, setting it to music and producing your own CD helps you see yourself as literate, creative and organised. Teaching drawing skills to disadvantaged kids can make you feel worthy, grown-up and responsible.

Such activities can even give you something to talk about in the first, awkward minutes of the interview, although the response will depend on your degree subject. The fact that you directed your school's drama society production of "Blasted" will impress an English don far more than an Engineering one. Your membership in a junior mountaineering club could thrill a Geography don, but not a Philosophy one.

And don't automatically assume that, however useful, such an involvement will take much of your precious time. We are only talking about a couple of hours per week at the most, and not always spent away from home. The road from first year A-level work to Oxbridge interview is quite a long one.

In the meantime, don't be overawed by the potentially scary words "brightest and best". Just like in a washing power ad, this is a promotional term, rather than a straightforward description of the product at hand. Oxbridge has a high proportion of very smart young people, but when your son goes on his taster visit, he is sure to discover that most are pretty normal, nevertheless. There are not enough genuinely driven, charitable, opera-singing, cricket-playing, leadership-oriented, microscope-fixated geniuses in this world to fill a university, never mind two.

3

GCSEs, AS and A-levels

Beyond brightness, interests and certain character traits, applicants also need some official bits of paper such as exam results. Taking note of school exams is not, contrary to popular belief, an ancient Oxbridge tradition. Until 1939, Oxford and Cambridge admitted students without any formal entrance qualifications. Any young gentleman with enough schooling to read a few Greek and Latin texts was welcome – assuming he could pay.

Until the middle of the 19th century, most students didn't sit any finals either. They simply claimed their degree upon an attendance certificate from their college. If you could afford Oxbridge you were entitled to all the blessings it could bestow.

Less well off young men with a grammar school education could apply, once an academic had recommended them, but acceptance often depended on them also gaining a small grant from a church, charity or Oxbridge itself. Most grants went to prospective clergymen. Competitive tests were only for the handful of very poor candidates admitted each year. A.L. Rowse, the son of a clay miner, started his career as a historian by winning the sole Oxford scholarship place available for the whole of Cornwall.

The result was that Oxbridge fell behind continental universities like Paris and Marburg once those had started to prefer qualified students. A steady flow of reforms, fiercely resisted by public school heads and many university dons, was gradually pushed through so it could regain its intellectual lead. From 1940, grammar school pupils willing to stay an extra term could get in by passing the new Oxbridge entrance exam. Well off candidates, however, were still accepted on the nod of a college head.

The Oxbridge entrance exam was resented by many applicants, mainly because it was conditional on them staying on at an often fee-charging grammar school, and because it did not apply to everyone. In 1987, a new system was introduced, covering all applicants, although colleges retained some discretion to offer places to exceptional applicants.

Since then the academic school exams, GCSEs, AS and A-levels have become the standard qualification required by UK students applying to Oxford or Cambridge. This seemingly puts Oxbridge on a par with all other British universities, which have been using these qualifications since they were introduced. Still, great differences in what is acceptable remain and pupils need to be clued up about them very early on. So, below is a guide to Oxbridge thinking on exams, based not just on official publications but also on dozens of private conversations with college dons.

A-LEVELS: HOW MANY AND HOW GOOD?

Today's UK pupils take an infinity of exams, but what formally counts at Oxbridge are only GCSEs, AS and A-levels. Scottish Highers and the International Baccalaureate, long accepted too, are evaluated in line with those. This group of exams will count even if aptitude tests, currently not widespread, are one day introduced for all degree courses.

What exam record, then, does your son or daughter need to stand a real chance of success? And how much allowance is there for the different types of schooling?

The answer, in terms of GCSEs, is simple enough. Oxbridge candidates are expected to have the normal number of GCSEs taken by students at their educational establishment. In practice, this can mean eight at a comprehensive or 12 plus at a public school.

When it comes to GCSE grades, allowances are again made for the type of school: at least half of a state school candidate's grades should be As or A*s, the rest Bs, with perhaps the odd C in a practical subject. Those sitting the exam in the private sector need to aim for at least As. Oxbridge is willing to concede that, at the GCSE stage at least, someone in a class of thirty-five pupils cannot be judged exactly like someone in a class of fifteen. As we reach A-levels, though, this awareness disappears. The rules become more complex and are shrouded in mist.

One of the worst bits of misinformation I encountered came from the education department of my local council. I had phoned them on behalf of a new neighbour. The woman, who speaks little English, had wanted to know whether there were any extra classes her teenage son, listed by his comprehensive as "gifted and talented", could take in preparation for Oxbridge. A female voice of authority replied crossly: "There are other universities, you know. All the applicants there have five A-levels at A or A*. They are all gifted."

Almost everything in the council dragon's statement, except for the first sentence, is factually wrong. To start at the end: the National Association for Gifted Children (NAGC) estimates that 2 per cent of the population are of exceptional ability, which means "gifted." The total number of "gifted" entrants among the 300,000 new students accepted by British universities each year is likely to be 6,000. Not all of these, by any means, wish to go anywhere near Oxbridge. Even if all of them did, there would still be places left over for other, fairly bright kids. Oxford and Cambridge, between them, absorb around 7,000 new undergraduates every year.

Now let's deal with A-levels. On these, too, myths abound. The official requirement for Oxbridge entry are three A-levels, as for most other universities, and half of all successful candidates have sat no more.

However, candidates from the private sector, where an entire Year 12 may apply for Oxbridge after a decade of being taught in small, single ability groups, are usually advised by their teachers to sit four A-levels. So are many students at the remaining state grammar schools. Five A-levels are pretty rare and are never demanded anywhere.

MAKING THE GRADE

But what about grades? The answer is, for the moment, pretty straight-forward. To get an Oxbridge interview, a student's predicted A-level grades should ideally be AAA (once the new A* grade for outstanding A-level work is introduced in 2008, however, this too may be expected). If a teacher foresees BBB or less, instant rejection is likely. A student with predictions of AAB or, once in a blue moon, ABB, may be asked up, but if her course requires her to sit an aptitude test, she'll have to gain pretty high scores.

However, the story does not end there. While grade predictions need to be very high, hesitant teachers and parents should be aware that a place offer made after an applicant's successful interview can be slightly lower. Individual Oxbridge colleges (a subject we shall get to) have always been entitled to admit the odd candidate with modest grades, if they so wish. How else would Prince Charles have spent his undergraduate years at Cambridge?

This discretion now tends to be used at the opposite end. Truly disadvantaged candidates from comprehensives may be offered a place based on AAB. A famous college that has been pilloried in the press for having few "ordinary" students will suddenly make its sole working class applicant an offer of ABB. Cambridge publicity material mentions even BBB offers, though none of the many schools I contacted had heard of such a case. In practice, nine out of ten current Oxbridge students got in with three As.

AS levels, once dismissed by Oxbridge dons as too easy, now play a growing role because their results are available by application time. Admissions tutors do not just look at AS grades but often at each individual module mark to find the most able pupils. GCSE grades matter hugely too, as they have been shown to more accurately predict academic success than A-level results. Students who get top GCSE marks often do best in their university finals.

So, it remains true that no amount of talent will get a student into Oxbridge unless their school can provide them with decent exam results. This is a rule that sets it apart from other Russell Group universities. One inner city teacher I interviewed proudly told me that one of his brightest but poorest students had just received an offer of CCC to read medicine at Queen Mary College, London. Such unconditional offers, made to express a university's trust in an applicant's outstanding potential, don't really exist at Oxbridge.

MORE RULES AND A FEW MATHS SECRETS

Oxbridge will be specific about the subject in which it will accept a B. If your daughter expects to read History and is taking A-levels in History, English and Biology, for instance, then any B-grade offer made will be in the unrelated subject, Biology.

It is also worth being aware of one pitfall for students aiming for the Oxford or Cambridge Maths course. Most teachers will suggest they apply only if doing both Maths and Further Maths. The problem is that the university will then usually demand A grades in both subjects. Further Maths requires intensive coaching if pupils are to reach top grades, which is not available at many state schools. So, their candidates might not get in. Pupils from comprehensives who choose to take only Maths and two other science subjects sometimes stand a better chance. Once in, they'll just have to work extra hard in their first year.

Applicants whose school does not even offer Further Maths (inner city ones rarely do) will certainly be considered. What they need is a strong, active interest and a firm but not always very broad knowledge base. One Oxford admissions tutor stated that pupils who did well in his Maths interview had a grasp of calculus, a method of writing a good proof, and a more abstract notion of what 'a function' was.

Both Oxford and Cambridge now put applicants through written Maths tests in their own schools first. Information and test papers can be found online. Still, the best way to prepare, by general consent, is by trying to solve lots of challenging problems on a good Maths website such as NRICH (http://nrich.maths.org/public/index.php) and by reading Plus magazine (http://pass.maths.org.uk/), Both are run by Cambridge.

A-level Physics, dons say, can also help with the two universities' Maths tests. Unfortunately, since 30 per cent of those teaching Physics in state secondary schools do not have a degree in the subject it may not help much. This takes us further along the admissions route, into A-level subjects.

PICKING THE RIGHT SUBJECTS

Once upon a time, this was a simple matter. Candidates needed only Latin and Classical Greek. By sheer coincidence, these languages were the sum of every young gentleman's education. They were not studied by anyone else. By keeping them compulsory, Oxbridge excluded both women and working men for 700 years.

Almost all of today's candidates have studied other and more practical subjects. A-level choice, though, can be a horribly confusing business for those without Oxbridge links. After all, comprehensives and sixth form colleges offer up to forty A-level subjects. How can your stressed daughter, faced with all those exciting options in her school's fat, brightly illustrated course brochure, possibly decide which ones to take?

Well, the choice is far smaller than both of you might think. What you need to know is that both Oxford and Cambridge prefer applicants to take three A-levels in academically demanding "hard" subjects like English, Maths, Chemistry or History, which they have studied at school in considerable depth and over many years. This is why even the most expensive public school will offer no more than twenty A-level subjects, including a range of languages.

This rule applies even if the "soft" A-level subject is also the one your daughter is planning to do at university. For instance, a student dreaming of a future as a psychologist might think that A-levels in Psychology, Sociology and, perhaps, Drama would be the ideal qualification. She would be wrong. What Oxbridge would expect is at least one "hard" science subject such as Chemistry or Maths (because Psychology involves scientific work) plus one "hard" humanities subject, such as English. A third "hard" A-level further improves a candidate's chances. A-level Psychology is fine but not essential, so don't worry if the girl's school does not offer it.

The same applies to Law. A-level Law is rated as not intellectually demanding enough at Oxbridge, so applicants for any Law degree course offered there should go for more traditional subjects. English is almost a must, plus perhaps History and some "hard" science subject. Oxbridge Medicine too (on which there is a whole chapter later on) will normally consider only candidates with three "hard" A-levels, whatever their background.

Oxford's degree in Politics, Philosophy and Economics (PPE), which churns out a steady flow of MPs and is the only media studies course as far as broadsheet editors are concerned, cares less about A-level subjects. It is keen on History and likes Maths (which helps with the statistics), but will consider any "hard" A-level or even a "soft" but smart and relevant third. The Cambridge course in Social and Political Studies (SPS), its version of PPE, again likes the first two A-levels, but will let some applicants combine them with "soft" Sociology.

Cambridge can be more particular than Oxford here and actually lists those A-levels it will accept on its website. While this is very useful to know, the list may come as a shock to some teachers. Even a subject like Critical Thinking, which is brilliant at developing students' reasoning skills, is defined as unsuitable.

None of these are iron rules. Faced with a child genius who has taught himself nuclear physics while caring for his dying grand-mother on a condemned housing estate, a college may choose to accept him, whatever his A-levels or grades. A politician's son from a distant British interest zone much in the news could find himself invited in with any odd qualifications.

However, if your son or daughter does not fit this bill, but is just the clever child of non-university parents, they will need to play it safe. They can certainly not take their cue from any student profiled in Oxbridge promotion material: some of these, with their clutch of mainly "soft" A-levels, are very untypical.

ARTISTS AND SCIENTISTS

Oxbridge sciences, as already said, include Psychology; Oxbridge arts are everything from languages to History and Philosophy.

While the arts/science divide continues to exist, it is not as rigid as it once was. Successful science applicants very occasionally have a mix of A-levels, but most admissions tutors at both Oxford and Cambridge far prefer three science ones. Having less may be read as a lack of scientific commitment. If your daughter has built her own mini computer lab, but is also interested in baroque paintings, Fine Art might therefore have to be A-level number four.

The arts are more flexible. A set of A-levels consisting of History, English and something clever like Maths is now a highly acceptable qualification for almost any non-science course. Very rarely, a student sitting History, Maths and Physics might be considered for a History course, but she would need to convince the interviewer that her interests really have shifted.

Students wishing to study Archaeology and Anthropology or Geography have perhaps the widest range of options when it comes to A-levels. Here, one "soft" A-level alongside two "hard" ones is usually acceptable, and sometimes even two.

When it comes to languages, the rules are different yet again. Those wishing to do a modern language course, such as German, need a top grade A-level in the subject. However, candidates wishing to do an Oriental language, such as Chinese or Thai, do not need to have studied it at all. Their four-year course will include intensive language training and a year abroad.

Latin and Classical Greek are today essential for only one subject: Classics (know at Oxford as "Greats"). Both Oxford and Cambridge, however, have turned this into a four year BA course, which allows applicants from comprehensives to pick up those dead languages as they study for their degree.

HARD CHOICES

So, what should you advise your wavering son? The admissions tutors I interviewed had no doubt: go for almost any "hard" A-level mix in, perhaps, either science or arts. Once an applicant has proved that he can think via his A-level subjects and grades, Oxford especially can be flexible about precise course requirements. Tutors in the arts (but less so in the sciences) often perceive A-levels largely as proof of an applicant's capacity to learn. They do not expect fully fledged experts. Only students planning to take a degree in one of their A-level subjects need to show detailed prior knowledge.

Certain combinations, though, maximise a student's options. Science fans with A-levels in Maths, Physics and Chemistry can apply to a huge range of courses from Engineering to Medicine. A-level English, History and Maths (or a foreign language) are a sound basis for most arts courses, in the way Latin and Greek were once.

Remember too that three top A-level grades are easier to obtain than four, and that three As will make a state school candidate attractive to all colleges, including the most famous ones.

What if your daughter has independently made up her mind? Going through the school's large range of A-level subjects on offer, the smart and curious girl has picked the ones that seem most exciting and fit her wide interests. Unfortunately, all three are "soft" A-levels, chosen not because they are easier but because she has done enough English, Maths or Biology, she feels, and does not plan to do these subjects at university.

This, of course, is her choice. She is almost an adult now, as she will no doubt remind you. There is no point in trying to impose your will. Getting any A-levels is a long, hard slog, and I was warned by several sixth form heads that unless a student selects their A-levels on the basis of at least some real interest, they could well drop out. Many top universities acknowledge this fact.

If your daughter really wants to go to Oxbridge, she will have to compromise. Don't browbeat her into changing her A-levels, just get her to accept that candidates who get in with three "soft" A-levels are as common as hen's teeth.

Then look at which of her "soft" subjects might still be worth doing. Media Studies and Textiles are definitely out. Oxbridge defines them as non-academic. An A-level in General Studies doesn't count either, but it greatly broadens pupils' understanding of the world and so helps with some entrance tests. Other subjects, especially Politics, Economics, Sociology, Religious Studies, Computing and Drama, are fine in the context of a relevant degree.

Now do the figures. If your daughter's state school has links with a certain college, she can certainly get into several degree courses with one "soft" A-level and might just be considered for one of their less prestigious courses with two. However, in a competitive environment these are not really very good odds. Colleges have been known to suddenly drop "their" comprehensive in favour of some other worthy cause. Candidates need to be acceptable to more than one place, in case their chosen one has more talented applicants that year than it can take.

Your daughter might also have a horizon so broad that three "hard" A-levels cannot possibly satisfy her. If the girl really wants to write English well, learn about sociology in some depth, live in Spain and be a historian, then she does need to do four A-levels.

There is one other good reason for taking four A-levels. This is if your hard-working son is willing to give up midweek nights out (though not, of course, football practice) for good grades, but is unsure if the degree course he has picked will suit him. Oxbridge is fairly easy-going about students changing subjects in their first weeks, but if he wants to make a bigger switch than, let's say, from Ancient History to Modern History, he will still need relevant A-levels. A set of four A-levels broadens the field.

However, do keep the grade issue in mind. It is no good ending up with the results BBBA if your teenager could narrow his aim and gain AAB. And be aware that while Oxford will only insist on three specific grades, however many A-levels you take, Cambridge has been known to specify the grades it wants in all four.

FOUR LEGS GOOD

Let's say your ambitious daughter has come round to the idea of four A-levels (as long as one of them is Spanish). Unfortunately, her problems are far from over. Many comprehensives cannot deliver them. This is not because they don't want to, but because of under-funding. A shortage of qualified teachers and pressure from other duties result in many students finding that the A-level options that they had chosen are only offered in one particular time slot. This may not be when the student is actually free. Those wanting to combine science with arts subjects such as languages frequently discover that their timetables clash. This is one more reason why the vast majority of applicants doing four A-levels come from private schools.

Now the truth is that missing out on a language A-level is far from fatal for adult life: students who have a grounding in French will have no difficulty becoming fluent in the language later on by means of evening classes or videos. Others acquire fluent Portuguese by working in Brazil or fluent Urdu by marrying someone whose family speaks nothing else. Brains do not actually suffer total melt-down at the average graduation age of twenty-two.

When it comes to other subjects, though, being unable to take a fourth A-level can close your options. This is because the Oxbridge attitude remains highly ambiguous.

One the one hand, all the dons I spoke to insisted that it is not necessary to have four A-levels, never mind five, in order to follow even the most demanding course. After all, almost everyone managed fine with three until about a decade ago. On the other hand, many of the same dons declared themselves impressed that nearly half of recent candidates "were bright and hard-working enough" to get four A-levels. This does imply that four A-levels count as a major achievement.

THE A-LEVEL MARKET

A-levels are not simply the reflection of a teenager's talent and hard work. They are also consumer goods. It is more difficult to buy a top grade vintage car in this country than a top grade A-level. The market supplies what the consumer wants and can pay for: so, if Oxbridge wants its applicants to have mainly As, whether they studied for them in a rural crammer with five pupils to a class or in a comprehensive in which the Maths teacher has a Geography degree, half the pupils have English as a second language and the crumbling science lab predates Apollo 11, then those parents who can afford it will reach for their cheque book.

Almost any public school nowadays, especially if it has boarding facilities, will steer your reasonably bright child towards a clutch of good A-levels. It has the language and science labs, the qualified teachers, the single ability groups and the one-to-one tuition that will do the job. There will be lots of support and few distractions. A-levels will be carefully matched to a pupil's perceived ability, to ensure top grades. Young people's own interests often count for rather less, but the end result is in the bag – if you are willing to pay £10,000 upwards per child per year, that is. Got two children? Tough luck. Advantage, as far as Oxbridge is concerned, is a term used in tennis.

But is there any other way of looking at A-levels? Steve Allen (not his real name) the head of science at a sixth form college whose pupils come from poverty line homes and include many refugees, has no doubt. "Oxbridge," he argues, "is not contextualising our pupils' achievement. To them an A is all that counts, and four A-levels are better than three. They don't understand that the young people we send have made enormous gains. We have students who live in a bedsit with their whole family, yet get very good grades, despite their insecure existence and family problems."

Would students with less than three top A-levels be able to keep up? Steve suggests that his do even better than that. "Once accepted into a good university, our students often become top of their year and the university is pleased it took them. They are hard-working and resilient. Oxbridge should take more of a chance on kids like ours, they overshoot once they are accepted." As an example, Steve cites one of his students, the son of a packer, who went from a C at A-level Physics to a First in his finals at King's College, London. A-levels, Steve argues, tell you about a disadvantaged applicant's past, not their future.

Every year, Steve and his fellow teachers at the school encourage a dozen of their most promising students to apply for Oxbridge; they are determined to maximise their potential. And their students do get Oxbridge offers, at least some years, but these are nearly always based on AAA or, at best, AAB. Such offers, the staff feel, are so unrealistic they might as well be rejections. Oxford is not comparing like with like, the teachers complain.

It is a view echoed by many colleagues elsewhere, invariably off the record. Teachers who have no qualms about shouting at their school's 6' 6" Karate champion for running on the stairs will drop their voices to a whisper and glance nervously over their shoulder when criticising Oxbridge. They are desperate not to offend the universities that can do most for their pupils. Each of them, though, knows of a gifted mathematician or other scientist interviewed at Oxbridge who then failed to get the required AAB. Maths, Chemistry and Physics require intensive, daily, small group teaching for top A-level results. Research methods have to be explained, findings interpreted. These are not teach-yourself subjects.

In public schools, it is almost unknown for a student not to get the required grades. This is not because state school pupils are lazier. Those who do get in tend to have educated parents who can help. They also often attend selective grammar schools or successful comprehensives in comfortable neighbourhoods.

Some of those working with exceptionally able children are also unhappy with A-levels being given so much weight. One of these is Deborah Eyre, who heads the National Academy for Gifted and Talented Youth (NAGTY) at the University of Warwick. Professor Eyre shares the view that A-levels are an unreliable predictor of university success. The current trend towards grade inflation, she believes, is working against many talented pupils. A scheme adopted some years ago at Warwick led to the acceptance of students from the most poorly equipped and funded institutions, further education colleges, on lower grades. The result confounded its critics: the FE group actually got more Firsts in their final degree exams than the best A-level students.

A study by the Government's Higher Education Funding Council (HEFC), released in July 2003, lends further weight to such views. Having tracked the progress of all 18 year old A-level students who entered degree courses in 1998 and graduated in 2001–2, its researchers found that, on average, a state school pupil performed as well as a private school one who had up to four A-level points fewer, the equivalent of comparing AAA with ABB.

The fact that A-level success must be seen in a socio-economic context is gradually dawning on some Russell Group universities and has already led to more realistic offers, even from departments academically rated just as highly as Oxbridge. Some actively seek out new types of candidates. At a seminar about medical school entrance organised by London universities, which was attended by the careers teacher of a "tough" London comprehensive, an admissions tutor recited the usual mantra about medical schools wishing to attract the very best students.

"Just tell us what you want, we'll send you candidates with six A-levels, if that's what it takes!" was the instant response of a private school head.

"It is not your students we're interested in here at this point," replied the tutor with obvious irritation, "we're trying to achieve a more representative intake, doctors who can empathise with more of their patients."

The careers teacher left in good spirits, but also aware that no such views have yet been expressed by Oxbridge.

Even worse, when another university with a high public school intake, Bristol, announced in 2003 that it would make slight A-level level allowances for disadvantaged pupils, there were howls of protest in the media. Frantic voices warned that letting in some state school students on lower grades was not only discrimination but a form of "pernicious social engineering" or "inclusion by the back door" and, as Simon Heffer put it in the Daily Mail of March 5th 2003, "an assault on the most hard-working people in Britain". In London's Evening Standard, Stephen Pollard from the Centre for the New Europe suggested that "in America such thinking has come close to destroying the very basis of academic standards".

One education expert wheeled out by the Headmasters' and Headmistresses' Conference, which represents the heads of private schools, actually claimed that "to go for such crude rebalancing at this level will create more unfairness than already exists".

Beneath the hysterics, you could just detect the gloom of a father who had been paying thousands (frequently £100,000 over a school career) to ensure that his son got into one of Britain's top universities, only to find that "his" place had gone to another kid.

ADVANCED EXTENSION AWARDS

But how do you prove that you're really the smarter applicant? A student keen to show that he has more to offer than just(!) top A-levels and wide interests can now take yet more exams. The new Advanced Extension Awards, known as AEAs, are especially designed to identify high ability applicants. These written tests, replacing the old S-levels, are currently available in twenty different subjects. Passing one or two course-related AEAs with a distinction is a sure way to impress Oxbridge admissions tutors, as well as other universities.

WHAT DOES IT ALL ADD UP TO?

The answer, despite all these grim tales, is that success is possible for state-educated students from even the poorest backgrounds, and today more than ever. One reason for optimism is that both Oxford and Cambridge are officially committed to widening the range of their candidate's backgrounds, undoubtedly out of idealism but also because future Government grants to Oxbridge may depend on it. Even more importantly, every year nearly four thousand state school students, including several hundred from working class backgrounds, already enter these universities.

Almost all of these students have managed to get top grades, so it is worth helping your child to do the same – perhaps in between lobbying Government for a regulatory body that will actually ensure a more representative intake.

But how is it done? Your teenager can find the answer in every basic study guide. To get top A-levels, a sixth form student should pick A-levels for which he has at least some aptitude, pay attention in class, establish a home study routine and plan out his work carefully, so all of it will be completed. He should also seek help from teachers, textbooks, websites (such as www.bbc.co.uk/schools/ sosteacher) or any knowledgeable adult, rather than hope that what is still unclear to him will not come up.

There are also things that mothers and fathers need to know. Below is the best A-level advice from the parents of highly successful students and education professionals. What will be relevant depends on your circumstances and on the time left.

WHAT NOT TO DO (AND HOW NOT TO PANIC)

Don't go on at your son about how he really must get top grades for his A-levels. Grading is what other people, namely the examiners, will do. He does not really have the power to determine their decision, which will depend not just on the quality of his work, but also on the standard set by other students. Instead, calmly encourage him to cover all the ground – a realistic and far less scary target. It simply means working through the books, chapters, problems, hand-outs, sample papers and/or revision notes he has been given.

Don't be swept along by his inevitable moments of despair. If he is about to chuck all his books into the fire, don't just agree with him that perhaps Oxbridge is really not for the likes of you. Instead, suggest a break and gently remind him that young people from his background do get through this frustratingly heavy work load every year. If he's still stressed, take him out for some fun, to buy a small gift for someone you both know, or perhaps for a sporting event. Then, find a moment to ask whether you can help. Are there any books he needs? Would he like you to video a relevant programme for him?

Keep reminding the lad that there is help in class too. Seeing himself as an independent young adult may have prevented him from requesting it. If a teacher's explanation still leaves him confused, it may help to consult shop-bought revision guides or websites like www.mathsnet.net and mpn.meikleriggs.org.uk.

Real exam panic calls for more active steps. An A-level student who has not uttered a word for days or bursts into tears as soon as he takes out his course-work will not simply snap out of this. So, don't keep this problem in the family: ask his teacher whether she knows what state he is in. Can she think of any specific reason? Are there any short-term tasks she can set him to move him on? Sometimes one seemingly impossible task paralyses an able but insecure student.

If the panic does not subside, you might want to address it more directly. Suggest that the lad takes a day off for an intensive dose of football or swimming. Physical exercise helps to reprogramme the mind towards a more focused state.

Then, if necessary, get professional help. A session with the school counsellor may reassure your son that his goals are realistic. Alternatively, he could try listening to a relaxation tape, or watch one of those "achieve your aims" type self-help DVDs which use mild hypnosis. These can be remarkably effective. Using psychological aids does not mean that your son is crazy in any way.

While trying to help, make sure you're not impersonating a bull-dozer but the AA, a service for emergency break-downs. Move the lad along, then let go. Accept that some mornings he will spend an hour staring at the wall, or kicking a ball into it. It's all part of the study process.

Lastly, don't encourage your son to see his A-level work as a competition with his class mates. True, some kids thrive on rivalry, but for many exams are the time when they need peer support most. His sixth form will be going through this mix of slave labour and adrenalin rush together and, rather than worry whether his best friend is getting on any better, he might want to team up with him. The two might waste some time discussing chart hits rather than studying Chemistry charts, but having company takes the panic out of revision. This often enables a student to arrive at previously missed solutions himself.

A-LEVEL TIPS

1. It helps to understand the real A-level time scale. While pupils will be preparing for their A-levels two years in advance, the last year is the most crucial. So, try not to schedule a big family trip abroad, the renovation of your home or your messy divorce for this period. Also avoid moving home halfway through the sixth form years, if that involves a change of schools for your child. Adjusting to new class mates, a different syllabus and exams set by different boards can be very tough.

2. Studying is work and saps your energy: that teenager stretched out on a book-covered floor with his eyes half closed and listening to what cannot possibly be music is (hopefully) memorising the church structure of Old England in between worrying about whether his girlfriend will like his radical new haircut. He might well be too exhausted to look for food, so coach him gently towards it at regular intervals. He'll protest that he is not a kid anymore, but probably appreciates the effort.

3. Make sure that your daughter doesn't use up too much of her precious energy in this period on paid work. If she currently has an after-school and weekend job to fund her clothing habit, this will probably have to go. Otherwise, she will be far too tired to concentrate properly, either at school or at home. She might be able to earn a little money: a Saturday morning at the supermarket till or a Saturday night sitting an exceptionally calm baby are fine, but anything more is likely to affect her results. The poor girl will probably be distraught at the idea that her new spring wardrobe might have to wait until after June, but you should stand your ground. People are not actually being evicted from clubs for wearing a six months old crop top. Could you perhaps offer a new bag or a Hennes voucher in the meantime? If nothing else, this will prove to her that studying can pay off.

4. If your son is working not for extras but in order to keep your family afloat, the answer is not quite so simple. First make sure all of you receive the benefits you are entitled to. The Education and Maintenance Allowance (EMA), introduced by the government in 2004, offers pupils £30 a week to stay at school, if their annual family income is £20,000 or less. Child benefit, which is paid to parents, normally stops at sixteen, but you can claim it until your son leaves school.

   There is also a new Child Tax Credit, introduced in 2003, which will be paid directly into your bank account if you are responsible for the children. You don't need to be in work to qualify for this. If you work at least 30 hours a week but are on a low income, you may, in addition, be entitled to the new Working Tax Credit. To find out how to apply, phone the tax credits helpline on 0845 300 3900 or go to www.inlandrevenue.gov.uk/taxcredits. You can also visit or call your nearest Inland Revenue office.

   You must also discuss your financial situation openly with your son. Make it clear that you thoroughly approve of his university plans and that you don't resent the cost of keeping him: you'd be surprised how many kids think that their parents do. Try to also get across that the drop in his own after-school income is only a temporary blip. Good grades will get him into a good university, which in turn should lead to a good job and an income which, if you are hard-up at the moment, may be almost beyond his imagination.

Make sure, though, that the lad does not try to bridge the gap with credit. Some card issuers will happily sign up 18 year old non-earning pupils The result can be urgent, massive debts, a bad start for his university life.

However, if your family finances really will collapse without your son's contribution, don't give up on the idea of Oxbridge. Just make sure that his school is fully aware of your family circumstances and mentions them in its Open Reference. Alternatively, he himself might want to talk about his paid work and why he needs to do it in his Personal Statement. Family poverty is not a character flaw he needs to be ashamed of. Allowances are made for seriously disadvantaged students and an admissions tutor genuinely committed to "widening access" (there are quite a few) might be impressed with the lad's persistence.

4

Getting the exam experts in

Having said all this, I must point out that none of the above steps willget your son into Oxbridge if the school's teaching is poor. If his school's results are consistently below the national average because its teachers do not have degrees in their A-level subjects or because of severe discipline problems then no amount of hard work by your talented lad can tip the balance by itself. He'll need external help.

What help you'll be able to get depends largely on the time your teenager has left. Nobody will have any magic solution to offer if you find out a fortnight before the crucial exam that large chunks of the syllabus have remained utterly incomprehensible to him. As the drunk, sitting in a puddle, told the lady who had asked him the way to the local savings bank: "Madam, you don't want to start from here."

On the other hand, if school reports or test grades indicate earlier in that year that the boy, who might even have been defined as "gifted or talented" by his teachers, is achieving well below his potential, then a revision course can be one way forward. It is best not to wait for the results of his springtime mocks; by then most courses will be booked up.

REVISION COURSES

Easter revision courses are run by some state schools, local education authorities and private institutions. None of these courses are a substitute for a student's own hard work. Nor can they provide a student with a full understanding of his or her subject. Some subject mysteries, though, will be resolved and study priorities established. Mainly, revision courses teach students to provide what the examiners really want. Teachers explain to them what they need to write, then make them practice writing under exam conditions. At the end of what is usually a week's intensive work, participants should have picked up enough study skills and exam techniques to show themselves in the best light.

What lies behind this is the assumption that exams are not just about knowing your subject, but also about preparing and packaging what you know in order to do well in exams. Some pupils can do this unaided, but most need to learn. This results in better and, in case of able, hard-working students, in excellent grades.

SCHOOL-RUN COURSES

An increasing number of state schools now run their own revision courses, sometimes financed by the Government's Standards Fund. These are free, voluntary and aimed at encouraging students who the staff feel might benefit most. Teachers seek to ensure that students have worked through the relevant course material, rather than blindly thrashing their way through everything they were ever taught. There may also be another mock exam at the end. Often, however, there is only limited emphasis on exam technique.

Still, your teenager should at least be given a copy of the examiners' mark scheme, which tells her what exactly the crucial extra marks that will take a student up to an A-grade are awarded for; in English, for instance, this will include putting a literary work into its historical context; in History, examiners reward students, amongst other things, for providing a "web of causation", rather than just a sequence of historical events. (The mark scheme can also be downloaded from the website of the relevant examination board.)

How much time there is to resolve individual student's queries depends on the revision course structure. Some individual concerns can certainly now be addressed, since classes will, at least, be smaller than in the school's term time A-level group. The classes might, though, still be fairly mixed ability and run by the students' regular teachers.

A few state sixth form colleges also run such vacation courses and some of those are open to outside students. If your daughter has been unhappy about the quality of some of her teaching, then a highly rated sixth form college (its Ofsted report will be on the college website) could be a better bet, assuming that its pupils are studying for the same board.

PRIVATE COURSES

Private revision courses, once the preserve of the rich and dim, are a growth industry. Some are run on a Saturday basis all year long, but most are holiday ones. Such courses, advertised around three months in advance in local papers and *The Times*, offer intense revision work in very small groups, albeit at pretty large fees – anything between £200 and £700 for a week. The cost depends partly on the number of subjects to be revised and partly on whether it includes accommodation. Day school courses are just as good as boarding ones, though you may not have a choice if you live too far away. Courses are often run on the premises of private schools and might employ some of their teachers. Students here will usually be guided towards a deeper understanding of their subject. They will also be reminded of fundamental principles and teachers will try to sharpen key skills, for instance grammar in the case of languages. Nevertheless, in most short courses the emphasis will be on what one revision college principal described as "technique, technique and more technique." Some revision courses are actually held inside colleges in Oxford and Cambridge. These are based on boarding and explicitly aim to make your son or daughter at ease there, as part of their preparation for the Oxbridge entrance process.

Before you part with such serious money, though, ask a few questions and don't be swayed by the freshly painted buildings and lush green lawns. It will take more than a generous application of Growmore to turn your teenager into an A-grade student. As a start, you need to know the qualifications of the course teachers. Reputable revision colleges will list those on the publicity material: John Smith, B.Sc. Biology (Cantab.) tells you that Mr. Smith has a Bachelor of Science degree in Biology from Cambridge. If it was a degree from Oxford in an arts subject, such as English, the qualification would be BA English (Oxon.). The letters M.Sc. or MA after a name indicate a higher qualification in most cases, but former students of Oxford and Cambridge can claim this title automatically a year after graduation. Some revision courses are taught by university lecturers or teachers who also moonlight as examiners.

You also need to know whether you are booking your son into a new or established revision college. New tends to be bad until proven otherwise. How big are their classes? Will they prepare your daughter for her specific subject exam and examining board? Do they specialise in helping their students to pass or to get As? And how many hours a day does the teaching actually take? The answers, you will discover, can vary extremely widely.

What you would, ideally, want to hear is that they teach a single subject in groups of no more than six, for at least two hours a day, with extra time set aside for exam practice, feed-back and advice on further revision work the student can do at home. It would also be nice for your purposes if the revision college took lots of bright students aiming to get into Russell Group universities and, perhaps, Oxbridge. Generally, smaller groups are far better value than longer hours. By this stage, your son needs personal attention. In this spirit, a good revision college will want to hear about the GCSE and A2 exams your son has already taken, plus his current grade predictions. These details enable them to fit him into the right course. If the principal is trying to make you sign a cheque without showing any interest in the boy's record – don't. You are probably being sold a pup.

I am less sure about the apparently rather well taught A-level courses at Oxford and Cambridge. Tempting as these may sound if your daughter clams up when confronted with quaint old university towns and the clipped vowels of their teaching staff, such a course does imply that Oxbridge is her sole possible destination. If she then fails to get in despite her very best efforts, the disappointment can be harder to bear.

HOME TUTORS

Getting one-to-one attention, even for a fairly short period, can dramatically raise a pupil's achievement. A good tutor will explain previously incomprehensible bits of the syllabus, focus on those aspects of a subject which are likely to come up in tests and, in an ideal world, suggest wider reading. He can also make even the driest subject sound exciting, thereby coaching your son towards doing more work.

To get the best results you must spell out the basics. Is the tutor there to help improve your kid's general grasp of a school subject or just to prepare her for an imminent exam? If exam performance is all you are after, the tutor will have to be familiar with the type of questions likely to come up. If he is not currently a teacher, this means that he needs to be given copies of previous years' papers, available from your son's school. The tutor may or may not cover exam skills such as timing, ordering material and clarity of expression. Unless you make clear what you want, no tutor can provide it.

(A word of warning: tutors can make a difference, but cannot magically transform a middling pupil into a top student. If that is what you hope, I'd drop the idea of Oxbridge. For the sake of family peace and your teenager's self-esteem, it would be better to focus on another university. Having two fairly strong subjects is the minimum requirement not just for getting into Oxford or Cambridge, but also for surviving there.)

So, where do you find a tutor? Well, Prime Minister Tony Blair found his sons' tutor at the nearest public day school, and there is no reason why you should not copy him. It is quite OK to ring up yours, picked from the Good Schools Guide, and tell the school secretary that you are looking for someone to do a few weeks' private tutoring. If their own staff are too grand to take the extra job (in the era of huge mortgages, few are) they might well have a friend or a former pupil just down from Oxbridge who is keen.

Don't be put off by a potential tutor's youth. When it comes to exam coaching, someone who left school only a few years earlier and so may have worked through the same syllabus as your son towards very similar exams could well come up trumps. And don't be ashamed to ask the young postgraduate student earning his rent in your sitting room what grades he got and how he got into Oxbridge himself. Is he keeping in touch with staff there? It's a good sign if he is. He might have picked up gossip about new priorities and admissions policy or might even be able to put in a good word.

Alternatively, A-level tutors seeking work advertise in may local papers. They are often retired teachers and some have worked in both the public and the private sector. Ask how long they have been retired (because A-levels have changed much in the last decade) and if they give the school as a reference, follow it up by phone. You never know whether you'll hear songs of praise or some tense, embarrassed waffle. The latter can mean he left under a bit of a cloud – drink or perhaps a taste for under-age boys. Schools rarely prosecute.

There are also lots of tutorial agencies offering their services in the papers. Told what kind of help your teenager needs, they'll try to come up with someone suitable. It's best to insist that this means a tutor who has graduated in the subject he will teach. The kind of person registered with the agency is often an Oxbridge graduate still looking for the perfect city job or for enough bookings as a comedian. A few are young academics trying to pay their mortgage. Some agencies check tutors' references, others are just groups of university friends sharing out the work.

As for the practical side, this is pretty straight forward. Expect to pay between £20 and £25 per lesson, and settle for between one and two lessons a week, depending on the amount of time left. A good tutor can massively improve a willing student's understanding of a subject and his exam skills in two or three months. The emphasis is on "willing": if you have scheduled the tutorials in place of your son's weekly football practice the tutor will be as popular as Bayern Munich.

Before finally striking the deal, clarify with the tutor how long a lesson will be and if you have to pay his fare on top of the fee. Then, fix a time and place and don't allow circumstances to alter them. The time should be after one of your daughter's easier school days or a quiet weekend afternoon. The place, ideally, around your bare kitchen table or your daughter's tidied up room. Being able to spread out reams of paper work is what matters here. This is not the moment to show off your new, extra-soft three piece leather suite.

In some cases, the tutor may suggest to hold lessons on the school premises or elsewhere. This may be tempting, especially if you feel embarrassed about your home, but it is worth keeping in mind that the tutor himself was probably not raised at Buckingham Palace. I'd certainly agree to this only if you can be sure that other, trustworthy people will be present. If the person who will be spending private time with your son was not vetted by anyone, you might even want to remain at home (but not in the same room, of course) during lessons. I'd also make clear to the girl that the tutor, however nice, is technically a stranger, which means not a trusted family friend whose invitations she can accept.

Lastly, it may be wise to review progress after two or three lessons. Ask your daughter how she feels about the tutor. Is he good at explaining a problem? Approachable? Responds to questions? Does she feel that she is learning anything or is she just watching a dopey stranger scoffing the chocolate biscuits you thoughtfully put out?

If things go wrong, don't be shy about starting again. Tell the tutor you are moving away (or whatever), then quickly look for another one by the same route. Tutors are just human beings and vary tremendously. The next one might be a teaching genius.

MOVING SCHOOLS

If you conclude that your daughter's school is not good enough already at the GCSE stage, you have different options. She might agree – or even be thrilled – to move to another, more successful comprehensive school for her sixth form studies. What you need to work out, though, is when and where.

The answer to the first question is simple: no later than the start of year 11. The best comprehensives want all applications in by January or February of the previous school year, which means eight to nine months ahead of entry. As for where to move your daughter, the choice is, on first sight, considerable. Legally, you no longer need to live near a child's school to apply for a place there, and your daughter is now old enough to travel considerable distances.

Picking a good school also seems simple enough. Obviously, both you and your daughter will want to attend the school's open day for sixth formers, which will be in November of the year before or in January thereafter. This is the time to check out the basics. Does it have the facilities and/or labs she might need? Are you struck by the positive attitude of the pupils who are showing you around? Do the teachers impress you as qualified, likeable and ambitious for their pupils? Does the school send pupils on Government-funded schemes designed to broaden their horizons, such as Excellence in the Cities or Access? Does it prepare its students for the Oxbridge entrance process and do any of them get in? A good school will send you home with a pile of bumph that will tell you the rest, notably what subjects it offers at AS and A2 level and where they might lead. It should also show the previous year's exam results and which universities, if any, their students have been accepted by. There will be some mention of class size, which in the A-level group should be 20 or less.

A well-structured school brochure will also contain extracts from the school's Ofsted report, although I'd treat those with caution. For instance, it is nice to know that its community links have been rated "excellent", but if your daughter is planning to do English, you really need to know the rating given to the school's teaching in that subject.

Also, "good" sounds fine in an Ofsted report, but actually isn't. The Ofsted range goes from "very poor", "poor", "satisfactory", "good" and "very good" to "excellent". So, "good" is actually pretty middling and you'd want it to be better than that. If the school won't tell you these things, you can go directly to Ofsted. Either phone for the report or go to their website, www.gov.uk and search for the name of the school.

Then, if you're happy, go ahead and fill in the application form, remembering to emphasize your daughter's academic abilities. You have done what you could and must now hope for the best.

Unfortunately, such steps have a really good chance of success only outside the big cities. In London, certainly, top quality comprehensives are hopelessly oversubscribed. When it comes to the sixth form, most take in only a small proportion of outside pupils. While it worth trying hard, which includes making sure that the school is aware of all your daughter's strengths and potential contribution to the school's academic glory, she may have to consider other options. The most obvious one is a sixth form college.

SIXTH FORM COLLEGES

State run colleges of this kind have a poor reputation, mainly because they often cater for a very mixed intake of young people. Some may come from failing schools, others from disadvantaged homes. This means that their overall exam results cannot equal those of a school in some executive suburb. However, the college might still be great at developing a pupil's individual potential. And don't be automatically put off by the presence of refugees: some of their parents may well have been teachers or civil servants before they had to escape and will encourage their children to study hard.

Most importantly, a huge amount of Government money has gone into this sector in recent years, which has been translated into state-of-the art facilities from language labs to IT equipment. The funding has also attracted more and more highly qualified teachers. As a result, your local sixth form college may well be better geared towards sending your son to Oxbridge than the struggling comprehensive down the road.

Having said that, the same rules as above apply: attend the open day, go through their bumph with a fine-toothed comb and check whether the staff are actively involved in preparing pupils for Oxbridge entrance. I would, perhaps, add one reservation, which is no reflection on the professionalism or the dedication of their teaching staff. Although some students from sixth form colleges get into Oxford and Cambridge every year, the two universities rarely accept them for Medicine and Law. Partly, this may be due to the rigid A-level requirements for these courses (three "hard" subjects at grade A) and partly, perhaps, just a case of Oxbridge being toffee-nosed.

IF YOU CAN'T BEAT THEM...

You may, in fact, dream of being toffee-nosed yourself, of sending your son to one of those schools which, in exchange for annual school fees well above the national minimum wage, smooth their pupils' path to Oxbridge. If you could afford to do so, you would presumably not be reading this, but don't give up quite yet; some private sixth form education is available at little or no cost, at least if your child is really talented and you play your cards right.

What you need to know is that almost all private schools have scholarship schemes. Most of these cover a proportion of a child's fee, usually 50 per cent. The traditional function of this is to enable those of their old boys who have fallen on hard times to send their kids there. Quite a few schools, though, also have 100 per cent scholarship schemes. These have quite a different purpose. They enable a private establishment with a mixed ability intake, which is what most public schools except for a tiny group of highly selective ones really are, to strengthen its academic base. The top A-levels won by its hand-picked scholars will ensure that the school retains its place near the top of the annual league table. Once this has been achieved, it can hike up its fees as much as it likes. In other words, scholarships are not a form of charity and you need not be embarrassed about accepting one.

There is only one problem. While these schemes might even get your son into some of the grandest boys' schools, including Eton and Harrow, full scholarships for girls are like gold dust. A drive to raise more money towards private school bursaries for talented girls, which was launched a few years ago by an educational charity, the Sutton Trust, has so far been unsuccessful.

Most existing schemes are aimed at pupils entering at 13, but big schools set aside about half a dozen full scholarships per year for sixth form entry. Created after the abolition of the Government's assisted places scheme in the 1990s, these are usually means-tested. In other words, they are aimed at those parents of a gifted child who are on the dole or earning little more than £12,000. If you are slightly better off, the school might drop part of the fees.

The scholarships usually cover all costs, including tuition and, if applicable, boarding. If asked, most schools will also find a way to fund the scholar's absurdly overpriced uniform and other kit. And when your son has lost his flannel blazer and cap for the third exasperating time, a kindly teacher will reveal to you that the annual school fete always includes a "good as new" second-hand uniform stall. Then watch the most genteel of middle class mothers get into a scrum so the money saved can go to Harvey Nichols.

When do you throw your child's name into this particular hat? The answer is very early. While state sixth forms do not usually decide on admissions until February of the year in which the sixth form course is to start, private schools think fourteen months ahead. This means you probably should first contact their admissions officer in July or August of the year before your teenager will be starting her sixth form. Below is a sample letter I suggest you send in order to set the process in motion, but you may want to tailor it slightly to fit an individual school. As you will discover by looking at a school's brochure or website, expectations from scholars can vary; some schools like to find the perfect all-rounder, the boy who performs equally well in all subjects without obvious preferences; others look for exceptional ability in one academic field. Most schools like a pupil who can offer extras like sporting ability or an outstanding musical gift. CHECK WITH ST. PAUL'S.

LETTER TO A SCHOOL (SAMPLE)

Dear . . . (phone to find out the name of the head),

I am the parent of a child currently attending Year 10 of his comprehensive school. My son has been assessed as gifted by his school (or an educational psychologist, or some other expert), especially as far as the sciences are concerned. He works hard and has consistently good exam results. He is also a keen athlete and plays basketball for his school.

His gifts, I feel, would be best developed in a school such as yours. I would therefore be grateful if you could advise me about your admissions procedures. Unfortunately, I am a low earner and unable to afford current school fees. Perhaps you could let me know whether there are any scholarships or bursaries available for boys in my son's position.

Yours sincerely,

If the school is interested, an application form will be in the post. The school might also ask for documentation such as school reports or teachers' comments. All being well, the boy will then be invited to an interview and exam session lasting anything from a few hours to two whole days the following November. This is a promising outcome, but don't count your chickens yet: a large private school may be offering up to 20 of their sixth form places to non-pupils, but will interview between twice and four times that number. If possible, your son should therefore sit exams for more than one school.

The exam itself usually consists of several parts. A chat with the applicant, perhaps combined with some sort of brief IQ test, will seek to establish innate ability. A set of longer, written tests will determine how much the lad knows about the subjects he has been taught. Some schools favour giving the applicants a kind of lecture, then quiz them about the contents; others ask them to write an essay on a non-school subject, often involving a story in the news. If you meet any current pupils, don't be put off by the unfamiliar way they speak. Obviously, your son's accent will be different, but accents change fast at that age and six months into the school year, he may well shock you by sounding like them.

The school may or may not wish to talk to a parent, but if they do, don't be nervous about this either. They are not looking for airs and graces, but for a commitment to your son's academic goals. This means that you will encourage him to work hard at home if an exam is looming, that you will not disappear abroad just before he is due to go home at half term or that you won't keep him away on holiday long after term started. They get quite enough of this behaviour from the fee-paying parents, thank you.

They will also expect you to back the strict school rules. You'll have to make your son understand that there will be little tolerance of misbehaviour. Private schools maintain discipline and try to prevent breaches of the law, such as drug-taking, by mercilessly expelling culprits. Parents of rebellious pupils, however bright, have reasons to fear the headmaster's dreaded phrase: "He would be happier elsewhere."

Can you prepare for this entrance exam? The honest answer is, most applicants do. You can start by asking the school for more details. Many will offer some information on exam contents, or even previous papers. Obviously, your son should be having another look at his GCSE notes in those subjects he intends to continue with. It may also be a good idea for him to do some newspaper reading. After a few weekends of immersion in The Observer, The Sunday Times, The Sunday Telegraph or the Independent on Sunday, he should be able to express a personal opinion on a few issues of the day: strikes, global warming or plastic surgery are just some examples. Remember, there are no "correct" views on such things, only arguments backed by facts.

Although few schools conduct proper verbal interviews, your son will probably be asked to talk a little about his interests. These might have to include cultural or sporting ones, depending on the school. Make sure he can rattle down a short list!

When it comes to the written work, it is obviously important not to overlook any of the mandatory questions by mistake. Most crucially perhaps, an applicant needs to be able to complete an essay within a set time, usually 45 minutes. This means acquiring the skills of timing, structuring and summarising. Check he's got a working watch!

If you're uncertain whether your son is properly prepared, consult ISIS, who might be able to tell you which sample papers your son might want to look at before sitting for a particular school.

WILL HE BE HAPPY THERE?

The answer is, it depends. I've rarely heard of a day school pupil on a scholarship regretting the choice they made. Sleeping in a different world can be more stressful. An outgoing teenager who likes group activities and understands that he is contributing to the school's fortunes will probably settle in fast. Large boarding schools tend to have separate scholars' houses and your bright son might really enjoy living with lots of other fast learners.

On the other hand, most private schools are single sex, and living an hour's train ride from the nearest place selling hair gel does not suit everyone. Having less freedom than at a comprehensive can be a pain, although boarding schools are no longer the prisons which earlier inmates remember them as. Physical punishment and fagging, the public school version of bullying, were abolished nearly a generation ago. There is some privacy and a universal youth culture has reduced the once enormous gap in pupils' lives. One Eton teacher, quoted in the Daily Telegraph, insisted that it can now be hard to tell who comes from where: "By the time you've opened a few doors, you see that everyone has the same rickety CD system and the same posters."

The range of well-resourced leisure activities can thrill a newcomer. Still, a very shy teenager may be thrown by the unfamiliar environment and not everyone fancies the wide open spaces, which may include dormitories, as well as playing fields. There can be other problems: a small school's intake may be too white to make an ethnic minority child feel at ease, or too intellectually average to stretch a fast learner. A few schools get so obsessed with A-levels that they (metaphorically) stamp on the more original pupil who is doing work outside the curriculum. To invent a game, design a machine or write a poem in school time can be seen as betraying the struggle for top marks.

In short, private education, even if you can get it, does not meet every gifted child's needs. There has to be a fairly precise match between abilities and facilities. Anecdotal evidence suggests that mixed boarding schools work best for working class pupils (think Atlantic College or Bedales) but a current A-level student should not get too excited about these options. While a couple of top public schools are in the process of raising huge scholarship funds, the number of free six form places currently available remains very small. There are only about three hundred a year, which does not quite make them a superhighway to Oxbridge.

5

What degree course?

Picking an Oxbridge degree course is something many pupils do in the first, exciting weeks of their A2 year, almost as an afterthought. The forms arrive in September, and finishing a class essay in time can, at this point, seem far more important to your son. So might finding out whether leggy Jessie from Maths has really broken up with her naff boyfriend in the holidays. Other pupils are probably not even discussing courses yet. After all, entrance applications to most universities need to be submitted over two months later. So, why worry? If you fuss now, you might well get your head bitten off. "Filling in the form just means applying for a course in what you're best at, right?" Wrong, actually.

Course choice is fairly crucial for enjoying university life, as well as for getting in. The problem is that by the time they fill in their Oxbridge application form, most pupils are perfectly clear about theirs. They want to study the subject in which they got the highest marks at school. Teachers may strengthen this idea by telling the proud dad on parents' day that "she is a natural mathematician" or assure a mother that "he has a real gift for English."

For the pupil with at least a trace of doubt, the school's careers adviser may be the next port of call. Some are wonderful at making even a timid but clever science pupil see herself as a future Professor of Medicine. Others, though, are overwhelmed by the requirements of so many new pupils, universities and courses. In a school which does not normally sends students to Oxbridge their focus might well be on making disadvantaged pupils consider any university at all. So, while all careers advisers have a shelf full of dog-eared books and booklets to lend, only a few will explain to an Oxbridge applicant while she, especially, should take time over them.

Nor is there much emphasis on the link between careers and courses. While it is pretty obvious what you can become with a degree in Law, the same is not true of, for instance, Linguistics. Its name alone sounds like a sexual practice. To a pupil nervous about striking out into the alien adult world in general and Oxbridge in particular, sticking with a familiar school subject also provides some reassurance. So, Maths or English (or History or French) goes on the application form.

WHAT'S ON OFFER

This is a great pity, as a start because your son will never know what he could be missing without a leisurely study of the Oxford or Cambridge undergraduate prospectus, available over six months in advance. Not only has this once dreary document at last caught up with the lively and colourful booklets issued by the former polytechnics, it also no longer assumes that every reader knows what Economics is or what jobs it can lead to. Every year too it contains more non-school subject courses, a few of them entirely new, others newly combined or newly opened to candidates without Latin.

Admittedly, the number of courses offered by Oxford and Cambridge is not huge. After all, for most of the two universities' long history, only three subjects, Classics, Divinity and Law, were taught there. Even the introduction of English Literature was fiercely resisted for decades but, once its academic supporters had won the day, the subject was, in true Oxbridge style, elevated to a national mission. Speaking after his election as Oxford English Professor, George Stuart Gordon announced in his 1922 inaugural lecture: "England is sick, and . . . English Literature must save it. The Churches (as I understand) having failed, and social remedies being slow, English Literature now has a triple function: still I suppose, to delight and instruct us, but also, and above all, to save our souls and heal the State."

Academics elsewhere tend to see their role in slightly more modest terms and so managed to create a wider choice earlier on. The new universities, in particular, try to cover every possible student taste, with some offering up to a hundred degree options, from Accounting to Culinary Arts (Pastry), both taught at Thames Valley University. Cambridge, in comparison, tends to list only around thirty degree courses in its prospectus. Oxford lists just over fifty.

Oxford and Cambridge have also taken seemingly different paths. While Oxford has gradually added a small but interesting set of combined courses, such as Mathematics and Philosophy, Modern History and Economics and Classical Archaeology and Ancient History, Cambridge has not, or so a quick skim though its prospectus suggest. Here the early 20th century range of academic disciplines, topped up by one newcomer, Computer Science, survives almost intact.

This impression is misleading. Once a Cambridge student has done her initial year, working hard to absorb a single subject at great depth, she has an amazing range of study options. Thanks to the many experts and expert libraries on tap, a History undergraduate interested in, for example, North African History, will be able to explore even its most obscure angle with a world-renowned expert. And if she wants to combine this with another discipline, say Cultural Studies, this is not just fine but actually encouraged.

In other words, although History and Culture is not a Cambridge degree course, you can actually do it, and probably to a higher level than elsewhere. This so-called "Tripos" course structure means than a student is sometimes even able to move from his official course subject to a fairly unrelated one. If your son has started off in Oriental Studies, but wants to broaden his outlook (or is struggling with Hittite grammar) by year two, he might be able to move to Social Anthropology, Law or Management Studies and continue with this into year three. This means he will end up, in practice, with a combined course.

In science too progress options are huge, though usually only when you have completed the first year of what in Cambridge is called Natural Sciences, but in Oxford comes under either Earth Sciences, Biochemistry, Materials Science or Physics. Other science courses, tend to offer the student either a wide module choice or at least some subject combinations. Teaching methods can vary too and you need to remember that, unlike in many other universities, the science approach here will be theoretical rather than applied. If Robert Stephenson had gone to Oxbridge, he might have been encouraged to explore the scientific principles making a steam engine possible, before building one.

It is also worth knowing that some subjects are absent only in name: "The word sociology, being a Latin–Greek hybrid, was not used in polite academic society," recalled Cambridge don Thomas Howarth. So, must you go elsewhere for this popular hybrid? Actually, no. Nowadays all Oxbridge Anthropology courses, as well as the Cambridge SPS course and Oxford PPE (see below) put their students through the Sociology reading list, albeit in between lots of other books.

No subject is today out of bounds to state school pupils. As mentioned before, this includes Classics, which now accommodates the study, from scratch, of Latin or Greek, or both. The Oxford

Classics course, a tour de force through Greek and Roman literature, history, languages, thought, art and culture, is not even terribly hard to get into. The only problem is that applicants from comprehensives need to do more independent reading than others to prove their interest. Private and grammar school pupils plough through loads of Classics-related stuff at school.

THINK BEFORE YOU JUMP

As a result of there being so much on offer, working out your course options from the prospectus alone can be hideously confusing. Don't even think of signing on the dotted line before you have read the clearer but also much more detailed information on the course website. Keep in mind too that two courses of the same name may be quite different at Oxford and Cambridge. Oriental Studies at Oxford, for instance, is largely language-oriented. At Cambridge it has a substantial history and culture element.

All admissions tutors I spoke to emphasized that it is absolutely fine for students to contact staff with further questions. This really should be done by your ambitious teenager themselves, either by email or (good practice for the interview) by phone. All the telephone numbers, email addresses and websites you might need to contact a faculty or college are listed in the university prospectus. The best person to ask for is the undergraduate studies secretary, a goldmine of information on exciting but unfamiliar courses.

On the other hand, simply sticking to the school subject he knows may well disappoint your son intellectually. For instance, doing school Maths eight hours a week is not at all the same thing as doing the more abstract Oxbridge version for thirty hours a week. Reading fiction for pleasure and writing essays about the narrative of your book is very different from concentrating on literary theory, as you would with Oxford English Lit., or on literary structure, as you would at Cambridge. Of course, some bright students absolutely thrive on this approach and will spend endless blissful university hours discussing iambic pentameters in English or Fermat's Last Theorem in Maths. Others, though, will love the inspiration found very much further afield.

So, encourage your son or daughter to take their time. It's best to think of course choice not as the automatic continuation of a student's school career, but as a new and carefully considered beginning.

PICKING TO GET IN

Course choice at Oxbridge also matters greatly (and far more than at many other universities) in terms of acceptance chances. What does this mean in practice? Well, let's say that your daughter has returned from an Access trip to Oxford or Cambridge determined to live for three years under the ramparts of a medieval nunnery, but also to study her favourite school subject. Unless she is a really outstanding pupil, this can be a problem. Each year, there are vastly more Oxbridge candidates than places for English, Maths, History and courses involving French. Poor teaching too often handicaps candidates for school subjects more than other.

If your daughter is determined to go to Oxbridge, but also to do French, the only foreign language taught in all English schools, she might have to choose between these two perfectly reasonable ambitions. Suggesting this to her could trigger a tantrum bigger than the one she threw, aged three, when she couldn't take home the deep hole she had dug in the playground sand pit. And, if she has read her way through the French novels shelf in your local library or is beginning to take an interest in Parisian existentialism she is quite right to ignore you.

Clinging to French just because it comes easy to her and she is curious about the world, though, might be the wrong decision. Oxbridge offers lots of alternatives – and we are talking mind stretchers, not cheap substitutes here. A pupil who fearlessly walked the horrifying tightrope of French grammar may actually find it more rewarding to tackle a new modern language or two. Or, if she has a more theoretical bent, the girl might consider the science of languages, Linguistics. A harder, non-European language with a whole alphabet of its own could also challenge her. Future explorers, meanwhile, will find themselves inspired by a course with lots of unfamiliar historic or cultural angles, such as Anthropology or Oriental Studies.

All these are stimulating, often extremely well taught courses and they have another very attractive feature: they admit the majority of those who apply. Many do not even require prior knowledge of another language, certainly not a non-European one. Others have admissions tutors who will be delighted to hear that your daughter speaks Polish to her grandmother or learnt Arabic in the mosque. She will still have to prove her interest in the course by reading around it, but her background can give her that slight edge.

And if the girl does get in, she might get a very good degree. Many a language student finds herself alongside some of the classic Oxbridge "coasters", rich but less academic students who have picked their mother tongue as a course subject and coast along on the strength of that. But to do well takes more than basic language skills, and if she works hard on all aspects of the course, your bright daughter might well overtake the coasters and get a First. On the other hand, if the girl insists on clinging to her school subject, she might not even get into Oxbridge.

TARGET PRACTICE

One of the open secrets of Oxbridge entrance has always been that you can get in by targeting a course which has a high rate of successful applicants. Rates vary greatly: courses such as Economics and Law accept less than one in five candidates, while History, English, French, Experimental Psychology and Medicine accept about one in four. The success rate of Chemistry, Materials Science and Classics applicants, on the other hand, hovers around 48 per cent. Nearly half of those who apply are likely to get in.

For unusual language combinations, success rates can be even higher: only Oxford and Cambridge can afford to run courses which, during certain periods of history at least, hardly anyone wants to attend. Some of these courses are relics of the British Empire, which exported thousands of young men with a grounding in the various "native languages" to the Colonies. Elderly Oxbridge dons still recall the frantic War Office search in 1941 for graduates in Serbo–Croat who could be dropped behind enemy lines in German-occupied Yugoslavia. Younger dons will talk of a similar search in 1999, when the British Government prepared to enter Kosovo.

Until recently, few people would have thought that Sumerian, the ancient language of what was Mesopotamia and is now Iraq, had any public use. However, the looting of Iraq's museums in 2003 deprived the world of valuable ancient documents and made the study of the remaining ones crucial.

As a result, courses which combine language training with historic or cultural studies are kept going even if there are very few applicants for them. After all, the dons teaching the course are around anyway, engaged in their own specialist and highly reputable research. What this means is that while it can be murder to get into Law, there are few barriers to the students wanting to do Sanskrit, or a language mix including Czech (with Slovak). Here, a bright applicant willing to broaden his horizons might well be greeted with open arms.

Why don't more state school students go for courses like these? The answer lies in the information available. Neither Oxford nor

Cambridge will tell you, for instance, what the acceptance chances of a candidate applying to do a particular language course are. Instead, the success rates listed are overall ones, based on all the degree courses run by an individual faculty. This was fine when a candidate could always call on a cousin or family friend who had been to Oxbridge and knew what was on offer there. Alas, times have changed and, without such key data, how can a student from a non-academic background possibly decide?

Families also like to know about the practical value of courses. Without this information, parents may not feel that they will be spending their hard-earned cash on something worthwhile. Actually, when it comes to languages, it's a case of no worry. They are amongst the most popular degree subjects in the eyes of top employers. However, while French remains useful to diplomats, business now loves Spanish, Chinese and Russian.

All these facts, of course, are exactly what public school teachers, who are usually Oxbridge educated, have at their finger tips. They are aware that relatively few people apply to do a combination of German and Turkish, or Arabic and Portuguese, even though these courses require only a prior knowledge of the European language. They know the success rates for Egyptology at Cambridge, and the chances offered to their particular students by the existence of so many Oxford courses involving Classics.

These teachers will also tailor their suggestions to the individual student by explaining that Materials Science (once called Metallurgy) at Oxford is not as academically demanding as Engineering and Materials, that Land Economy at Cambridge is less of a tough intellectual slog than Economics. They are aware that Cambridge Theology turns out graduates interested in comparative religion, while Oxford Theology suits potential vicars, and that very few eighteen year olds aspire to become either of these things.

One of the main reasons such a disproportionate number of Oxbridge students come from their kind of schools is that they apply to a far wider range of courses than state school students do. Public school teachers also realise that being flexible about your degree subject does not make for a disappointing outcome. Many of their students return to recommend their course to others, not only for intellectual satisfaction, but also on career grounds.

This does not, of course, mean that a student should completely disregard her own instincts in order to get in. If you hate languages, don't apply for a course requiring full-body-immersion in two of them. If you hate scientific research, looking at flow charts all day could make you feel sick. Most students, though, do not have preferences quite as strong as this and a little open-mindedness can be very rewarding indeed.

If you are wondering whether you should consider a course which is in no great public demand, the answer is probably yes. Do look at previously unconsidered options like the mysteries of Assyriology and, if they even vaguely spark your interest, skim through one of the relevant course textbooks listed on the faculty website. The excellence of Oxbridge teaching often makes a not (as yet) loved subject a highly stimulating experience.

Equally importantly, the student will still have access to the lively intellectual scene which characterises Oxbridge. Not only do students mix socially by college rather than by course, but the brightest often attend lectures in a subject other than their own. There is also nothing to prevent an interested science undergraduate from joining many of the Oxbridge arts societies and vice versa. More than one lost Engineering student has found his spiritual home on the university's drama stage.

So, your son and you should certainly take a close look at non-school subjects. If a course description baffles you even after you explored the relevant faculty website, try to discuss it with his teachers or encourage him to look at some introductory text in the library. By all means encourage him to do a further search on the net, but remember that it is awash not just with facts but with the outpourings of aggrieved individuals: a key word like Archaeology will bring up a several specialist magazines, but also dozens of personal websites in which students criticize their course. Your son could well have a completely different experience. At this stage, he needs proper direction and the confidence to be broad, rather than narrow, in his choice.

PICKING FOR A CAREER

The psychologist and ability expert Joan Freeman discovered that very bright children can find it especially hard to make career choices. To a quick, thorough mind, Latin and Persian, or Maths and Medicine, can seem equally manageable and attractive. Even ambition is not necessarily a good guide. Your son may want to become a successful, well paid young professional, but teenagers outside the educated middle classes often know too little about real jobs to link university learning with the work people do. The gifted sixteen year olds interviewed by Professor Freeman thought that bankers handle money, or that chemists hand out medicines at Boots.

Knowing more about the reality of work helps pupils to make better choices. It is useful to realise that a banker, for instance, benefits from knowing about politics. He might have to decide where money should be kept, and a bank's investment decisions will have to take into account political developments.

Then there is the historic precedent. Britain was, for hundreds of years, ruled by white men with an Oxbridge degree often known as "Greats". The idea behind this was that a politician needed a good grasp of the moral principles taught in Classics courses – if only to disregard them. Today's politicians are more likely to have done Politics, Philosophy and Economics (PPE), which elderly dons call "Modern Greats", a course only available at Oxford.

If you are after an academic reputation, it helps to know that this does not depend on the subject an Oxbridge don has specialised in. Cambridge Celtic is taught by people who are no less world renowned than those teaching French or, say, history at the same university. By choosing a less popular course, your son is likely to get personal, undiluted attention from some of the best minds in the field.

Parents doubting that their son has the potential to become a don may not be convinced of such a course choice. Aren't Celtic, Oriental Studies or Medieval Languages peculiar interests which lead nowhere? Surely, a solid, familiar subject like Maths or English is a far safer bet? You want your son to have a career, after all, not to be on the dole.

Luckily for the lovers of deeply obscure Oxbridge courses, this is not so. For instance, Oriental Studies degrees built around complex, demanding subjects like Japanese, Chinese or Egyptology, appeal to top employers in finance or law and supply Britain with a steady trickle of ambassadors. So do Classics, perhaps because they really involve moral judgements or perhaps because so many people in a position to offer highly-paid jobs got a First in them and still feel deep loyalty to the subject. Classics graduates make the Mafia look like a loose-knit group.

In short, by choosing his degree subject, your son is not automatically embarking on a "till death do us part" relationship with Norse or Chemistry. He might remain faithful if he becomes a teacher or lecturer. Otherwise, his degree course will have served as a kind of mental fitness gym in which he can practise unloading cartloads of jumbled facts, writing reports that need to be ready by dawn and having polite, informative chats with people he never met even over the most disgusting sherry.

What about the business world, though? Cambridge Economics may well sound less useful to a budding tycoon than Business Economics, a subject widely offered elsewhere. The world-famous Cambridge course will, in fact, cover this aspect alongside others, but will stress the subject's theoretical base and its historic and political context. Once a student is able to produce sound essays on all this to sharp weekly deadlines, many employers will assume that he can learn how to actually trade in bonds or beer cans at work.

Oxbridge Economics is not all about making money either. Exploring the causes of poverty may be as important as pointing the way towards wealth. The groundwork for the British welfare state was laid in Cambridge by the economist John Maynard Keynes.

Lastly, we must tackle many an English student's secret dream, that of becoming a writer. Don't you need an English degree for that? Well, actually no. Some experts even argue that you might be better off finding something to write about instead.

You can certainly remind your budding literary star that neither Jane Austen nor Charles Dickens, George Orwell, Virginia Woolf or Doris Lessing had any university education. Of Oxford writers, Evelyn Waugh, who celebrated its upper class students in Brideshead Revisited, did History at Hertford. Shiva Naipaul did Chinese at University College, John Le Carré did German at Lincoln, Julian Barnes did French Lit. at Magdalen and Marina Warner did Italian at LMH. Salman Rushdie read History at King's, Cambridge, and J.G. Ballard Medicine at the same college.

Other famous and prize-winning literary authors are non-Oxbridge: Pat Barker read International History at the LSE, London, Anita Brookner did her degree at the Courtauld Institute of Art and Hanif Kureshi did Philosophy at London's own King's College. The poet Linton Kwesi Johnson has a sociology degree from Goldsmiths' College, London.

So, don't be too narrow in your choice. All Oxbridge degrees, especially if they are "good", which means a First or an Upper Second, will open up a wide range of interesting careers.

WHAT NOT TO DO (ABOUT COURSE CHOICE)

Quite a few parents, delighted at the thought that their son or daughter might indeed stand a chance of getting into Oxbridge, will now be tempted to impose their own dream. More often than not, this is for their daughter to become a medical consultant or for their son the family's first-ever lawyer. There is no denying that these are indeed satisfying and financially rewarding careers. They might even happen if your teenager is very smart and hardworking and actually fancies one of them.

If he'd rather do History or English, though, forget the idea. Telling the boy about the sacrifices you have made by keeping him at school and saving for his tuition fees is unlikely to make him change his mind. Nor will constant hints about the pleasure it would give his dear old gran to see him in a doctor's scarlet graduation gown. Today's young men pick their own colour schemes and careers.

But let's say your more soft-hearted daughter obeys your command, drops her plan to do Oxbridge Philosophy and applies for the "sensible" subject. All well? Unfortunately, not. Medicine and Law are highly competitive fields. Admissions tutors look not just for innate ability, but for genuine, bubbling, information-packed enthusiasm. Faced with a sullen, wistful teenager secretly pining for her abandoned pet subject, they'll rapidly move on to the next candidate. So, there goes the poor girl's Oxbridge dream – and yours.

This is not to say that, in the case of Law, you need to totally give up hope. Many lawyers reach the profession by following up a first degree in another subject by a conversion course leading to a qualification called CPE (Common Professional Examination). This involves the cost of an extra year's study, but is an entirely respectable route in: not only are there always too few good Law graduates for the legal profession to choose from, but solicitors' firms and barristers' chambers actually welcome the variety of intellectual approaches other graduates bring along. Most importantly, science and engineering graduates in particular have the kind of expertise that can be highly useful in court.

You might also find it reassuring to know that even if your girl scoffs at this option, your dream of having a lawyer in the family need not go into the dustbin yet. The Open University offers an excellent Law course, open to applicants of all ages. All it takes are a few undisturbed hours a week, perfect for a parent whose children have flown the nest...

WHAT IS BEST WHERE?

What subject, though, is best studied where? Well, as a start the old saying that Oxford is best for arts and Cambridge for sciences is hopelessly out of date. Oxford regards itself as tops in Medicine, while Cambridge points to its excellence in Maths. Both have world-famous English departments. In real terms, there is little to choose between them. The Government assesses the quality of teaching and research at British universities and regularly lists Oxford and Cambridge among the top three in these fields, which means both have extremely high general academic standards.

What about the best colleges, though? Well, since each of these famous universities is made up of colleges, it is fair to assume that no individual college will be completely useless (we'll deal with the Oxbridge college, a mysterious beast with some very odd feeding habits, in the next chapter). Not every college will take students doing every single subject and you must therefore work out which one offers what from the university prospectus. A college not offering your degree course subject may still accept you, which is nice if you have picked it for its great church organ or badminton court. However, you will then be taught by academics who are fellows of other colleges, while the staff of your own college will take little interest in you.

Experts will tell you that some colleges are the best in the world for some subjects, for instance Trinity, Cambridge, for Maths and Magdalen, Oxford, for Classics. While this is probably true, it is most important for the ambitious postgraduate student seeking to become an expert. An undergraduate might not worry about this or might have other priorities: different colleges specialise in very different aspects of a subject, which means that a student interested in Human Geography will get the best tuition at one college, but someone more interested in Physical Geography is better off at another.

How do you find out where to best study your preferred subject area? The answer to this question was once jealously guarded by private school heads who dined in their old Oxbridge colleges several times a year and kept up with developments. Nowadays, all you need to do is go into the Cambridge Geography course website. This will tell you that many of the fellows (lecturers) who specialise in Physical Geography are at Sidney Sussex, while others specialising in Human Geography are at Emmanuel (www.geog.cam.ac.uk/people/academic.html). That's college choice sorted.

On the other hand, if your teenager is open-minded and likes to explore new directions within a subject, any college that enjoys a good academic reputation will do him fine. Many students I met had picked a college without worrying too much about its course specialisation and none regretted the result. It can be thrilling to discover aspects of a subject you never knew existed at school.

In other words, the option is either to look quite thoroughly into the subject angle taken by specific colleges or to be fairly relaxed once you've made a general subject choice and go with the flow. In either case, you will end up in a place that has a library, a lawn, a supervisor with a doctorate and a wardrobe without any decent coat hangers.

This, however, takes us to the subject of Oxbridge colleges, which is dealt with in the next chapter.

6
College daze

One of the decisions Oxbridge candidates are asked to make as part of their application is which college they would like to attend. Once upon a time, this was a simple matter. Writing in the "National Review" of October 1906, an anonymous public school headmaster issued this firm advice:

> A parent who asks "which is the best college at Oxford" means "where would my son fall in with the most desirable companions." If your son is a clever boy, send him to Balliol. Even if he does not appear clever, still send him to Balliol, as that is where any latent abilities which he may possess will be drawn out. But if you cannot, will not or do not send him to Balliol, why then send him to New College, Christ Church, Magdalene, Trinity or University (College), and he will have every chance of spending two or three, or even four, completely happy years.

Nearly a hundred years later, the bit about sending a clever boy to Balliol remains pretty valid. But there are lots of other places at Oxford and Cambridge which that boy (or girl) might like to consider for happiness and intellectual stimulation, as well as to improve their entrance prospects.

How do you, though, choose between fifty-nine different Oxbridge colleges? As the college system hardly exists outside Oxbridge, this question can flummox even university educated parents. To make matters worse, there are quite different places called Trinity, St. John's, Pembroke, Magdalen(e), Jesus, Corpus Christi and St. Catherine's at both Oxford and Cambridge.

As a result, some candidates would rather not to pick at all. Both the Oxford and the Cambridge prospectus make clear that this is perfectly OK. All students need to do instead is to submit an "open" application. This will leave the decision as to which college, if any, their application will be passed on to the university itself. But is that wise?

It can certainly be tempting. As some dons will point out, almost every college now contains some undergraduates who had ticked this option. However you need to know that open applications have traditionally been far less successful than targeted ones. The reason for this is unclear. Perhaps colleges do like to be chosen or perhaps candidates who shrink from such a choice come from schools academically less geared than others towards Oxbridge.

Certainly, sending your application form to the university rather than a specific college should not be taken as an obvious way out. It does work, but mainly "for excellent candidates with exam scores in the top percentile marks", as one admissions tutor put it. In other words, if what you have to offer is more mixed, pick your own college.

One way to do this, of course, is by putting down a name at random. Another, traditionally suggested in the Oxford prospectus (and echoed in the Cambridge one), is "not to worry too much about choosing a college," as this is mainly about "your living environment". To the uninitiated, this could suggest that the size of the snooker table in the student common room is all you should care about.

Candidates might want to take this advice with a large pinch of salt. For a start, not all colleges take students for all courses. Also, more famous ones may have more applicants but not necessary more places. While a college not interested in a student can recommend her to another one perceived as a better match at Oxford, or put her on a university-wide shortlist (the so-called Pool) at Cambridge, it is not obliged to.

Most importantly, each college has its own ethos and, to some extent, admissions policy. While none today contains less than 50 per cent state school students, the type of state school (inner city comp or suburban grammar) which those students come from does vary, as can their home background. It's not a deliberate policy, but college dons can be quite a cohesive group, seeking similar academic standards and sometimes traits in their candidates.

Such details are never spelt out, but a college which describes itself as "exceptionally informal" or stresses its students' varied social and educational background is really saying that it would love to find yet more smart applicants from modest homes. This information can narrow your choice, while still leaving you with a decent shortlist.

LOOK AT THE FOUNDATIONS

One way to understand what real options you have is through a potted history. Oxbridge colleges started off as separate monastic foundations in the 13th century. Religious scholars gathered there to study philosophy and theology, as well as to train clergymen. To fund themselves, they also took up training pious students in law and, later still, less pious ones to become gentlemen. Great minds beavered away at great works along-side this job for a good few hundred years, but college scholarship gradually declined. Some colleges became little more than finishing schools for any 14 to 18 year old boy whose father could pay. By the early 19th century, standards within the two college clusters which made up the universities of Oxford and Cambridge varied shockingly. Their better academics often did not teach and in some colleges bored students fought or vandalized halls to pass the time. Lord Byron arrived at Trinity Cambridge with a live bear and complained: "College improves in everything but learning, nobody here seems to look into an author, ancient or modern, if they can avoid it." When it became clear that the more academic universities in Germany, Belgium and France had overtaken Oxbridge in reputation, there were calls in Parliament for British standards to be raised. Changes followed, but as they were up to individual colleges, they did not produce identical results. Instead, colleges evolved into three distinct types.

At Oxford, Benjamin Jowett created a "nursery of public men" as Master of Balliol. The college picked the most intellectually hard-working students and turned them into civil servants, diplomats, politicians, colonial governors, judges and law lords. Trinity College, Cambridge, a centre of mathematical learning which had produced Isaac Newton, was bitten by the science bug and began funding research and laboratories.

Other college masters emphasized character development through sport. Identifying with the Athenian philosophers, they saw college as a place to watch "our young barbarians at play", which meant having lots of jolly sporty chaps and the odd classics scholar. Training clergymen was now a minority pursuit.

Colleges did not have to account for their choice to the university, because they lived on their own endowments and the fees they charged. Like local councils making up a town, they cooperated at times, but more often defended their independence tooth and claw. The subjects a college taught, how it taught them and whom it chose to teach were its own business, and each had its own Royal Charter to prove it. Some Oxbridge colleges taught nobody at all.

An endless series of reforms, sometimes imposed by the Government but more often by the colleges themselves in order to pre-empt greater Government regulation, have narrowed college options. The reward has been Government funding. Public money allows Oxbridge to spend about twice as much per student as other universities because it tops up the funds most colleges have accumulated over the centuries from benefactors and property investments. The result is that Oxbridge students, as well as dons, enjoy a stunning environment. Most study and dine in priceless antique surroundings and relax in beautifully kept gardens closed to the general public. Even first years get their rooms daily cleaned by college servants. One Midlands student told me he felt like a lord at his Cambridge college when told he wasn't even expected to lick his own stamps (porters there frank all students' mail), but this shows a slightly warped view of peers' privileges.

The price of reform has been a degree of standardisation. Today, all colleges must comply with Government teaching standards, equality laws, health and safety rules, etc. Out went poorly qualified, non-publishing academics and in came lots of women students. Ethnic minorities, taken as one group, must also be represented, at least if enough of them can be persuaded to apply. Accommodation too has improved. The damp, medieval student rooms, so cold that older graduates recall sleeping in their coats, have been replaced by spacious, electronically equipped bedsits.

Oxbridge colleges, though, remain a mixed bag when it comes to levels of academic success, atmosphere and social composition. Pupils asked to list their preferred college on the application form therefore need to find out as much as they can before picking up their biro. They should certainly disregard the advice given by both Oxford and Cambridge that these places are all alike and so students might as well leave the section blank if they're unsure. This hands the choice to the university, which may push such applicants towards a less renowned college. Measures are being taken to counter this trend, but a 2004 Oxford study revealed that nearly all self-selected "open" applicants were allocated to four of its colleges.

But what can your poor confused daughter, stuck with two parents who stubbornly insisted on earning their living from an early age, do instead? Take her time is the most immediate answer, but below are some methods people use to arrive at the right choice.

ASKING FORMER STUDENTS' ADVICE

If you are considering a college, it is tempting to ask the opinion of someone who went there. For people who don't move in Oxbridge circles, this is often a teacher, the family doctor or a clergyman. Elderly chaps with fond memories of Oxbridge tend to wax lyrically about the unique character of their college and its unique features, telling you categorically: "Sidney Sussex is the only place to be. Nowhere else has such a jolly crowd, once threw a chap into the Cam for wearing the wrong bow-tie."

On the other hand, quite a few who went there from disadvantaged backgrounds have very bitter memories of their college as a place of loneliness, braying public school boys and no respect for hard work. I was struck to discover that several of the working class students I interviewed turned out to have a father or uncle who was accepted by Oxbridge, but dropped out because he absolutely hated the place. Forget the fun of the Footlights: there were no Swinging Sixties in Oxbridge and, a generation ago, some college boys still wore plus fours. The younger students I met almost didn't go because they were put off by such accounts.

In the end, all were extremely glad they had gone. The Oxbridge of the 21st century, a place where women and state school pupils make up half the undergraduate intake, works even for students who don't know what plus fours are (for those who care: they are knee length sporting trousers). Some quaint college customs, like the annual May Ball, remain unchanged. Some dons still like to say grace in Latin. Some students are still very much richer than others and strangle their vowels. A surprising number know how to jet-sky. All Oxbridge students, though, now wear jeans and communicate by that unique social leveller, the text message.

This is not to say that college life is a vision of perfect harmony. You can still become a hate object, only it will not be for your strong Yorkshire drawl but for pinching other people's chocolate mousse from the fridge. Old men's tales are not a reliable guide to the Oxbridge of today. Its colleges have strong, not always lovable individual traits, but none remains the idle public schooler's haven or the working class student's nightmare of yore. So, you might as well choose your new abode by whichever positive features are most relevant to you.

PICKING BY ACADEMIC REPUTATION

The general fame of a college, often based on the writers, scientists, TV historians or brilliant spies it has produced, is no reliable guide to what it can offer the undergraduate.

Brilliant minds regularly pack their bags for the stratospheric salaries of Princeton or Yale. Dons become bestseller writers and decamp to the Georgian mansions of Hampstead. And even if they keep living opposite your side of the quad, they will probably be far too eminent to teach greenhorns like you.

Academic reputations certainly need to be date-checked. Trinity College, Cambridge, proudly reveals on its website that it has won more Nobel prizes than France, and a little research will reassuringly tell you that the last time it indeed garnered one of those prizes was in 1998. On the other hand, some colleges still base their reputation on educating a famous philosopher, poet or scientist who has been dead and buried for well over a hundred years.

There is, however, a league table of colleges, which tells you at which Oxford or Cambridge college students get the best grades. The better the grades, so the theory goes, the better the teaching offered there. Traditionally, the top half makes up a kind of academic college elite, so here are the respective lists for 2003.

There are some problems with relying on this information alone. As a start, the Norrington table, thought up by a 1940s don while in the bath, is largely based on how many Firsts the students an Oxford college obtained, with little weight given to the next-best degrees, Upper Seconds. The same is true of the Cambridge version, the Tompkins table.

The difference between the top and the 30th ranked colleges can be a mere handful of Firsts here and there, which can radically change the table from year to year. Pembroke College, Cambridge, which topped that university's 2002 table, for instance, was seventh in 2001 (but should not be confused with Pembroke College, Oxford, which was 25th). Balliol took the top Oxford place in 2001, but found itself tenth in 2002.

Another problem is that Firsts can also be the result of careful student selection. A college which picks all its candidates on the basis of great intellectual promise, ignoring singing skills or rowing stamina, will find itself higher up on the table, whether or not its teaching is brilliant. Degree subjects can affect the outcome as well. In colleges offering mainly Engineering, a subject that can attract less academic candidates, 35 per cent of graduates may get

Lower Seconds or Thirds. Very few Oxbridge English or History graduates do.

Still, this gives you some idea. If a college is somewhere in the top half, it will be harder to get in. On the other hand, once admitted, a really bright student should be in her element. So, if you are dreaming of an academic career or want to spend three years in the presence of truly brilliant and influential minds this is what to go

---

COLLEGE TABLES

Cambridge 2006	*Oxford 2006 (adjusted)*
1. Emmanuel	1. Merton
2. Gonville & Caius	2. Balliol
3. St. Catherine's	3. Magdalen (joint 3)
4. Pembroke	3. New College (joint 3)
5. Trinity	5. St. John's
6. Christ's	6. Christ Church
7. Selwyn	7. Wadham
8. Corpus Christi	8. Lincoln
9. Sidney Sussex	9. Corpus Christi
10. Jesus	10. University
11. Downing	11. Queen's
12. Clare	12. Trinity
13. Churchill	13. St. Edmund Hall
14. Queen's	14. Worcester
15. St. John's	15. Brasenose
16. Trinity Hall	16. Somerville
17. King's	17. Hertford
18. Robinson's	18. Jesus
19. Fitzwilliam	19. Lady Margaret Hall
20. Magdalene	20. St. Catherine's
21. Peterhouse	21. St. Anne's
22. Girton	22. St. Hilda's
23. Newnham	23. Pembroke
24. New Hall	24. St. Hugh's
25. Homerton	25. Exeter
26. Lucy Cavendish	26. Keble
27. Wolfson	27. St. Peter's
28. St. Edmund's	28. Oriel
29. Hughes Hall	29. Mansfield
	30. Harris Manchester

---

for – at least in the humanities. Aiming low may feel less risky but that does not always make it wise. State schools students, especially, often underestimate their abilities.

There are also changes ahead. From 2008, Oxford will be piloting a new admissions scheme designed to make applicants' success less dependent on college choice. The way it has been devised means that every realistic applicant will be seen by two colleges, rather than just one, and a student might even be offered a place by a college she never applied to. Cambridge too is broadening college contact. However, the new arrangements are quite complex and until they are actually shown to improve the odds, students should think hard about their college choice.

College choice is slightly less crucial in the sciences. The 20th century growth in scientific knowledge forced Oxbridge to centralise. Many science students now treat their college as what one professor I spoke to called "a bed and breakfast establishment." Rather than sitting all day hunched over a little Bunsen burner in their college, they will spend it at one of the new physics or chemistry laboratories built with millions of pounds of taxpayers' money. These faculty labs are shared by students from the entire university. Much of the students' progress is assessed by staff working there, although tutorials will still be held in their own college.

So, if your chemistry-mad son ends up at Cambridge, but not at Trinity, his college of choice, do tell him to cheer up: it does not mean he won't make professor, invent a new wonder drug and/or win the Nobel Prize.

PICKING BY STUDENT TYPE

Pupils unsure whether Oxbridge can really want someone like them often try their luck at the colleges with the highest state school intake. This means that Wadham, Oxford, and Kings College, Cambridge, places with fine academic reputations which also have around 70 per cent state school students, are engulfed by such applicants. As a result, many have to be turned away.

If your daughter really wants to get into Oxford or Cambridge, she might, in the current political climate, be wise instead to walk straight into the lion's mouth. It is the larger colleges with the most conservative entrance policies which are being leaned on to change, so let her target them. One of those castigated for always picking candidates who happen to be fourth generation Oxbridge might love to snap her up. The college will, of course, be doing so because it values her intellectual gifts, but accepting her will also save it from having its knuckles rapped by a nervous university administration.

But how do you find out which college is on the prowl for students like your girl? The answer is that there are two ways. One is by sussing out who might be particularly keen to change their intake. Ever so often, a news story appears about a college criticized for having too few state school pupils and this sometimes is followed by a wider recruitment drive. This does not mean that you need to scan the education press for Oxbridge stories every day. Colleges seeking to change their intake proportions tend to be extremely pro-active. If a college keeps adding to the Access initiatives listed on its website, bombards your daughter's inner city school with information and welcomes the girl on her Access visit like a long lost friend, it is what is called by dating agencies "ready to commit."

In practice, this means it intends to take perhaps a dozen pupils like her and it would therefore be a good idea to get an application in, even if she is not sure of getting three As.

Another way to check for promising colleges is the traditional "minor public school house master's route" to Oxbridge: if a college is small, poorish, far from the town centre and low down on the relevant league table, tell your boy to make a beeline for it.

The natural prey of such a college is the rural private school chap who rows, has been in the cadet corps and plays the bagpipes. As a result, it will have far fewer really bright candidates than the rest. Relegation to the bottom of the league constantly threatens this college, and in these days of "Widening Access" even applicants from bog-standard comprehensives are welcome if their presence can avert this fate. They no longer need to be male or middle class, but it helps if they are all-rounders with a good singing voice.

Another last chance saloon are, sadly, the original women's colleges, even if they have gone mixed. Low down in the academic league tables because they are relatively poor and few of their dons are eminent enough to set the exam questions, places like New Hall and Newnham in Cambridge and Somerville and St. Hilda's in Oxford can't afford to turn away too many applicants. Before you opt for one of them, though, read the chapter on Oxbridge women.

BUT WILL SHE BE HAPPY THERE?

Some colleges can be hell for some students. Many a young Oxbridge feminist has been furious to discover that her lovely college gardens are infested by rugby players barking sexist ditties and trying to bear hug every passing girl. A quiet, non-drinking male student will loathe to share his JCR with teams of drunken rowers listening to what one such wretch described to me as horrible Welsh Indie Rock. If you want to avoid these experiences, don't pick Oriel College, Oxford or Peterhouse, Cambridge. These are the favourite haunts of sporty boys from small public schools.

If, on the other hand, you combine academic interests with a real talent for a major college sport, you'll find a warm welcome in such a place. Don't worry about your background; a winning rugby team knows no class distinction.

This is not to say that you will feel the same way. Your rugby mates may, after all, be pretty brainless and only got in because their school coached them to the hilt. Even in this day and age, a "young barbarian" can still melt the heart of a sporty admissions tutor. So, while your college mates will be half-heartedly aiming for a third in some undemanding subject, you might be trying to pick up top professional skills and a good degree in between games. Such misfits have spoilt the university experience of quite a few male working class students. Female ones tend to cope. Perhaps girls just get on with life.

Some colleges can, on first sight, seem far more scary than others, but don't assume that the grandest places are the ones you'll feel most uncomfortable in. A good example is Oxford's by now much mentioned Balliol College. This has age, beauty, money and a stunning academic record, yet works very well for some state school students. One of the reasons is that here a very sharp mind really is all that counts. The other reason is the presence of a large number of foreign students, mostly from continental Europe. Thanks to a blissful ignorance of the British class system and its linguistic quirks, this group somehow defuses the tension between the two English camps.

In fact, most Oxbridge students, whatever their background, display a remarkable affection for their own college. As long as the place actually has a substantial state school presence, even people from non-university backgrounds tend to cosily settle in. Fears about being among all those terribly posh kids often fade as soon as students meet. Very few privately educated students have parents who are aristocrats or millionaires. So, don't be automatically put off by a college's reputation as popular with public school cricketers or piano-playing southern girls. There will be some such students about, but they might well be nice, and outnumbered too.

Having said this, a good social life in your college is undoubtedly harder to build if you are black or from a solidly working class background. Breaking into a group of students who may have known one another from age six (which can be true of comprehensive school girls from smart urban areas, as well as for public school boys) sometimes does feel like mission impossible. And you'll be more tempted to give up, convinced you are being snubbed, if you're the only girl from Moss Side or an Afro-Caribbean boy from Liverpool.

More often than not, such fears are unjustified. These people are just used to hanging out together. They also tend to study different subjects and so will gradually grow apart. By the end of the first year, students usually have far more in common with those struggling through the same enormous reading lists than with their bosom buddy from nursery school. Their best friend now will be the person they share their tutorials, seminars or college microwave with. Others bond over drama, student politics, football or darts – though if you're really shy, getting past the bonding process can feel like a long wait.

HOW TO BE HAPPY

Happiness at Oxbridge is often a function of understanding what you are meant to do there. The answer is certainly not just "get a degree". Instead, dons vaguely mumble about wishing you to explore both different ideas and different activities in the company of your peers. Foreigners are often best at translating such waffle. In his wonderful account of how he made his way from a Burma guerilla camp to Trinity College, Cambridge, Pascal Khoo Thwe says that being there was not simply about competing; nor was it just a means to an end:

> It was a place where you were given the gift of an "interval", a time of leisure, where you did not have to make up your minds about your beliefs, and learned as much from conversation as from lectures and books.

(*From the Land of Green Ghosts*, Flamingo, 2002)

Annie, a giggly Danish friend who came to stay with me after doing a placement year at a very famous Oxford college, put the same thing rather more simply: "They have all these funny clubs and societies where students meet. At first I couldn't understand why, but then I thought it's a bit like Legoland: you're meant to play with all the little houses, not just to swot. The university put them there as a kind of practice for grown life, I think."

87

So, try and persevere in finding new playmates. Beth, a nurse's daughter from Northern Ireland recalls that she walked into Fresher's Week at Hertford College, Oxford, shaking with nerves, but forced herself to think: "Excellent, here's 115 potential new friends."

It worked for her, but if your college is really useless at supplying friends, remember that there is always the university. Just treat the college like a plush but rather boring hotel and join the university's student union, drama group or choir. Talk to people in your faculty lab, offer to write for a university mag, volunteer for charity work or political campaigns. There are over 10,000 people roughly your age and ability in the place. Surely, you are not so unique that you have nothing in common with any of them?

This is not to deny that college life does stink for some. In fact, I have spent many hours over the years listening to former students who have been utterly miserable. Until the mid 1980s, this was almost entirely a matter of class: the tone at Oxbridge was set by a wealthy, privately educated majority of students and those without their kind of manners or money had to be quite assertive to survive. Also, quite a few of the older college dons were horrible snobs or misogynists.

But we're talking about your parents' or even grandparents' generation. If an Oxbridge student is constantly unhappy now, there may well be other factors. Often, these are personal, and it is worth knowing that student counselling and health care are pretty good. Both Oxford and Cambridge have come to accept that students can be badly thrown by events happening elsewhere: it is hard to settle into college life when you've learnt that your best friend is now sharing a hammock with your former lover in Goa, the family dog is sick or your father has left home to have the op and become a lap dancer.

Alternatively, a student may just be doing the wrong thing. One exceptionally bright working class student tracked by Professor Freeman in a study of gifted children had been used to being always top of her class. Finding herself surrounded by people who were at least equally smart, her response was to rush back to her books. Rather than enjoy the company of her intellectual peers, she tried to out-work them until she collapsed with exhaustion.

Depression can also be the result of a student not acknowledging that she really needs more cash. Which brings us to yet another way of choosing a college.

PICKING FOR FINANCIAL SURVIVAL

Today no student drops out of Oxbridge due to genuine poverty. The poorest have university grants, currently between £500 and £4,000 a year, as well as loans designed to cover the basics. Many also receive a college grant, bursary or scholarship.

Older, richer colleges, though, can be rather more generous, and this can affect how well you do academically. A student needing to improve her French language skills because she is studying the subject, but has never been abroad, will have no trouble securing a travel grant from one of the older colleges. These may also offer substantial bursaries for book purchases. College rents there may be kept low by subsidies and students will usually be able to live in for three years, rather than move into more expensive private housing after the first year.

In addition, there are many other types of bursaries, often funded by grateful former students. Some are essentially a cash prize for a good essay on a specific topic dear to the donor's heart. Others are designed to fund small scale research projects. All colleges make provision for helping needy students, but the older the college, the wealthier it is likely to be and the more generous its help. For instance, the average hardship grant in 2002 was £560 at Oxford's ancient Christ Church College, but only £45 at the far newer Keble College up the road. If many students at a college are well off, moreover, there will be little competition for such grants.

So, the poorer you are, the more you might want to apply to a grand old Oxford college like Merton, which has an annual endowment income of £2 million, or to Christ Church, academically ranked 7th in 2002, which earns a whopping £4.5 million a year from investments alone. Another wealthy Oxford college, St. John's, used to own so much land in the 1930s that people claimed you could walk from Oxford to Cambridge without ever leaving college property. (The Cambridge equivalents of these rich old colleges are Trinity, Gonville & Caius and Corpus Christi.)

There is, of course, another and even more crucial consequence of a college's wealth: it will be able to attract the best, and therefore most highly paid academics – albeit sometimes in exchange for a promise that they won't have to teach beginners. Its libraries too will be better stocked and they may have a smaller students per tutor ratio. Wealth and academic glory often go hand in hand, at least in Oxbridge.

PICKING FOR POWER

While Oxford and Cambridge like to present themselves, at least to the general public, as purely scholastic institutions, they are also something quite different. Politicians, industrialists and journalists will regularly make the weekend pilgrimage to their old college, rather like a medieval lord would visit his fiefdom's learned abbot or a 19th century Jewish industrialist his wise old rabbi.

This is not merely a sentimental journey. While sipping port from cut-glass goblets in a college's panelled dining room, the Oxbridge men – rarely women – who run the country will discuss public affairs, form alliances and take crucial decisions. They will also graciously mix with a few promising undergraduates brought by their tutors. This (to the entirely justified fury of non-Oxbridge graduates) is where to pick up news of top jobs coming up, of Government reshuffles and of business developments that may shake the finances of ordinary people.

But which colleges hold the power key? The answer used to be that there were two: Peterhouse, Cambridge, which produced much of Margaret Thatcher's various Cabinets, plus Magdalen, Oxford, the intellectual cradle of most Prime Ministers. To this had to be added All Souls, a postgraduate college which raised editors for The Times.

Times, though, are a'changing. Many of today's top Labour figures have bonded during their years at Carlton TV rather than at Oxbridge. Even the reputation of Magdalen, Oxford, as the cradle of political leaders is fading. Former Conservative leader William Hague did go there, but his successor, Iain Duncan Smith, studied in Italy and Michael Howard at Peterhouse, Cambridge. Theresa May was at St. Hugh's and Ann Widdecombe at Lady Margaret Hall, Oxford. Margaret Thatcher went to Somerville, then an Oxford women's college. David Cameron studied for his Oxford degree at Brasenose. Labour is not quite redbrick either: Prime Minister Tony Blair was at St. John's College, Oxford, Patricia Hewitt at Newnham, Cambridge, Geoff Hoon at Jesus, Cambridge and David Miliband at Corpus Christi, Oxford. Charles Clarke's former college is King's, Cambridge.

So, any Oxbridge college can kick-start your political career, though it helps if you also get elected President of the Oxford or Cambridge Union. This, as said earlier, is the university's main debating society – not to be confused with that champion of under-graduate interests, the students' union. Anyone is free to become a member of OU or CU by paying the membership fee, if necessary by instalments.

PICKING FOR BEAUTY

Budding aesthetes in flowing silk scarves will have no problem picking their perfect college: it has to be St. John's, Cambridge, with its Bridge of Sighs spanning the river Cam, or Christ Church, Oxford, with its Tom Tower, Christopher Wren's masterpiece. While other colleges spoilt their appearance by adding on nasty modern fripperies such as labs and snack bars, both remain pure examples of Britain's Classical architecture. There can be no more perfect backdrop for the photo the aesthetes plan to email to their world-wide chat-group on English life.

On the other hand, one future architect I met confidently opted for Robinson College, Cambridge, a 1970s redbrick structure. An outstanding example of the modernist approach seeking to mix clear lines and varieties of shape, it is much loved by its residents, mainly future research scientists and veterinary surgeons. Robinson is also unique in Oxbridge by having one feature perhaps more conducive to beauty than anything else: students' en suite bathrooms.

7

Accessing Oxbridge

What can make a student decide against applying to Oxford or Cambridge at the last moment, sometimes even after he has found a course he really likes, is not what he knows about these places, but what he thinks he does. One 2002 survey, for instance, found that many comprehensive school pupils put the number of Oxbridge undergraduates from their background at below 10 per cent. The actual figure, mentioned before, is 55 per cent.

Others have heard strange and deeply off-putting rumours. One boy proudly told his father's boss of his university plans, only to be told "Cambridge? Well, it wouldn't have been my thing. Do they make you wear them jackets with the long tails only in class or do you have to wear them to the shops as well?" (For the record, Oxbridge students wear jeans during the day, and dark suits or two-piece outfits to formal occasions. It is Eton pupils who pre-pay for a lifetime of privilege by wearing the naff tailcoats at school.)

Schools deal with Oxbridge during careers advice, but this can mean anything. The sixth form head may well give your son a detailed pep talk, based on his own Oxbridge years or on a teacher's workshop attended at one of the two universities. Such a talk will help a pupil understand what is special about studying there, as well as cover entry requirements, subject options and the tutorial system. At best, it will also address the most common fears: "Can I afford it?" and "Is it for people like me?"

More likely, though, your son will have the following experience:

Teacher (slightly rushed as she has to explain university choice to 90 first-generation higher education applicants before tea): Well, John, you've had excellent GCSEs and your AS level work is going well. Have you considered Oxbridge?

Pupil: No, not really.

Teacher (brightly): Well, you might want to. Anyway, let me know what you decide. You might also find a leaflet on the sixth form notice board, if nobody has taken it down. I'll get you the application form in case you'll want it.

Pupil (keen to end this obvious waste of time): Sure.

The above conversation, reported to me by quite a few people, is the end of many a promising Oxbridge career. How, though, can your son, who has never given a moment's thought to Oxbridge or, worse, tried to find it on the map, work out whether he wants to spend three of the most important years of his life there? One obvious answer seems to lie in a family visit.

WHAT NOT TO DO (ON A SUNDAY)

Having seen the odd colour snap of your son's potential university, you may think that it is enough to let the place speak for itself. Just set aside a Sunday afternoon, check out the train time table or pile into the car. Surely, walking through a pretty town like Cambridge or Oxford will help the boy make up his mind?

I once tried this myself, with my goddaughter. A 17 year old with body piercings and a prediction of top A-levels, she needed only a bribe of double pocket money before agreeing to tag along. While her mother and I then gushed over every gothic building and ornate bridge before settling down to a traditional cream tea in a wood-panelled shop, she sulked on an iron bench outside one of Oxford's most famous colleges. It was raining and, as this was term time, strangers were banned from entering colleges or libraries, even for a quick glimpse. On the drive back, the girl summed up her views: Oxford was boring and old, as well as weird, three of the worst traits in her value chart. She put Sussex at the top of her UCAS list as soon as she had walked through her parent's front door.

A disaster? Not quite. She had some regrets in her student days, feeling she would have been more challenged at Oxford, but ended up with a First and is now a young financial journalist. Her best friend, who did choose Oxford, has yet to settle into the perfect job. Best not to get too worked up about university choice.

How else can you help your son or daughter to make up their mind? Luckily, you don't need to. There is a glut of publicly funded projects designed to do just that.

ACCESS, OUTREACH AND ALL THEIR FRIENDS AND RELATIONS

Public concern that too many students still come from the same class background has generated a veritable supermarket of widening access initiatives. Most of the Oxbridge-linked ones are funded directly by the Department of Education, which between 2000 and alone spent around £2.4 million a year on three projects, called Aspirations, Summer Schools and Widening Participation.

Oxbridge also draws applicants from the various Excellence projects aimed at promoting higher education among inner city pupils, which is funded by the Department to the tune of £63 million per year.

The result has been a myriad of university projects under ever-changing names. Most, but not all, of Cambridge Access activities are now run under the Widening Participation label. Part of Oxford Access has become Outreach. Excellence in Cities, the Department of Education scheme which used to run an Oxbridge link-up, has been re-launched as Excellence Challenge.

These initiatives which, for simplicity's sake, I shall call Access, are aimed at a wide range of targets from primary school children to FE students and from mature students to ethnic minorities. They are also run by a variety of bodies. Admissions departments, university faculties, colleges and students unions have projects of their own, aimed at encouraging specific groups of potential students. The Department of Education and at least one education trust run separate schemes.

Some of the most imaginative Oxbridge projects are student-led, and the enthusiasm which these young men and women exhibit for their university is so great it makes you think of those bright-eyed moppets in Disneyland ads. Many talk with almost touching grati-tude about the life and opportunities given to them.

So, how does your teenager find out whether he, too, might want to try for Disneyland? The answer is that he can do so in a dozen ways and, even better, without cramping his style. Initially, the idea was that teachers would suggest Oxbridge schemes to suitable pupils, but this has now changed. Finding that many overstretched schools did not respond, Oxbridge has started to encourage indivi-dual pupils to book themselves in. Those interested in what Cambridge university has on offer will find most details on the Target Schools, Widening Participation or Open Days websites listed at the end of this book. Oxford's main Access projects can be tracked down in the same way.

If you're a student interested in a particular course, say Law, you may want to phone the Law faculty of Oxford or Cambridge directly. This will lead you to discover that they not only hold an annual "Law conference" in which sixth formers explore the subject, but may also have a Law lecturer giving talks in your town. Below you'll find a selection of what else is on offer.

A TASTE OF OXFORD

Oxford runs some 100 open days each year, targeted at different groups and aimed at dispelling different anxieties. At some, students chat to visiting school kids about university life in terms of workload, nightlife and general atmosphere. An growing number of events, though, focus on academic fields such as science, or on individual subjects. Visitors can find out which subject areas will be covered by a course and how it will be taught. Talks are often held in colleges keen to increase their state school intake and include tea and biscuits, lunch and a tour of Oxford. All this, including the meals, is entirely free, and you can get even your travel paid through your school. Some colleges even welcome accompanied parents.

Oxford also organises events covering similar ground in towns which have traditionally sent very few students. Both open days and the more course-oriented information days usually include workshops on the admissions process for visiting teachers.

In addition, Oxford runs a school visiting scheme in which dozens of its state school students go and tell pupils about their university experience. The assumption behind this project and most others is that state school students don't apply in large enough numbers because they feel shy. Much of it is designed to break down myths and stereotypes about the university being a posh place and replacing them with a vision of Oxford as a world in which students from all backgrounds enjoy life in a "work hard and play hard" sort of way.

In this spirit, questions on open days are often taken by a working class student. If you ever wondered what it's like for a girl from a mining town to share a tutorial with someone who misses her horse, here you will find out: apparently, it is absolutely fine, because she might well share your enthusiasm for philosophy and Garage. And if she doesn't there are, literally, thousands of other people to make friends with. Most Oxbridge students, like the horse lover and you, will have gone to state schools. (Surprised? Given the current level of school fees, few parents can afford to buy their privately-educated daughter a horse.)

What isn't on offer from Target Schools is much help with preparations for the Oxbridge interview, but even so these are useful projects because they are open to all. Although its student

95

organisers advertise events by writing to all schools and FE colleges in February, no teacher involvement is required. Pupils whose school has not organised a day trip for them can book themselves in directly through the website www.targetschools.com.

A GLIMPSE OF CAMBRIDGE

Cambridge admissions staff and student groups run projects very similar to those at Oxford. There are open days and information days, visits designed to counter students' misconceptions about the university and academic introductions to unfamiliar subjects or courses. Some open days are specifically aimed at students attending further education colleges or access courses, rather than comprehensives, grammars or private schools. There is also at least one event targeted at ethnic minority students.

Excellence Challenge, a Department of Education scheme designed to raise aspirations, funds inner city school initiatives that bring their students into contact with dons from various universities, including Cambridge. The idea is to offer more young people a taste of university subjects such as or Philosophy or Engineering, plus information about the application process.

Teachers sometimes have to drag their pupils to such "stuffy" events, but do encourage your son. To be gently introduced to a new subject by a brilliant thinker in their field can be a life-changing experience, even if the student does not end up at Cambridge or Oxford. To find out whether your son's school is participating, look at the government website www.dfes.gov.uk/excellencechallenge.

Cambridge is also involved in running special introduction days in education action zones, which are usually the neglected parts of big cities. These aim to convince pupils that the university welcomes applicants of all sorts and offer courses that might be of particular interest to them. Some information about course contents may be included and there is ample time for questions and answers. Even larger events, open to all Year 12 students, are organised by Lifetime Careers, a joint venture with Oxford. To widen their appeal, some of these events are held in football stadiums. Book for this and other Cambridge initiatives by contacting access@cao.cam.ac.uk.

SUMMER SCHOOLS

A further inroad is provided by the summer schools run annually at both universities. Many of these are organised by the Sutton Trust, an educational charity which encourages able Year 12 pupils from a poor, non-university background to aim high. Places go to "plausible applicants for university places with a minimum of five A/A grades at GCSE".

Sutton Trust events last five days and aim to introduce participants to non-school subjects such as Medicine, or to the university version of other subjects, through lectures and workshops carefully tailored to their age group. This is combined with sightseeing and various leisure activities.

These much praised events are run by Oxbridge academics and are completely free: the Trust covers all travel to and from the venue, food and accommodation and also trips and activities. Pupils can apply directly to this scheme, but are advised first to visit the Trust's website, http://www.suttontrust.com.

The Higher Education Funding Council for England (HEFCE) has set up a series of residential summer schools at universities including Oxford and Cambridge, which are aimed at Year 11 students from non-university families. Run under the umbrella of the government's *Aim Higher* scheme, they offer pupils a general introduction to the academic world, including sessions about costs, degree subjects, college societies and the prospects of graduates. The scheme is restricted to specially chosen schools to ensure that only pupils from the most disadvantaged sectors benefit. Anyone unsure whether their school is participating (or keen to go although they have not been picked) can check out www.dfes.gov.uk/excellencechallenge. Cambridge also runs other summer schools aimed at mature students, ethnic minorities and pupils at FE colleges, details of which can be found on its website.

Shorter stays can offer valuable insights into the most avidly fought-over course subjects. Law and Medicine weekends allow pupils to find out not just what such a course would involve, but also what qualities and skills each of these departments seeks.

COLLEGE INITIATIVES

Quite a few individual colleges at Oxford and Cambridge also run their own schemes, either in cooperation with *Aim Higher* or under their own *Target School* s label. Some of these are focused on areas of low educational attainment. Jesus College, Cambridge, which has a partnership link with Newcastle, organised a 2003 visit by seventy Year 10 students from the town to the university.

Other Cambridge Colleges are working with specific local education authorities in deprived areas. For instance, St. Johns' College has a scheme in Lambeth and Clare College in Tower Hamlets, while Sidney Sussex and Fitzwilliam are active in Greater Manchester and the North West. For pupils wanting to take the initiative, many colleges also hold a free open day to which anyone who has booked can come.

Some initiatives are based on a more scatter-gun and at times rather defensive approach. When Brasenose, one of the richest colleges in Oxford, was publicly criticised because its state school intake was (just) below half, its Warden responded in The Guardian of 26th January 2003 by revealing that it was now involved in no fewer than 51 events aimed at recruiting state school pupils.

So, if your son likes the sound of an Oxbridge college, the best way forward is for him to ring up its admissions office and ask whether there is a project which would allow him to have a closer look. Chances are there is and that someone is actually being paid to make pupils like him feel welcome.

SHADOWING A STUDENT

Both Oxford and Cambridge also run "shadowing schemes" in which interested pupils can follow an Oxbridge student around for a couple of days. The visitors get to sit in on lectures and tutorials, as well as visit a student pub, in order to find out how that mysterious creature really lives.

This approach can be immensely reassuring. Apart from proving to the young visitor that many of the turreted buildings contain not just libraries and labs but also state-of-the-art bars, cinemas and snooker halls, talking to a student guide can allay deeper anxieties. The guide may reveal that even Cambridge has a branch of HMV, point out those local businesses which give skint undergraduates part-time jobs and, by his very normality, suggest that most Oxbridge students are neither geniuses nor geeks. To become a Cambridge shadow, go to www.applytocambridge.com. Potential Oxford shadows should look up www.oxford-access.org.

DOES ACCESS WORK?

The honest answer is: some of it does. Projects involving a visit to Oxford or Cambridge are definitely worth doing. This is because they enable hundreds of pupils each year to spend anything between an afternoon and five days in a different world and introduce them to exciting new fields. While there is a wide choice, subject-focused events are of most use. Once on site, a visitor can poke the university's ancient chairs, find out whether a cutting-edge interest area will be covered by its course or even ask for a few useful reading suggestions.

Any Oxbridge visit, though, will be of some advantage to the student invited back for an interview. Walking up to those ivy-clad towers and stained glass windows next time should feel less like approaching Dracula's castle and more like returning to a place of nice memories like Blackpool or Benidorm. And a relaxed interviewee is more likely to impress the admissions tutor.

The hometown events held outside the university may be less trouble to get to, but they lack this psychological hook. Your daughter might come away eager to apply and with a clearer idea of the various courses, but seeing Oxbridge for the first time at the interview can still put her off. So, do encourage her to apply for a visiting scheme. If the one she is accepted for does not offer academic details (perhaps because it is a shadowing scheme) there is nothing that says that she cannot also attend a local open day to find out how, for instance, Cambridge Physics is taught.

On the other hand, an intellectually very secure pupil who is just wondering which course to pick may benefit most from the introductory workshops offered by different college dons on their subject.

Do the projects also ensure that "the brightest and best" succeed? This is more doubtful, despite the great effort put into them, especially by the unpaid student volunteers. One reason is the total absence of talent spotting. You may have a young Isaac Newton in the family, but nobody at Access is in the business of finding out. Although university lecturers are involved in many events and may spend up to a week with a small group of pupils, they are not expected to even guess at an individual's ability. The Access brief is strictly to encourage applications.

This means that while your son might be a deep thinker asking super-smart questions in his summer school, no formal note has to be taken of this. So, when it comes to having his application considered, he is in the potluck bowl with everyone else. Rumour has it that the odd don may quietly suggest to a particularly impressive participant that he should perhaps consider an application to her college, but this actually is against the rules and as far as it goes.

The opposite approach is taken by America's most prestigious academic institutions. Over there, the top universities' talent scouts visit schools and summer camps not to encourage the most doubtful kids, but to identify the most talented ones. The latter are then asked whether, subject to passing their SATs, they would honour the university by becoming one of its students. Which situation would you rather be in?

The main flaw of Oxbridge Access, though, is the underlying assumption that the problem lies with the pupils themselves. The schemes, I was repeatedly told, were necessary because state school pupils "are hesitant to apply because of low self esteem". So, the stated aim is to give them the confidence to apply – not to ensure that more state school pupils actually get in. Access does not even have a numerical target when it comes to raising the proportion of state school entrants, rather than just the number of applicants, to a more representative level.

When I asked Access officials if widening participation might not also require a change in the current entrance procedures, the response was embarrassment. People emphasized that they were not campaigning for any such thing, heaven forbid. Both paid Access staff and student volunteers insisted that entry remains a matter entirely for the university's admissions tutor. They had no views on whether the system was fair or could be improved. Pupils' university choice was all that mattered – and was clearly the only thing they could influence.

So, Access concentrates on broadening the field of applicants. Colleges keen to admit more state school pupils, and especially more working class ones, now have a much bigger pool to draw from. Many take advantage of it. Access cannot, however, force a specific college to abandon the idea that Winchester public school is the main source of intelligent human beings nor curb its enthusiasm for fresh-faced kids from genteel country towns. Colleges are independent bodies or, to put it disrespectfully, college admissions tutors are a bit like horses: you can take them to the water, but you cannot actually make them drink.

Government expenditure of some £10 million on Access in the four years leading up to 2003 had little impact. In fact, the proportion of state school students entering Oxford actually dropped by two per cent that year. Cambridge acceptance figures for this group rose by the corresponding percentage, but the cart remained stuck. By 2005, only 53.4% of new Oxford undergraduates came from state school backgrounds, down 0.4 percentage points from the previous year. At Cambridge, the corresponding figure was 56.8%, which was a little better, but still 0.1 percentage points down.

What this means is that the two universities' annual intake has been made up of roughly 55 per cent state school students since 1999. As the benchmark figure which the government had set for Oxbridge is 75 per cent, progress could fairly be described as non-existent.

WHY ACCESS IS WORTH DOING

Despite their undoubted flaws, Access projects, which vary greatly in focus and scale, work for some teenagers. Merely attending an Access event will gain your son some brownie points if he decides to apply and he might well do so because Oxford or Cambridge now seem less alien. The rest depends on brains, careful subject and college choice, good interview preparation and a bit of luck. Reassured that Oxbridge is the place for them, boys and girls from urban comprehensives and rural council estates handle the entrance process right and get in.

But how many do? There are no official data about the success rate of pupils attending the big Oxbridge Access events. It is not even clear what proportion decide to apply after attending. Sutton Trust schemes run in Cambridge in 1999 resulted in nearly a third of participants getting in. Students running a smaller, more socially focused scheme, which includes expert talks on general interview skills, told me that between 3 and 5 per cent of their pupils were now Oxbridge students. Of those attending a medical summer school, for which all participants had been intellectually cherry-picked, 10 per cent, or five out of fifty, were accepted.

In other words, while such figures give applicants some hope, they don't exactly amount to a cast-iron guarantee of success. So, don't let your teenage whizkid get too fixated on the idea of spending the next three years doing PPE in a manor with its own tennis court. He needs an attractive second choice, just in case. Greater certainty would be nice, but it may have to wait until Oxbridge introduces new entrance quotas (if it ever does) or an entrance process that works equally well for all.

8

The paper trail

The most crucial thing to do, if you'd like to study at Oxbridge, is to actually apply. This involves submitting a batch of forms, some but not all online. You will need to do all this in good time. Don't even dream of leaving the job to the night before the deadline. Try to paste up or photo-copy everything you plan to send. This way you can write draft versions first and also mark what documents or information you still have to ferret out.

Oxbridge candidates usually have to supply five separate bits of information, six if they are applying through the *Cambridge Special Access* or *Oxford Additional Support* scheme for disadvantaged students. Cambridge applicants also need to send a photograph. There is a further online form for students required to take a pre-interview test at their school, which includes everyone applying for Medicine, Veterinary Medicine or Law.

Daunting as this may sound, most of the information requested is perfectly straightforward: what you are being asked for are relevant personal details. Surely, somebody in your family remembers your date of birth? The exam details requested are also simple enough.

Candidates still at school will normally be supplied with UCAS, Oxford and Cambridge application forms. Once you have looked at yours, you might want to approach a teacher or careers advisor to help you with the factual bits (this is not a job for parents). External candidates will have to assemble exam information from the records they have kept.

Still, there is quite a lot else to do, and we'll go through it bit by bit.

FORMS TO FILL IN
To be considered for a university place, you will have to comply with a whole series of information requests:

1. UCAS Information
The first thing to fill in is the main body of the UCAS form, in which you give your personal details and list all the university courses you

have picked. If you are member of NAGTY, don't forget to tick the relevant box! You can currently list up to six, but if you are applying for Medicine, Dentistry, Veterinary Medicine or Veterinary Science, this drops to only four. Most of the information requested here is of a pretty general kind, as pointed out above, and advice on how to fill it in can be found on www.ucas.co.uk, together with the form.

2. The UCAS Personal Statement

The UCAS form, which changes slightly each year, also requires you to provide two longer bits of writing. One of these is your Personal Statement. This is your very own promo, in which you are trying to sell yourself as the kind of student any course leader might like. Are you hard-working, imaginative, a born linguist or a lover of abstract thought? The resulting document, which should be upbeat, persuasive and perfectly spelled, must adhere strictly to the word limit set.

The best way to achieve this is to write crisply, without labouring your points. You don't need to use old-fashioned language in order to communicate with an old university, but make sure your grammar is correct. Oxbridge candidates need to be a little creative in what they write, so don't just adapt the dull Personal Statements found on the internet. This is especially important if you are applying for an Arts course.

While one way in is to describe how you approached a school project or A-level topic, keep in mind that more is expected here: you must show a strong, active, academic interest, ideally in subject areas beyond the syllabus. What got you interested and how are you pursuing them? What are you hoping to understand and what have you already learned? Do make sure that the field you express most interest in is related to your course choice.

This is also the place to mention some wider but still course-related activities, so for heaven's sake don't forget that you are involved in the Maths Olympiad. Try to point out what skills you have developed as a result and don't be too modest:. Describing your academic side does not count as showing off.

Some factors mentioned can be personal: medical students, for instance, are often led towards a particular scientific interest by an illness in their own family. Mainly, though, this is an opportunity to mention the book(s), article, play, lecture, etc. that prompted your current academic interest. With a bit of luck, you will be asked to expand on this information at the interview. Students need to be quite specific here, so ensure you give the correct names and titles.

It is also sensible to give the reader some idea of your home circumstances if they affect your work. Parental unemployment, poverty, homelessness or the need to care for an invalid relative are in this category. Try to avoid vague phrases if you would like to convey the personal consequences. Writing that you spend much time helping your parents tells the interviewer nothing.

Spelling out that you help out on weekday afternoons in the family's Chinese takeaway or each Saturday at the supermarket suggests that you are conscientious in your commitments and have achieved your present academic record against considerable odds. Such information will not demean you in the eyes of the university. Staff really do look for a good mix of candidates and I have met Oxbridge students with backgrounds like these.

So, anything you spend lots of time on might be worth putting in your UCAS form and if it's a bit unusual and memorable, the better. Do, however, beware of exaggeration. Having seen a TV film about George Stephenson does not yet qualify you to state that you are passionate about engineering. Above all, don't mention that impressive-sounding book you were planning to order ages ago. You probably won't manage to read it in time for your interview and fibbing will do you no good. Oxbridge dons have had centuries of practice in getting to the truth.

3. The UCAS Open Reference

The next bit of writing your completed UCAS form must contain is an Open Reference, which is a recommendation from a teacher, tutor or head. This should mainly be a thumbnail sketch of the pupil's qualities, but should also include information on relevant outside interests.

The referee should certainly not only provide a summary of work done at school. She must also make clear how any qualities mentioned are reflected in the pupil's independent academic work. The idea is to impress all the universities listed, but also to ensure that Oxbridge sees the applicant as outstanding and suited to its learning style.

If the student has succeeded in his career so far against personal odds or great poverty, but has not referred to this himself (many disadvantaged students take hardship for granted), this should also be made clear. Generally, a candidate requires more than a cautious endorsement along the lines of "he is a good student and we recommend him". His tutor or head has to be a strong advocate for his cause and a few superlatives like "one of the best" will not go amiss.

Pupils are entitled to see this entry and can even make suggestions, if only to ensure that the Personal Statement and the Open Reference do not repeat the same points. If an Open Reference is particularly tepid, I do feel the candidate deserves an explanation. The referee might be quite right about his academic potential – or quite wrong about the kind of student Oxbridge, especially, might be looking for.

I would certainly not drop the idea of applying there at this point, unless strong reasons were given to me. Because the Oxbridge interview counts for so much, some clever students do get in with a less than brilliant reference.

The Open Reference should also describe the school. If it is not an average comprehensive, some details should be provided on its educational status and the nature of its intake. If a school has the kind of problems that are likely to affect student performance, all universities will want to know.

It is important, though, that anything that might interest Oxbridge is spelled out clearly at this stage. While referees can add an extra bit to their Open Reference when it is sent to its admissions tutors, not all do.

OPEN REFERENCE SAMPLE

John is a very bright and inquisitive student who takes an active interest in Physics well beyond the requirements of the school syllabus. His classroom work has consistently been above A-level standard and truly outstanding in several cases. Independent projects he has undertaken have impressed the staff as well-planned, imaginative and thoroughly researched. John is also involved in an online project by young people trying to set up their own science website. He is the kind of autonomous, interesting pupil we do not see every year.

Moreover, John has maintained this standard despite difficult economic circumstances. Unemployment within the family has required him to take on weekend work. This suggests that he is focused and determined, as well as bright.

Ours is a rapidly improving school, which has just been upgraded to become a Special Language Academy. Most of our intake comes from the local neighbourhood, which is one of the most deprived in London. 50 per cent of our students qualify for free school meals and an even higher proportion (70 per cent) have English as a second language.

So, what are Oxbridge admissions tutors looking for? Well, it depends partly on the individual, college and course, but quite a few of them agreed that the kind of Open Reference which would make them feel particularly well-disposed towards a student might be a variety of this.

4. The Oxford or Cambridge Application Form

In addition to the UCAS form, every Oxbridge candidate also needs to fill in a Cambridge or Oxford Application Form. Again, this seeks out general data, as well as some specific information, such as your college choice.

The Cambridge form also asks for an Additional Personal Statement, called Additional Information in the Oxford form. This is yet another promo, but one in which the student needs to create a closer link between his A-levels, his interests and his chosen Oxbridge course. If that course is rather different from the ones he picked elsewhere, he'll also have to explain why. Oxbridge likes to feel that the course you have chosen is the love of your life. Any dithering between the respective attractions of Maths and French and you could be dismissed as a wrong 'un.

Filling in this bit is not mandatory, as your UCAS Personal Statement will be passed on to Oxbridge together with the Open Reference, but it is wise. Candidates who can show how everything in their personal history leads up to their Oxbridge course tend to do best. You may find it reassuring to know that the Oxbridge statement will not be shown to any of the other universities you're applying to.

Style, too, particularly matters in the Oxbridge forms. Clear, concise English goes down well with science, as well as with arts tutors. The fact that you are applying to an old university does not mean that they want you to go all stuffy or formulaic on them. Try to describe yourself in your own voice. This can mean a lot of rewriting at the draft stage, so set aside a few evenings for it.

(Oxford forms are available to external applicants from
www.admissions.ox.ac.uk/forms.
Cambridge forms can be downloaded from
www.cam.ac.uk/cambuniv/ugprospectus/applying).

5. Candidate's Work Sample

A university interested in a candidate may also want to see one or two samples of her work in the subject she is planning to study or a related one (which can mean History, if she is applying for a course in PPE or SPS). This sample can be a completed project, an extended essay or a piece of work done in class during a 45 minute test. Although the school can send any of these, admissions tutors like you to include class work. Its advantage, they feel, is that one can be sure no one else has been involved in producing it. The work sample(s) should be sent with a cover sheet filled in by the applicant and a teacher.

6. Oxford or Cambridge special forms for disadvantaged applicants

Candidates from disadvantaged schools and homes (or their teachers) are advised to fill in a special form. This needs to be sent to the university or college they are applying to. The Cambridge Special Access Scheme form can be downloaded from www.cam.ac.uk/admissions/undergraduate/apply/csas.pdf. For the Oxford Application Support form, go to www.ox.ac.uk/prospective/support/oasp.doc.

7. Applications forms for pre-interview subject tests

Other online forms need to be filled in and sent off by applicants before the UCAS form. Students hoping to study Medicine at Oxford or Cambridge or Veterinary Medicine at Cambridge need to apply to the BMAT assessment centre at which they'd like to sit the test. Details can be found on www.bmat.org.uk.

Candidates applying for Law at Oxford or Cambridge need to register for the LNAT test before filling in their UCAS form. This test too is taken at a special centre, but you can access the registration system through the LNAT site, www.lnat.ac.uk.

Cambridge Maths candidates expected to take the STEP test need to register with the OCR examination board which administers it. However, candidates for the Cambridge Thinking Skills Assessment Test (TST), may not need to be pre-register at this point. Students hoping to read English, Maths or History at Oxford also need to register for an advance test, to be sat at their school.

Not all of this is free. In 2007, UCAS was charging a £15 processing fee and Oxbridge applicants living in the UK or elsewhere in the EU had to send a cheque or postal order for £10. BMAT candidates living in the UK or elsewhere in the EU were charged £27.30. A UK student unable to afford it could ask the university to be reimbursed.

What students need to be most aware of is that rules about pre-interview tests and the course subjects that require them periodically change. They might even be replaced by one single entrance exam one day. Meanwhile, though, it is crucial to double-check all application details on the Oxford or Cambridge website.

CONQUERING THE PAPER TRAIL

This large list of requirements means that even the most motivated candidate requires a fair bit of assistance from her school. Private schools often manage the whole process for their pupils, right from ordering the forms to editing candidates' draft Personal Statements. Comprehensives which regularly send pupils to Oxbridge also often have a routine in place that smoothes a determined pupil's path. They direct candidates towards the right forms, offer advice on what they might write and ensure that the tight deadlines are met. One such school even arranged for a pupil with unemployed parents to have his processing fee paid out of public funds.

The most disadvantaged candidates, though, also often attend the least Oxbridge-oriented schools, and this is where the system breaks down. Even those few student run Access schemes which offer guidance on the applications process cannot change the fact that teachers may be unsure about what to write, or students unused to filling-in forms. Several student Access campaigners remarked that abolishing the separate Oxbridge paper trail was essential to attract more "non-traditional candidates". What was most urgent, they felt, was the abolition of the £10 extra fee for Oxbridge application. Although candidates could usually afford it, poorer ones resented the cost and concluded from it that the two universities were not for them.

Rereading all those forms, it certainly struck me as amazing that thousands of young people every year managed to return them at all. Even more amazing is that so many of them handled the process skilfully enough to be offered a place. Perhaps this is a measure of the qualities possessed by Oxbridge candidates (one admissions tutor certainly thought so) but, more likely, it reflects the sterling support provided by so many schools. What this book enables you to do is to maximize the value of that support, or to get by without it, in case it is not there.

10

What not to wear to the interview (and other worries)

Having received the completed paperwork, Oxbridge does a month of sorting. As long as your teenager has very good GCSEs, AS grades and A-level predictions, or did very well at a pre-interview test, he is likely to be asked up for an interview. Contrary to popular belief, the majority of candidates are.

While pretending that interviews are cool, your teenager will be thrilled, as well as panicked by this development. You may want him to get on the net immediately and track down the cheapest fare to Oxford or Cambridge, but he has more urgent matters to resolve. The first of these concerns his appearance.

What to wear for the interview can seem like a trivial question, but if both of you are nervous about the event you might be pushed into expenses the family can ill afford. So, forget that Paul Smith suit which you son says is a must-have for the great day. Hardly anybody wears suits for the interview anymore. If the admissions tutors who will interview him really cared about designer clothes, they would be working in a place with far better salary cheques than Oxbridge.

Even the message sent by a certain type of old clothes is out of date. Among the sixth formers fidgeting as they wait for their interview, there will invariably be one confident young man dressed in his father's frayed, greenish-blue tweeds, with the label of the best Cambridge tailor stitched into the silk lining. Unless, however, he also has a lot between the ears, he too will not necessarily get in.

This is not to say that clothes don't matter at all. Turning up in dirty, scruffy gear, with mud-covered shoes indicates a lack of respect for the institution your teenager is supposedly keen to join. So, smart casual is the order of the day. This means jeans are OK but should be in a healthy state, an ironed shirt might be preferable to a T-shirt and if it has to be a T-shirt, let it be plain. Anything imprinted with an even mildly obscene message is absolutely out.

The same basic rule, of course, applies to girls. They don't have to wear skirts, suits or dresses any more, but it probably does no harm to look nice. This does not mean showing masses of bare skin. Even the most heterosexual male don will take this as a sign of desperation.

Gay men, whatever their usual style, are wise to avoid looking wildly camp at their interview. It will only get you typecast as one of those idle, tiresome chaps seeking to relive Brideshead, Evelyn Waugh's great homoerotic novel, set among decadent upper class students in 1920s Oxford.

A light jacket might usefully complete the outfit of someone applying for Medicine or to one of the posher colleges, such as Magdalen, Oxford, or St. John's, Cambridge. Clean hair, needless to say, is a must. I would not go into a panic about nose rings or even tongue studs at this point. Students sporting them can be seen in a few medieval quads, so clearly they are not, in themselves, a cause for rejection.

Lastly, it is crucial that once these basic principles have been absorbed, you leave the choice of interview gear to your daughter or son. It's no good sending someone off to an important interview sobbing: "I look like a prat."

MANNERS

Most people teaching Oxbridge entrance include a smattering of manners. This usually means things like sitting straight, looking (at least occasionally) at the interviewer and speaking clearly, rather than mumbling. Most academics I have interviewed swear blind that manners don't matter one bit. What they are looking for is talent, and if talent bites its nails, that's OK with them.

I am not so sure these academics are telling the whole truth. Obviously, saying "may I sit down", rather than just sinking into the nearest chair is no longer an adequate entrance qualification. Equally obviously, a young Maths genius scratching his back as he rattles down perfect formulas, explanations or equations is rarely shown the door.

However, if your child is not a genius but is still rather bright, then sheer pleasantness may well tip the scale. After all, the interviewer will have to spend at least an hour per week in a small study with the applicant. This is a less attractive proposition if she cannot easily hear what the boy is saying, if she risks being showered with dandruff or if he does not show her any respect.

THE HORRORS OF FISH

One of the key anxieties I have heard expressed are about table manners. Interviewees eat their meals under the medieval eaves of the guest college's often very impressive dining room. One girl recalled her horror when served a whole Dover sole at her first dinner there. How on earth was she going to get this dead body into an edible state?

She need not have worried. The dinners are not a test of whether you'll fit in, just a way of meeting other students. Of course, if your son takes the opportunity to get drunk and abusive instead, it might be assumed that he is not interested.

Still, for the sake of reassurance, you might want to pass on the basic rule: treat the fish like a travel bag to be unzipped; cut round the edge, throw it open so you have two fillets, one of which should have the skeleton attached to it. Lift out the skeleton with knife and fork, put it on the side of the plate and start eating, preferably with your mouth shut.

And, by the way, the slightly deformed looking bits of cutlery next to your plate are the fish knife and fork, to be used much like the other kind. If there are several knives and forks are laid out, start with the ones at the outer edge, working your way inwards, course by course. The same rule applies to the row of shiny wine glasses to the right of your plate.

Conversely, Oxbridge dons keen on wider participation might also wish to learn something new. Fish is eaten by most of the population in the form of easily dissected, breadcrumb covered fillets without bones. Perhaps the hall menu in interview week could take account of this fact.

11

What to expect at the interview

Having resolved the big issues, like whether a micro-skirt qualifies as smart-casual and whether someone living on prawn crackers can define herself as a visiting vegetarian, your jittery daughter can now address herself to secondary matters. In other words, she can start wondering what on earth, Oxbridge actually wants her to go up for. Is the interview just a grown-up conversation?

To many non-university parents it seems logical that being such a grand place, Oxbridge has summoned their teenager primarily to see whether she will fit in. They will consequently advise her to be on her best behaviour and, perhaps, "to treat these great professors with respect".

If you are a teenager, you are likely to interpret this to mean that you must not talk too much, not query anything you will be told or, heaven forbid, disagree explicitly with any, however, objectionable statement. It also suggests that you should sound as posh you can and not dangle your legs in those hideous, freshly polished new shoes. The prospect is dire enough to make you want to miss the train up on the appointed day.

In fact, the purpose of your forthcoming visit is something completely different, so just forget this advice. The word interview is a misnomer which can trip up even the most talented students from non-university backgrounds. What awaits you is a verbal ability test, supplemented in a few subjects and colleges by a short written test, set by the interviewers. Only candidates for a handful of courses also sit a proper, scientific exam, devised by outside experts. It is very much easier to get into Oxbridge once you know what to expect.

Most British universities no longer routinely interview potential students. Only those whose record is defined as "borderline" are still invited in for a chat. That tense half-hour in which a terrified 17 year old, who had probably never talked to adults outside her immediate family before, faced three men in corduroy trousers sitting behind a shabby wooden desk bit the dust in the 1970s. A friend who started his academic career then and is now a sociology professor at a popular university, recalls it as a supremely pointless exercise. "What on earth do you ask somebody applying for a subject they haven't done at school?" he had asked a fellow interviewer. "Beats me," was the reply, "but we always pick the girl with the longest legs."

Oxbridge, though, has an almost religious belief in the magic of the interview. Combined only occasionally with any scientific test, it is meant to establish the candidate's ability to think. Few state school candidates, of course, get this far without such an ability, but displaying it while balancing on a 16th century armchair which keeps tilting backwards can be a different matter. Not all of us spontaneously do our best thinking among the oak-panelled set of a period film.

So, how do you cope, apart from by reminding yourself that you are there because Oxbridge was impressed by your potential? The answer will be obvious to every pint-sized boy scout: be prepared. Find out as much as you can beforehand.

DOING THE GROUNDWORK

Before setting foot in Oxbridge, it is wise to do yet another bit of light reading. Start by skimming through the essay you sent and your personal statement, so you're prepared to talk about anything mentioned there. Look at the university prospectus again, then re-check the course details given on the faculty website. You want to know where you are going and why.

Applicants should also find out in advance what exactly the structure of the interview will be. As every college can choose its own, this can vary considerably. Take two Cambridge candidates: if your daughter applied to read History at King's, she will have to sit a written test at her interview. Her classmate, interviewed for the same subject at Jesus, may get only oral questions. If the invitation or prospectus does not tell you what to expect, it is perfectly OK to ask the college by email.

Next, it helps to know that "the interview" may consist of up to three separate conversations. A candidate is usually interviewed by an admissions tutor, who teaches the course he is applying for, in her college room. A second tutor may be present, especially if the candidate has mentioned a personal interest in a field she is unfamiliar with. For instance, a History tutor expecting a candidate who has done a project on Northern Ireland may bring in an expert on the

Province from another college. An English tutor specialising in Victorian poetry might ask an expert in modern American literature to sit in on the interview with a young Alice Walker fan.

At Oxford, a tutor to whom a good candidate does not appeal will pass him on to a second one, picked in advance. This does not necessarily reflect a low opinion of the lad. Tutors and colleges often have very specific approaches and they like candidates to fit in with them. A few candidates might even be interviewed at a third college in the hope that this, at last, will be the right place for them.

At prospective Cambridge student is more likely to have two interviews at a single college, occasionally even three. Should the two sides not hit it off but the candidate still manages to impress, he'll be put into a "pool" of shortlisted candidates. If another college with places to spare is keen, it will fish him out for a further interview.

Traipsing around between colleges or waiting for one's turn to be seen can be a nerve-wracking experience. So, try and remind your daughter before she leaves that her success does not, in fact, depend on her interview performance alone. The results of any pre-interview tests will certainly count. So will a good open reference from her class teacher, especially if he does not just praise her school work but also broader qualities such as motivation and a willingness to read beyond syllabus needs. The teacher should also mention any obstacles she had to overcome during her schooling.

If your daughter has attended any Access event, even if it was just a morning visit during an open day, this again will count in her favour. Attendance is interpreted as a sign of commitment, yet another quality Oxbridge dons like to encounter. And if she actually visited the same college she is about to be interviewed in and made a good impression there, even better.

Lastly, a good personal statement, crisply written and packed with details about her own interests and achievements, will direct questions towards areas in which she can shine.

TALKING THE TALK

Most interviewers start off gently with small talk unrelated to the course, often while your son is still in the waiting room. This is not the moment to show off, but to connect with a stranger by exchanging featherlight bits of information. The first question, especially if the interviewer is no creative genius, might well be: "Did you have any difficulty getting here?"

All your son is expected to do in return is to keep the ball rolling. "No," by itself, is a conversation killer. "No, but it's quite a long journey up here from Sunderland, what with half the points system not working," will do fine. Such an answer allows his conversation partner to ask questions about the boy's home town, his school or the state of British railway engineering. His answers will help to make him a real person to the interviewer.

Do tell your son not to fret too much about his answers at this stage. Anything said to him while he is still taking off his coat is unlikely to be a test.

Once everyone is seated, talk will rapidly shift to scholarly matters. Interviews have become less rambling and more academically focused, but neither of the academics present is likely to dwell on the candidate's A-level syllabus. Instead, he may want you to talk about a relevant project or bit of coursework you have done. Questions will centre on the research which you did to produce it, the texts consulted and the problems encountered on the way. Not only does this gives you a chance to show how you think, but it confirms that the document was really all your own work. Remember to mention what it is you enjoy about the course-related subject!

Another "easy" question sometimes used to kick-start the actual interview is: "Why did you choose this college (or Oxford)?" Fortunately, the traditional answer, "Daddy spent such a wonderful three years here" is no longer good enough. Still, it is probably best to avoid total honesty, if that would mean saying: "Because you're rich enough to give me a decent hardship grant."

A better idea would be to suggest that you had heard that it was best for a specialist field which you are becoming interested in, say Medical Physics or Civil Engineering. Candidates who have done their net research might even add that their interest in this field was prompted by a piece in *New Scientist,* contributed by one of their own dons. Remember, you can find this inside dirt on the college website!

Be cautious about bringing up your own ambitions here. Magdalen College, Oxford, has indeed educated most British Prime Ministers, but "because I want to run the next government" is still the wrong answer. While this might be true, your university chances will be far better if you focus on the academic training the college can offer. True, Magdalen has unbelievable connections and an old boy network that seems to run the world, but to mention this would be rude, proof that you don't understand the subtle strategies needed for political careers.

There is a further reason, of course, to talk about academic work, not networking: your future dons are human beings. They like to spend their time with people who enjoy their teaching and give something back, rather than regard their tutorials merely as stepping stones to power.

In any case, such questions mark the end of the warm-up. After that, things tend to get rather pacey. Transmogrifying into a more paunchy, less well-dressed version of Jeremy Paxman, the interviewer will start checking what kind of things, in or outside your field, you can understand, explain or make sense of. Now, question might follow question, without any feedback about whether you hit the spot.

This style can be quite disconcerting for some candidates. State schools have in the last two decades gone out of their way to communicate with students in ways that build confidence, rather than just implant knowledge. They emphasize the positive, try to be soft on delicate young egos.

Many Oxbridge interviewers, on the other hand, believe in the rapid fire approach, in tough questioning not interspersed with any reassurance or praise. After all, they have scores of candidates to see within a couple of days. By pressing on, they hope to quickly discover hidden strengths, expose weaknesses, get to the core.

This is not the moment for a candidate to feel shy. No intelligent guess or opinion is likely to harm her chances of acceptance. What matters is to take a stand, then back it up by giving good reasons or facts. Often, she will be invited to apply familiar theories or principles to new areas. A History candidate, for instance, might be asked the following question: if the appeasement of Hitler was a bad thing in 1938, would we be right now to appease North Korea's dictator?

Fortunately, the girl is not expected to issue the final ruling on this world-shaking matter. The interviewers are trying to extend her understanding of the subject by their questions, not trip her up. A promising candidate will be happy to speculate on whether the theory behind the first scenario might be effective in the second. The skill the interviewer is fishing for here is an Oxbridge favourite: lateral thinking, known to members of the computer generation as "mental cut-and-paste."

It is also important to realise that candidate and interviewer are playing a subtle game. A Politics tutor, for instance, might choose to put forward a quite outrageous proposition: "Could it not be argued that dictatorship is a natural form of government suited to many nations?"

A young candidate might seriously consider walking out at this point in horror. Are these ghastly old fogeys the people she had considered studying with? Best to suppress this emotion. This is not the time to run, but to hold your ground. Chances are, the tutor is merely playing devil's advocate. He'll want to hear why she would disagree, and will expect logical grounds and/or concrete examples. She is being invited to play intellectual tennis and should hit the ball back hard but politely.

Scoring a point here means showing that one would be responsive to this kind of teaching, has respect for its learned practitioners, is articulate and keen enough on the subject to have done some independent reading. The interview is a selection test for the ability to do academic work. Could this candidate, the interviewer asks himself, benefit from tutorials, engage in dialogue, contribute to college life?

WINNING STRATEGIES

While your son has no control over what questions he will get or how they are delivered, there are strategies he can adopt which will greatly improve his answers.

The first of these is to make sure that you have understood the question correctly. It's OK to ask for it to be repeated or rephrased slightly, if necessary. Don't spend too long wondering about the perfect answer, but it is best not to rush in either: often a question will contain subtleties that require a bit of reflection. And don't panic if you really do not know one answer or get it wrong: this alone won't fail you.

The second strategy is to always remember in what context you are being asked a vague or unrelated question, seemingly plucked from the sky. One example is: "Could you imagine the country doing without TV?"

If you are hoping to do Computer Science, you are probably expected to take this as an invitation to describe the various ways in which electronic signals can travel through air. If you are aiming at a politics-related course, say SPS or PPE, on the other hand, this may be the moment to talk about the role of television in education or about the shaping of public opinion instead. There is almost never a single correct answer here. A good answer, though, will connect the question to the course and allow you to display any knowledge you have.

The third strategy involves not being too set in your ways, a sin some of the smartest applicants are prone to. Not all of human behaviour can be explained through the writings of Karl Marx, Sigmund Freud or Virginia Woolf. Equally, great historic figures are sometimes revealed by later historians as liars or wimps. Great scientific theories, which seem to explain everything, turn out to be incomplete and are superseded by others.

So, temper your views with a good dose of scepticism. If your daughter has been holding forth on the evils of capitalism, it may be a wise thing for her to end with something like: "On the other hand, poverty might have a whole number of causes, and I'm really keen to learn more about those."

Much of this, it should be clear from the examples given above, applies not just in the arts, but also the sciences. While scientific facts are of a more definite nature and interviewers expect you to know the basic ones, you also need to be aware that assessments can change. This means you could get a question along the lines of: "What is wrong with Watson and Crick's views on DNA?"

THE APPLIANCE OF SCIENCE

A concern for the implications of scientific developments is often seen as essential. If a Natural Sciences candidate claims that her main interest is biology, for instance, she might well be asked her opinion on the possible consequences of genetically modified organisms (GMO).

Again, no ultimate judgement is expected of her. What she needs to show by her answer is that she has enough of a sound factual basis to speculate intelligently, as well as a grasp of the most important scientific principles. The idea is to apply these principles to the new information put in front of her, to notice connections, or differences, or rules.

Again, too, it is crucial to elaborate. The ideal answer to any question, no matter how short, will be long enough to show that you have a solid grasp of the subject, a positive hunger to learn more and a healthy awareness that certainty can be an elusive thing, even in science.

Some science subjects require a very hands-on attitude, and this should be reflected in your answer. In Engineering, for instance, a willingness to apply the knowledge you already possess in Maths or Physics to practical problems marks out the right candidate. If asked a question that starts with "Is it your sense that it would it be possible to..." don't ever think about answering yes or no. Instead, try to suggest an experiment that might work in response. If you have ever conducted a relevant one and can describe it, even better. The point is not to offer a perfect solution, but to show that you are willing to grapple with a problem.

Science interviewers, whether they are vets or physicists, also share a general appreciation of certain traits. High up among those is a numerical bent. So, don't just put all your answers into words. Instead, show your awareness that figure analysis is often a good way to tackle even a non-mathematical problem.

This need not be a scary prospect. Often, it just means doing mental calculations based on estimates, or suggesting a simple statistical inquiry. At other times, a verbal question may be best answered by scribbling equations, calculations or general diagrams on the nearest pad or board. But do talk about what your scribblings might mean; don't just assume that they are self-explanatory.

THE NEW EXAMS

To give applicants yet another way of proving they have brains (and to allay public concerns), Oxford and Cambridge have since 2002 introduced written aptitude tests for some of their most coveted courses. Students hoping to study Medicine or Law at either university and Engineering, Computer Science, Economics or Natural Sciences at some Cambridge colleges now sit a formal exam. So do candidates for History, English and Maths at Oxford. Each of these different exams tries to establish whether a student has the intellectual skills for a specific field.

The universities like to stress that as these are not subject tests, preparation is unnecessary. Still, candidates sitting an exam for a science course need to be at ease with their GCSE science and Maths. Having an AS level in Critical Thinking or the A-level in General Studies can also help, as may two useful books, *How to Pass Advanced Aptitude Tests* by Jim Barrett (Kogan Page, 2002) and *Mensa: How to Excel at IQ Tests*, edited by Robert Allen (Carlton, 2002). And, since an unfamiliar format or wording can throw a nervous student, always check for sample papers available online.

Don't worry too much if you really cannot work out an answer: the tests are meant to be hard and a few questions may defeat even a brilliant student. As these are long papers, though, it pays to work fairly fast. How much they will count for, exactly, neither Oxford nor Cambridge will say.

11

Becoming a great interviewee

Many of my readers will, at this point, throw up their hands in despair. How can a smart but inexperienced teenager possibly cope with such a complex scenario? Do those dons really expect a 17 year old from a comprehensive to shine in a kind of discourse they never have at home?

The answer is, of course, that it is much harder for those from non-academic backgrounds, and for the quieter kind of young person. Nor can you expect much help from Access. Only one of its myriad projects offers Oxbridge interview training. Some of the scheme's organisers say that this is because to do so would be unfair to other applicants. Given that almost half of those accepted will come from private schools which lay on intensive training, this seems pretty odd. Other Access staff argue that what matters more is to raise pupils' low self-esteem. The interview, from this perspective, becomes a minor obstacle, rather than the decisive event in the application process.

State schools can be very good at bridging the gap. The most crucial thing a school can do at this point is to provide enough interview practice. At some schools, sadly, the sole Oxbridge applicant, already feeling edgy about going on this jaunt, is matched up for one brief mock interview with the school's sole Oxbridge-educated teacher, who may not have been back to his old university for 20 years. This rarely goes swimmingly, leaving the candidate more anxious than before.

State school teachers who regularly send students to Oxbridge are adamant that three interviews, each of them followed by detailed feedback, are the minimum it takes.

Feed-back should be given not just on what to say, but on how to say it. One young Oxford English graduate, now teaching at a London specialist school and proud of sending a steady stream of students to her old college, is clear about what is required.

"My students," she says, "are encouraged to practise the long, explanatory reply, rather than the brief, correct schoolroom answer. This can involve speculation, examples, even an admissions that the girl does not know enough yet about the subject to be certain she is right. I also tell them that it's fine to question something that has been said, as long as you are willing to make clear why."

The teacher admits that if a pupil comes from a culture in which openly disagreeing with your elders or betters is just not done, this can seem an almost insurmountable challenge. Still, talented pupils faced with a sympathetic interviewer somehow do occasionally bring it off. "Of course," she added, "it might be fairer to allow our students to acquire such skills in their Oxbridge years."

Another state school teacher, educated at a northern university, concentrates on ensuring that her well-taught Modern Languages students are relaxed enough to display their abilities. Having visited Cambridge several times, not just on an Access day seminar, she can honestly assure candidates that "people like you" are already there. She also encourages them to feel that the visit to Oxbridge is already a special treat, a reward for their hard work.

Yet another teacher, an Oxford educated scientist, tries to keep up with scientific work done in the two colleges which he directs pupils towards. This helps him to recommend papers they can read in order to show that they are interest in the "cutting edge" approach taken by their chosen college. He also prides himself on knowing Oxford well enough to always pick one particular feature of the place, college or course that will appeal to the individual applicant. His pupils, as a result, manage to display genuine enthusiasm at the interview.

Not surprisingly, given the quantity of ground covered above, only a handful of state school teachers manage to do all these things in between marking, classwork and smoothing the path for six dozen university candidates applying elsewhere. The number of Oxbridge students going into teaching too has been steadily dropping, so pupils from urban comprehensives, in particular, cannot rely on their teachers alone.

How, then, can your state educated son walk in with a realistic hope of success? After all, being lively, brainy and enthusiastic in the presence of some terrifyingly eminent older figure does not come naturally to any teenager.

WHAT NOT TO DO (BEFORE THE INTERVIEW)

One temptation at this point, for some parents at least, is to assume that determination will do the job of preparation. In other words, if the lad will only understand just how important Oxbridge entrance is to them, they feel, he will study as hard as he can beforehand and concentrate as hard as he can on the day. Surely, this is enough to swing things?

One young man I talked to was actually told by his father, as they walked to the train, that as he was his parents' eldest son, the family's entire fortune depended on his interview. The poor man was not alone in making Oxbridge entrance a life-or-death issue: one girl recalled that her mother, a single parent who had been forced to leave university due to money troubles, spent weeks saying that she would be absolutely gutted if her daughter did not get in.

Unfortunately, telling your teenager that you don't know how you could possibly live with the disappointment is the worst possible thing to do. She needs to be at least tolerably calm to succeed, but can't be if you keep upping the stakes. Instead, the wretched girl is almost certain to panic on the crucial day and fail, crushed by a responsibility far too great for someone young.

THE DO-IT-YOURSELF INTERVIEW

Instead, it is best to concentrate on honing general interview skills. The interview is, above all, a talk between a teenager and a strange (in some cases, very strange) adult, so one of the most useful things you can do is to ensure that the experience is not totally new to your son.

But who can he talk to? With the demise of the extended family and the growing fear of "stranger danger", many children reach 18 without ever having talked to an adult who is not their teacher or parent. You want to provide a safe environment in which that is possible. So, invite a neighbour in for a cup of tea, or take the child along when you go to the tax office, doctor's or physiotherapist. Encourage him to answer the friendly questions unfamiliar adults there might put to him – only while you are present, of course. The crucial thing here is to let the boy talk, not to butt in and answer on his behalf.

If you can, send him then on a play scheme, to summer camp, to a youth club or to Sunday school, any place in which he will have to interact with people he hasn't known all his life. Older teenagers gain more that just confidence from an engagement with the community. Preparing a church service and picketing a multinational are equally good for mixing generations.

Sleepovers at same-age friends' homes are great confidence builders, too. You'll be amazed how many candidates spend a sleepless first night at Oxbridge, freaked out by staying in a bedroom not their own.

Academic talk will seem far less daunting after such enriching experiences. This is likely to pay off, as long as your son has done enough general work, of course, and is prepared to follow the route outlined by this book, as well as his own good sense.

While there is no way of accurately predicting Oxbridge questions, he can limber up for the interview by doing a few practice runs. This does not necessarily mean setting up a whole trial interview; even just preparing for a likely kick-off question can be worthwhile, because this will prevent him from going blank at this early, scary stage and in those unfamiliar surroundings.

But how do you prepare? Start by writing a brief profile of yourself. What are your university-geared interests? How are you pursuing them and what made you consider the course? Was it a book (remember its full name), an article or some fascinating programme? What key insights did you gain from it? Did it lead you towards any further research? Candidates need to know their subject, say dons, but should also be clear about their motivation and interests.

This information need not cover more than a quarter of a typed page or around a hundred words. Now, read it out to yourself, then take the three key points, write them on a scrap of paper and, drawing only on these, try to tell the whole story smoothly. Then do it without any notes. The point here is not to become word perfect, but to make sure you know what you want to say and are used to speaking up.

In an ideal world, you should practise this mini monologue on an adult, perhaps a neighbour, careers adviser, youth worker or family friend (not your mother, who might feel too involved and will only make you tense). Alternatively, the bathroom mirror will do.

Try to sound confident – and to feel it. There are good reasons for this. You've been invited to attend an Oxbridge interview because of what you have achieved so far, and your potential educators want to know more about how you think and what you might be capable of. They are already teaching students from backgrounds like yours.

DIGITAL LEARNING

Despite their often stern demeanour, dons conducting an interview do not perceive themselves as interrogating students but as debating with them. But what if you have done no debating before? Well, the next best thing to a real-life, fast-paced intellectual debate is a recorded one. Top of the range are the *Today* programme and *The Moral Maze* on Radio 4, accessible through www.bbc.co.uk. BBC2's televised *Question Time* is hectic and sharp. To discover a calmer, but more academic debating style, listen to one of the archived radio programmes of *In Our Time* (www.bbc.co.uk/radio4/history/inourtime/inourtime_archive_home.shtml). Here, a student can learn what our best minds disagree on, from imperialism to the impact of Tolstoy on the British novel. She can also get a sense of how real academics argue their points A weekly dose of this could turn a timid talker into an intellectual bulldog.

Once a student has concluded that highbrow arguing can be fun, it is time to see how Oxbridge interviewers do it. Students who attended one of their conferences held in major towns may have had a taster session, but for those who didn't, all is not lost. Clips of college interviews, albeit mocked up, can now be found on both universities' websites.

While your own experience may turn out to be different, as each interviewer has her own style, the clips can be helpful. Most importantly, they familiarize students with the very adult, formal terminology many dons use. A question starting with "What is your sense of..." or "Can you imagine..." is not meant to scare you into silence. Instead, it seeks to elicit both subject knowledge and your views. You are also meant to answer it at some length. Keeping up your end of the debate can be tough, but an able student truly interested in her subject tends to manage, or so Oxbridge dons believe.

Lastly, it pays to know that some of the worst advice you can follow will also be found online, or rather in some student chatrooms. Out there, privately educated students whose entire school life has been geared towards top universities regularly beseech others to eschew all interview preparation. Behaving naturally, they insist, is all that counts and it got them in. Often the persuader is genuinely unaware that years of intense coaching by teachers who speak just like the interviewers do aided his Oxbridge success.

BECOMING A SPECIALIST

Having decided what you might say during the first few minutes of the interview, you may wonder how to prepare for more specialised questions. Should you jot down yet more detailed notes? Well, it's best to have your school Physics or the rules of Spanish grammar at your fingertips, but cramming works only up to a point. There is no way of second-guessing the interviewer. She might, in any case, want to hear you talk about a subject area or topic you never studied at school.

Still, if you have expressed an interest in evolution in your Personal Statement, it is as well to double-check what issues keep popping up in the literature. This will mean you can offer an informed opinion when confronted with a question like: "Should all living species be preserved?"

Arts admissions tutors in particular like to discuss topical issues, so it can be worthwhile, yet again, to read at least a quality Sunday paper in the months before the interview. Look out for relevant articles written by experts, which will be on the features pages, as well as for news. The most useful ones will have headlines asking things like "should we go to war? or "should we give up the Pound?" before laying out the pros and cons of the case.

It helps to expect different types of questions. "Talk about biological success," for instance, is scarily open-ended, but this does not mean you are being asked to go on and on. Just list what you think might be its key features and then, if you feel confident, venture an opinion on whether the term is meaningful at all.

Often you'll need to decide quickly whether you are being asked to establish a fact or express an opinion. If the interviewer is fishing for facts, then try to respond in that vein. If it is your opinion which is being sought, don't just state it but give reasons too. This shows you are capable of analysing things. You'll get extra brownie points for making clear what you base your answers on: is it a theory, an observation, a principle or a book you have read?

Now give some thought to how you lay out your stall. A good answer is not a ramble. It will be fairly concise, which often means between two and four sentences long. Many interviewers also like you to use qualifying terms such as "perhaps," "in some circumstances," or "on the one hand" (don't forget the other!). So, draw up a few sample questions, no matter how far fetched, do a quick think and practice using these phrases as you write five line replies.

Lastly, what can keep you calm is not to expect the interview to have a steady rhythm. A tutor will briefly spot-check key points but may want to dig out every single fact you know about others. So, when your turn comes, be prepared to launch into a long, detailed reply, only to be interrupted after a few words.

The point of all this is not to try and have a stock of perfect answers ready, but to avoid being thrown by the way in which your interviewer talks. While a sound factual basis matters, of course, so does an awareness that questions may take you outside your field or beyond your subject knowledge. As long as you have those and practice the Oxbridge answering style, you are bound to come across well.

On the other hand, don't bother learning how to speak without your own perfectly normal accent. This is not a test about whether you can pronounce your h's. One or two former candidates have said that their voice suddenly sounded out of place to them at the interview, but they still got in. It helps to remember that nobody on earth sounds quite like an Oxbridge admissions tutor.

Instead, you want to sound keen, thoughtful and open to new ideas. The standard advice from Oxbridge publications is to "be yourself" but perhaps it is a more a case of being you "with added value." There are other options too. One very shy science candidate, whose textile worker parents had moved to Britain from Bangladesh, decided that she would field all questions by imagining she was the cool and smart Carol Vorderman. Reader, it worked for her.

THE BOOK

What, though, is the strongest factor which swings the interview for a candidate? Dons are unequivocal: it is his willingness to analyse, combined with some lateral thinking.

The successful Oxbridge candidates I talked to were just as unequivocal: it was "the book." Each of them had read (and mentioned in their Personal Statement) an adult work relevant to the subject they were applying for. By putting their subject into a broad, intellectual context, the book had enabled them to understand the questions and answer clearly. Reading only photocopied magazine articles or the key chapters of books produced far poorer results.

This is not to say that the candidates had necessarily read the same book, or the same kind of book, even if they were applying for the same course at the same college. The more determined ones had indeed patiently worked their way through a first year university textbook, in the case of science candidates something with a title like Modern Organic Chemistry or Advanced Physics.

Others had had their enthusiasm kindled by a more specific study, and below are some examples, again in the science field. Popular among biology fans were: *Genome* by Matt Ridley, *The Making of Memory: from Molecules to Mind* by Steven Rose, *Trilobite* by Richard Fortey, *The Lying Stones of Marrakech* by Stephen Jay Gould, *The Darwin Wars* by Andrew Brown or *The Human Brain: A Guided Tour* by Susan Greenfield.

Aspiring physicists had read: *QED* by Richard Feynman, *The Physics of Star Trek* by Laurence Krauss, *Chaos* by James Gleick, *Mr. Tompkins in Wonderland* by Russell Stannard and George Gamow, *The Restless Atom* by Alfred Romer or *The Physics of Ball Games* by C.B. Daish.

Aspiring engineers listed: *The New Science of Strong Materials* by J.E. Gordon, *The Engineer in Wonderland* by Eric R. Laithwaite and *Heat Engines* by J.F. Sandford.

Those interested in astronomy and cosmology read anything by Stephen Hawking.

An interest in science could also be developed with the help of a good biography, such as: *Marie Curie: a Life* by Susan Quinn, *Einstein* by Banesh Hoffmann, or *Genius: Richard Feynmann and Modern Physics* by James Gleick. A more spiced-up, fictional version of the scientific life, centred on ethical problems, was found in *Cantor's Dilemma* by Carl Djerassi or *The Swarm* by Frank Schatzing.

Even certain plays could make you a more interesting science interviewee. These included: *Copenhagen* by Michael Frayn, *After Darwin* by Timberlake Wertenbaker, *Arcadia* by Tom Stoppard, *The Life of Galileo* by Bertold Brecht, *The Physicists* by Friedrich Durrenmatt and *An Experiment with an Airpump* by Shelagh Stephenson.

Young mathematicians trying to bridge the yawning gap between A-level Maths and the Oxbridge version were helped by *Alice in Numberland* by John Baylis and Rod Haggarty. Those sitting the Cambridge STEP papers also need to work through *Advanced Problems in Mathematics* by S.T.C. Siklos, an OCR collection. They might then want to read *Dr. Riemann's Zeros* by Karl Sabbagh for fun.

Law candidates new to the subject's formal language and issues often have a go at *Learning the Law* by Glanville Williams (but warm up first by reading the weekly Law supplement published by The Times). Alternatively, books like *Eve was Framed* by Helena Kennedy, which deals with the courts' treatment of women, can prompt an interest in a specialised field.

In other arts subjects, and especially in languages, history and philosophy, the range of "useful" books varied so widely with candidates' personal tastes that there is no point in even giving examples.

A brief word about English Lit.: its candidates need to be the most voracious readers. Here, a familiarity with novels, plays or poetry well beyond the school syllabus is absolutely taken for granted. Avid fiction readers need to show a taste for a specific genre and must have some clear favourites. If your son claims to love Magic Realism, for instance, the interviewers will expect a list of such novels read (four's a good score, two will not do), plus, perhaps, some interest in their structure or social context. Real show-offs also try to understand Terry Eagleton's *Literary Theory: an Introduction*, or at least the first two chapters.

Interviewers for most Oxbridge courses are delighted to encounter a well-read candidate, which does not mean that you should be trying to impress them with a long list of half-digested famous works. In most cases, mentioning that you have read a relevant book or two will do fine. It does not need to be an academic work; detailed popular science books written by experts certainly count.

What the interviewer will try to do is establish whether the candidate has reflected on the tomes he has been consuming. The lad will be expected to voice an opinion based on his reading, make comparisons, mention what problems he encountered and show signs of lateral thinking.

A good bookworm, in other words, is a selective bookworm. Candidates who "skim" lots of material may have a wider range of facts at their disposal, but the best books teach you to connect.

BREEDING A BOOKWORM

So, the wise parent does not assume that never looking up from one's homework is the key to getting into Oxbridge. Discouraging hobbies and restricting a pupil's reading to school textbooks, as some well-meaning, non-university educated parents try to do, can produce a very dull candidate and make family life hell.

By the A2 stage, most teachers have produced a university geared reading list, but until then a wild dash through world fiction or a solid diet of electronics textbooks can work equally well. As long as it has a spine, its presence on top of that pile of dirty washing in your son's room is probably a good thing. All sorts of books, serious or funny, novels or nonfiction, highbrow or lowbrow, will broaden your son's outlook and introduce him to unfamiliar ideas, places and words.

How, though, can you support this expensive habit? The point is, you shouldn't even try. If your daughter is a serious reader, she will go through far more books than you could possibly buy. Instead, make sure that she acquires the library habit early on. Take her to your local children's library, let her pick her own books and go to the counter to have them stamped. Back home, establish a corner where only library books live, so they will never get lost. A working bedside light is not just a convenience but will protect a bookworm's eyes.

If she seems to lose interest after a while, consider that she might have outgrown the children's section, even if she is only ten. Ask the librarian for a map of the grown-up shelves. Then suggest that you might both potter around for a bit in what she thinks is the most interesting looking section. At this point any section, whether philosophy or photography, will be fine. And if your local council tries to "rationalise" library services by closing your local branch, tell them what you think – then campaign for the opposition.

Encourage your daughter to ask for advice. Once she has worked out what kind of books she likes, it's OK to ask the librarian or a subject teacher for suggestions. Only if the books have just come out or have been stolen from the shelves (a regular event in our local library) should you think of buying. Book tokens make excellent, lightweight presents and show that you trust the girl to make her own choice.

If your daughter gets interested in a subject via a TV documentary, she might want to read the book of the series. Before your buy it, though, encourage her to skim through to check whether it really expands on the subject, or just offers bits of recycled text in large print plus lots of film stills.

Dramatised fiction, on the other hand, will more directly lead to top quality books. The only problem of discovering a great story in this way is that the TV version remains in the mind. So, before talking excitedly at her interview about Dr. Zhivago and how the star-crossed lovers managed to escape at the end, your daughter had better cross-check what happens at the end of the book (the hero dies).

YOUNG OXBRIDGE

If your family's potential Oxbridge student has a younger sibling who shows similar ability, here are a few practical suggestions. You don't need to be brilliant or highly educated yourself to implement them. If the child has a good mind, the following strategies will help him on his way.

1. Let him experiment with his pile of bricks without rushing in to help and without sneering when things go wrong.
2. Tell him it's all right to say "I don't know".
3. Encourage him to ask "why" or to say "can you explain".
4. If you can't answer his questions, suggest that you both look for answers in a book.
5. Don't always interrupt what he is doing. It is important to eat, but it can also be important to finish drawing a picture.
6. Listen to his opinions with respect. He might be wrong, but has probably thought before speaking.
7. Ask his opinion about films, teachers, the state of the world.
8. Ask for advice. By ten, a child should know quite a bit more than you do about computer use, video-setting or recording CDs. By 15, he is probably lightyears ahead of you when it comes to the facts about hair dyes, online travel booking and modern music.
9. Encourage him to give his opinions and advice clearly and politely.
10. Teach him that there may be more than one right way of looking at major issues.

THE PITFALLS

No amount of reading can fully prepare you for the interview, and neither is it meant to. One of the key ideas behind the Oxbridge interview is the precise opposite: to discover how well a candidate will cope when faced with the unexpected. Elderly dons still fondly quote the first lines of Rudyard Kipling's poem, *If* – in this context. Oxbridge, so they imply, wants you:

If you can keep your head when all about you
Are losing theirs and blaming it on you,
If you can trust yourself when all men doubt you
But make allowance for their doubting too,

If you can wait and not be tired by waiting,
Or being lied about, don't deal in lies,
Or being hated, don't give way to hating,
And yet don't look too good, nor talk too wise . . .

Well, this is an impressive list, and the ability "to keep your head" was mentioned even by many dons without reference to the poem. The quality would certainly have been useful for picking a Victorian district officer who would be ruling over half of Burma or some pre 1948 Indian state with a million inhabitants and no other Queen's representative within 500 miles. Why it should be quite so crucial "to keep your head" for a future Music or Biological Science student, though, is anyone's guess.

Questioned about this by The Independent (1st October 2000) Susan Stobbs, the veteran director of admissions for Cambridge Colleges, said somewhat defensively: "We are not trying to catch people out. But our courses move very fast. We need to see that students can pick up and develop ideas fast."

Younger Oxbridge academics can be quietly critical of this. One female science tutor from a comprehensive insisted (off the record) that guiding a student through a set text, however complex, was a totally different process. She thought it wrong to put already intimidated young people on the spot and certainly never adopted the tactic herself.

Still, certain, often elderly admissions tutors continue to go for the *If*-approach in a big way and like to make sure the candidate feels surprised.

Often this is just a peculiar seating arrangement. One successful candidate recalls being made to sit at the far end of a very long table, while the interviewer sat at the other end, almost invisible in the gloom. Another one described how her two interviewers positioned themselves at opposite sides of the departmental office, so she could not look at both of them as she talked.

More disconcerting can be a swap between two related subjects. Sue, a grammar school girl who was hoping to read Chinese, found herself interviewed by someone actually teaching Thai, and was asked to apply her (as yet very basic) understanding of Chinese grammar to a line of Thai writing. As the two languages are closely related and she had followed her yoga-teaching mother's advice to do relaxation exercises before the interview the girl, somewhat stumblingly, managed to comply.

Tess, a comprehensive school pupil from a non-academic family, had applied for the Anthropology and Archaeology course after reading an article about a Japanese anthropological project. She was shaken when she found that her interviewer was an archaeologist. Her total ignorance of his subject, she felt, meant she did not stand a chance against "cleverer" applicants. Shrinking back into her seat, which was miles from the tutor's, she whispered: "I don't know a thing about this." However, when reassured that this was OK and invited to speculate, she decided she had nothing to lose. She is an articulate girl, and her off the cuff suggestions on how one might study a dead, rather than a living culture got her in.

Another popular tactic is the prolonged silence, which can be used in various and sometimes disconcerting ways.

Tim, a terribly well-read candidate, was faced with an elderly interviewer who failed to greet him, settled into a distant window recess and after several minutes barked "talk about your own subject" in his direction. The young man launched into an account of what he, out of nervousness, called Astrology, though he meant Astronomy. He quickly corrected himself, but felt so embarrassed he lost his thread. He stumbled on, expecting to be told when to stop, but instead was allowed to go on. When he eventually ran out of things to say, the interviewer maintained his silence. After what felt like an eternity but was, as the candidate later realised, only quarter of an hour, he was told that he could leave.

Grace, who had applied for Modern History, had the opposite experience. She had mentioned in her Personal Statement that she was the leader of a Brownie pack. One of her interviewer's first questions was about the founder of the scout movement, Robert Baden-Powell. Shaken, she admitted to having never heard of him, and prayed that they would move on to another subject. Instead the tutor gave her a little lecture about the famous man, which took up most of the interview. All she was expected to do, she realised after a moment, was to nod enthusiastically.

(Unlike the prospective astronomer, the Brownie leader got in. What can we conclude from this? Probably only that external factors, rather than the interview itself, determined the result: she was a Shropshire working class girl with top grades and a perfect mix of brainy interests and sporting skills, while he came from an already overrepresented public school.)

A more tricky approach can be deeply unsettling for vulnerable candidates.

Maher, an applicant from a poorly rated comprehensive, did well in his written science test, although he felt that had he been less nervous, he would have started faster and done even better. But faced with a plummy-voiced interviewer whom he found hard to understand he clammed up. He had never sat in a room with such precious old furniture before. Being fairly dark-skinned, he also wondered whether the fact that the interviewer made him sit at the end of the room was a put down. Did the professor not want to sit next to a dark-skinned person? Or did he think that he, Maher, smelled?

Or take Joseph, who came from a struggling urban sixth form college. He had applied to do a course based on Spanish, his mother tongue. When his interviewer explained that she did not actually teach the language, Joseph's first thought was: "So the Spanish tutor can't even be bothered to see me." Hurt and confused, he refused to play the game. He gave short, terse replies to any factual questions put to him and when asked what he thought was the most exciting aspect of European culture, he just mumbled: "No idea." He had, in fact, worked as a Saturday cleaner for a small record company that promoted regional music and was interested in its work, but felt that mentioning his lowly job would demean him in Oxbridge eyes.

Both applicants were rejected, which came as no surprise to them. Their respective teachers, though, were absolutely furious. Each of the boys had been carefully hand-picked by his school as a highly talented student.

So the result of such an überclever approach, although perhaps designed to transcend subject coaching and create a more "level playing field", is often counterproductive. It is bad enough being in an unfamiliar environment with someone speaking in a superior accent without being asked about a subject one knows nothing about. Almost invariably, the applicant's residual doubts about whether this venture into other people's world was a good idea will click in. The suspicion that he is undergoing a deliberate humiliation, rather than a fair test, may paralyse a student intellectually, so that he might fail.

12
Paying to shine at the interview

There is one obvious way to make the Oxbridge interview a cinch rather than a nightmare: this is to go there from the right school. While creating Oxbridge entrants used to be a mission restricted to a few public schools, fee-paying parents now expect this from every private establishment. They also tend to obtain it, and not just in terms of the intensive, small class teaching by qualified staff which the schools officially emphasize. One such establishment, once mainly known as a supplier of officer cadets to Sandhurst, includes in its weekly time table for Oxbridge entrants amongst other things:

- a 40 minute tutorial in which pupils go through old Oxbridge entrance papers
- A short essay on verbal interview questions pupils were asked in the past
- Verbal interview training
- A talk on an interview-related course subject given by an expert
- Half hour talks given by pupils on their own academic interests
- A problem-solving session
- Guidance on how to research a project to be mentioned
- "Six of the best" book club sessions in which pupils discuss with a teacher the half dozen books pupils are expected to have read in the holidays etc. etc.

The effect of all this has been to create what one young ex-Oxbridge lecturer now teaching abroad referred to as "a Sparkler", meaning a candidate who shines brightly at his interview, but might or might not soon fizzle out. The Sparkler would deliver all the "right" answers from the start. Asked why he picked his course, for instance, he would launch into a little monologue which suggests that he embodied all the qualities and skills admissions tutors were fishing for. To show you what this means, here is a (mildly satyrised) version of the Sparkler's performance:

"Well, I thought a lot about it before deciding. I was very impressed with your general academic reputation, of course, especially in Historic Anthropology (my housemaster told me about it), but I became really interested in the family structure of medieval Provençal villages when I went to the local museum near our French holiday home and found some old land records (actually, the careers teacher recommended that I go there, having steered me towards this unfamiliar subject, because he knows that two fellows here specialise in it). I am currently reading *Provençal birthing rituals* by Dr. Deepthought who is teaching here. It is absolutely fascinating.

Actually, I was so keen I started a Provençal Society in our school, and one of my friends has already become a member (after, that is, I agreed to join the Latin Grammar Society he founded so it could go on his Personal Statement).

Then, of course, there is the recreational side. Your team usually wins the inter-collegiate rugby final (my PE teacher translated the prospectus reference to 'lots of Rugby Blues' for me) and I am quite a keen forward scrum myself (actually, I find rugby terrifying, but it was mandatory at my boarding school and the headmaster claimed that playing the game went down awfully well with Oxbridge. I'll drop out of matches in the first term)."

Evidently eager, motivated and academic, the Sparkler seems to be the answer to even the most sport-hating don's prayer. But is he? The answer lies in the mixed intake of most fee-paying schools. While some parents opt for private schooling because they hope it will stretch their bright, fast-learning child, other parents see it as a way of giving a slow, under-achieving pupil the best chance in life.

So, a Sparkler could be anything. The best Oxbridge entrance training makes it impossible to tell whether you are dealing with a gifted youngster who will excel once on the course, or a carefully tutored but middling pupil who will struggle to keep up once his support system is gone and will finally leave, having barely scraped a Third.

Now contrast this with the (again mildly satyrised) answers given by another candidate, when asked why he chose the college:

Fred: "Well, I was told it was not too high up the league tables, so it might take more state school pupils. I wasn't too sure about this place at first, what with most of the buildings being so old, but apparently the student rooms are in a new block, so I figured that would be alright."

Interviewer: "Anything else?"

Fred: Well, of course that I could do Archaeology here. I got the idea from seeing "Raiders of The Lost Ark", and then I read a magazine article about what archaeologists do in FHM. My local library also found me a book that was mentioned there, even though I had to wait for three weeks, but it was really interesting. Not quite as good as history, mind you, which is what I like best at school. I even got to read out my holiday essay on Scottish war songs on local radio. Only Oxbridge History is supposed to be really difficult to get into and so my teacher suggested I settle for Archaeology instead. I'm halfway through the introduction he lent me. There's quite a bit of history in your course, isn't there?"

Interviewer: "You could say that. But archaeology is still hard work and requires excellent time management. Do you combine your reading with anything else? Rugger? Rowing?"

Fred: "Not really. My mate and I used to bum off for a fag when the rest got on the minibus to the sports centre at the other end of town. And we don't have any rivers in Luton. Mind you, I've heard that you got your own full size football pitch here. Would it be OK to have a kick about later on?"

Well, who sounds more like a potential Oxbridge student to you? The answer is not quite as clear-cut as it seems. A handful of colleges do have an intelligent, motivated, honest student like Fred. What makes the huge parental investment in school fees seem worthwhile, though, is that so many admissions tutors, including state school educated ones, still go for the Sparkler.

INTERVIEW TRAINING

What options do parents have if they cannot afford the fees that would transform Fred into a Sparkler? Until the appearance of this book, which was put on this earth to do exactly that, the answer has been precious few.

The cut-price option has, for the last decade or so, been a bit of interview training offered by an Oxbridge graduate doing home tutoring while he waits for his dream job, or a few extra sessions tacked on to a private A-level course in some private college. Alternatively, such training can be bought, in the form of about a week's coaching plus general guidance, from a small number of outfits specialising in this field.

Oxbridge absolutely hates these paid interlopers. Mentioning that interview training courses were now held in Oxford itself, one powerful admissions tutor told me with almost a hiss: "I am appalled to think that some genuine colleges here would agree to have their premises used by such people."

Anthony Smith, the President of Magdalen College, Oxford, went even further when he described the staff of one interview training company whose success in placing pupils had been much in the news as "just a bunch of grasping, meddling, money-grabbing young men" (The Times, 29th May 2003).

This is a quite extraordinary reaction. After all, the headmasters of most private schools are welcome guests at the dreaming spires. So, if a man who charges parents £10,000 a year to (amongst other things) get pupils into Oxbridge is regularly invited to dine at the dons' high table, why is the chap who offers to do this for a more affordable sum, between £250 and £1,000 a throw, treated as socially below a pimp?

There are two possible answers to this. One is that interview training companies, or at least those which work on the basis of a no-win-no-fee basis, will only accept the kind of students who would get in anyway and therefore, as Magdalen's President has also suggested, "make their money out of parents' social anxiety about Oxbridge."

This would indeed justify the Oxbridge disdain, if it were not for one thing: some dons are claiming the precise opposite. Far from agreeing that all those evil, venal young men always get their pupils in, they insist that interview training never works. They are convinced that they can always spot its signs (unless, presumably, it is done by a private school) and that this leads them to dismiss the candidate's own abilities.

In other words, just a tinge of snobbishness about the kind of training which is acceptable, as opposed to the kind which is not, might be a more likely explanation.

But if you buy, will you get value for your money? You certainly might. While interview training cannot impart a knowledge of facts, it can help a student decode the often mystifying questions asked by Oxbridge dons. Ways of neatly structuring your answer may also be taught. This may be enough to shift the balance in favour of a bright, well-taught applicant from a non-academic home.

The crucial thing is to watch out for the problems. One is that an outfit which prepares large numbers of students for Oxbridge during a very short time may indeed find it hard to avoid the production of clones. This will make it obvious that their candidates have been coached, and so interviewers may well spot and reject them.

And if parents only pay the interview trainers if their son or daughter gets in, that target can end up overriding others: pupils might be subtly encouraged to lower their sights in order to improve their entrance chances, for instance by considering less competitive fields than Law or Medicine. Alternatively, they might be directed away from the most academically renowned and hardest to impress colleges, in favour of the old "housemaster's route" outlined earlier.

The less popular a candidate's course and college choice is, after all, the more likely the candidates are to get in and the interview trainers are to get their money. The result of such a strategy could be an unsuitable course, or a miserable time at the wrong college and a career that does not live up to one's expectations.

However, there is no sight that any of this is happening and some students who had paid interview training certainly seem delighted with the results. If there is a real problem with interview training, it lies elsewhere. Many parents cannot possibly spare several hundred pounds, never mind several thousand, just to help a top university recognise their teenager's ability.

13

Grading the interview

Oxbridge students tend to be very positive about the interview process. After all, it enabled them to join "the brightest and best" in their delightful mini-world. Unsuccessful candidates, who went into the interview cold, are often more bewildered than cross. "I just couldn't work out what they wanted from me," was a phrase heard more than once.

Outside experts can be more critical. Deborah Eyre insists that identifying those who will benefit most from a top academic education is an expert job. Her organisation, NAGTY, seeks to establish prospective students' intellectual profiles on the basis of a whole portfolio of evidence, including a battery of scientific tests. The Oxbridge interview, to her, is "a very unscientific way of testing ability, made even more arbitrary by the variation in practices by individual admissions tutors and colleges".

Much of this is due to the fact that most Oxbridge admissions tutors have undergone no training at all. The universities have started to train new appointees, but veterans of the interview process need not join them. They can ask a candidate whatever they like and, if the spirit takes them, with both eyes closed. Only the admissions tutors for the Oxford medical course are somewhat restricted; their questions must cover specific areas, listed on a task sheet. How to cover them, though, is entirely up to the interviewer.

The result can turn the interview into a tombola; those candidates who get in and those who don't may have totally different interviews despite university guidelines.

Professor Eyre is also concerned about the distorting effect public school training has on interview outcomes: "What we see is that children in the private sector seemingly over-achieve. They are trained up to the limit of their potential, then groomed to come across as exceptional, whether they are that or not."

Nor is she happy that the blame for failure is, so often, attributed to a lack of self-esteem. "Some interviewers," she says, "are overbearing, and some young people just do not like to be interrogated. They find the encounter unattractive, whatever their ability."

Another problem has been pointed out by Joan Freeman. "The talented are not a homogeneous group," insists Britain's veteran expert on this group. She wants interviewers to be aware that a gifted young writer and a gifted young scientist will behave quite differently, and individuals within each group may do so too. The "brightest and best" can be dozy or sparkling, quick witted or ponderous.

No testing system is entirely value free either, warns Professor Freeman. This is true of the Oxbridge one, as well as of the standard IQ test and the American-type SAT. The shorter a test is too, the more the values of the tester will affect the outcome, and the Oxbridge interview is often very short indeed.

The new aptitude tests introduced for specific courses have also failed to reassure some experts. The Schwartz Report of May 2004, commissioned by the Government, warns that preparing and travelling to additional tests can interfere with a student's classroom work. Deborah Eyre feels that having subject tests that also vary from university to university "makes life more difficult for the student, parent and school". A set of generally accepted ability tests might, both suggest, work rather better.

Foreign academics, while admiring the intellectual glory of Oxbridge, are amazed at its entrance process. Graduates of top US universities like Harvard and Princeton, or of the Paris Sorbonne, are renowned within international organisations like the UN for their analytic minds, articulacy, lateral thinking and all the rest of the Oxbridge wish list, but they have not been entry-tested for any of this. Instead, a great university seeks to gradually develop these great qualities in bright applicants.

This is why American universities grade all applicants by a standard academic ability test, the SAT, which is regarded as fair, though you can bone up for it. The candidates with the highest scores are offered places in the most highly rated institutions. Applicants to even the most renowned French universities need only to have done well in their baccalaureate, an extended form of A-levels.

A VIEW FROM THE STAFF ROOM

How does another group, the teachers, feel about Oxbridge entrance? One group of sixth form teachers I spoke to were clear about the problem faced by large schools like theirs, with a mixed and often disadvantaged intake. It is not just that they cannot possibly provide the intense interview training offered elsewhere. Oxbridge also wants a candidate who is positively bubbling with enthusiasm about his subject and is actively pursuing it beyond syllabus requirements.

Now, although comprehensives seek to get all their bright pupils into university, "Oxbridge qualities" are a minority trait and pupils exhibiting them too publicly risk trouble from their peers. Winning a prize, or even choosing to compete for one can, in some schools, set the bullies on you. So can speaking up too much in class or knowing so much more about various subjects than your classmates do. Not until the A-level years, when these pupils are taught separately, does the classroom really become a place in which it feels safe to show off intellectually, or even to openly pursue unusual hobbies.

If a pupil has an articulate, educated family, this will balance outside factors and no damage is done, said the teachers. For many bright comprehensive school pupils, though, the interview becomes a place where they are suddenly expected to do what instinct told them to carefully avoid: show wild enthusiasm for their subject, be quickwitted and sparkle. The deliberate underplaying of their abilities perfected over the years now backfires. They undersell themselves.

To illustrate the outcome one teacher quoted the feedback he had received after the rejection of an outstanding pupil interviewed at a Cambridge college. The boy, the admissions tutor wrote, "got an A for his written exam, is serious and passionate about his subject. Unfortunately, he was nervous at the interview and overly defensive."

The head of the department, who had sent seven other pupils to various other Cambridge Colleges that year, all without success, quoted similar feedback from the university. His candidates, he was told, had been too tense and not fluent or expansive enough at the interview. To this was added the usual sop: "We had so many very able candidates this year."

A teacher at a more successful school nevertheless concurred with her colleagues. Oxbridge was clearly trying to broaden its intake, but there were still "social" entrance qualifications. Far too much, she felt, hinges on a pupil's ability to sustain a long, clever verbal exchange with a well-spoken, highly educated adult.

Oxbridge success must not remain merely the responsibility of schools, insisted the experienced teacher: "There is a need for a Joint Working Party made up of dons and sixth form heads in order to work out what precise qualities Oxbridge colleges can reasonably seek. It also needs to consider how entrance can be made a fairer process, given that some of these qualities just cannot be fostered in a large, mixed ability state school."

WATCHING THEM RUN

Ongoing changes in the interview process could be an attempt to forestall such intervention. Questions have become more subject-centred and an admissions tutor can no longer single-handedly grill two dozen students in a day. Now there are usually two interviewers present, both to guard against prejudice and against the exhaustion that might cause the talents of the last poor soul ushered in to be overlooked.

But will that be enough? Contrary to popular belief, it is not just outsiders who are wondering. Writing in the *Times Higher Educational Supplement* of 13th January 2006, Oxford don Alan Ryan claimed that he'd never understood the faith in interviews. "It would be better to set an entrance examination or get the applicants' A-level scripts to read," argued the warden of New College. "What students do at university is write; what they get a degree for is performance in examinations. You'd have thought that the way to decide which applicants to accept is to see how well they do what they will do at university. If you were picking a team to run in the Olympics, you wouldn't interview them about running; you'd watch them run."

14

Going for it

Despite all the criticism voiced of it in recent years, the interview remains the most crucial part of the Oxbridge entrance process. Most dons insist that although it may not be totally value-free, it is essential to help them find the right students for their unique face-to-face teaching system. Those found today include a (slight) majority of state school students, some from very poor backgrounds. Passing the interview means that you will be offered an internationally coveted university place, subject only to the kind of A-level results most candidates can expect.

To a bright teenager setting out for Oxbridge, these points should provide enough reassurance to carry her confidently past those manicured lawns, shiny iron gates and freshly painted stone walls into a room full of people wearing bicycle clips. Parents still toying with the Valium, though, may want a slightly more detailed summary, which goes roughly as follows:

That the interview structure does not compare like with like there is no doubt. There is just too much difference in pupils' academic and social background. Equally, there is no doubt that it does pick up on real talent in all sorts of candidates, and that many interviewers genuinely seek to broaden their course intake, albeit in oddly unscientific ways. Even if there is prejudice among some, this cannot be allowed to determine the university's overall outcome. Unwritten targets for a publicly acceptable proportion of state school students must, after all, be met. The alternative might be a – regularly threatened – cutback in Government funds.

As a result, interviewers can be surprisingly nice, and those whose fierce or peculiar manners flummox outsiders are gradually being reined in. Responding to criticism from headmasters, one admissions tutor argued that the treatment of applicants had been "a great deal more savage" in the past.

It should also be said that while some candidates find the interview nerve-wracking, others actually enjoy the rapid verbal to-and-fro and get an unexpected thrill from being able to show off their mental skills. For many a junior thinker, there is nothing quite like a famous senior thinker's quick, almost imperceptible nod of approval after a good reply.

Leaving you for the 9.43 train, your daughter should therefore take heart. Not only is Oxbridge committed to taking someone like her, but you and this book are on her side. Guided by the information given on these pages, she need not feel at a disadvantage compared with posher and seemingly more confident students. Quite of few of them will fail, because even the most meticulous coaching and the greatest familiarity with ancient buildings is not a substitute

---

ONE FOR THE ROAD

It you have come this far, you have probably absorbed enough information to get through the interview, or to prepare your teenager for it. Still, just in case it all seems too much, here is a basic summary in the form of ten simple commandments:

Rule 1: Be prepared to answer questions about your interests, activities, subject, course or college choice.

Rule 2: Accept that you might not be asked about any of this.

Rule 3: Treat the interview as a conversation in which ideas are thrown back and forth, not a quiz session with correct answers.

Rule 4: Say not only what you think but also why you think it.

Rule 5: Give longish, considered answers.

Rule 6: Speculate, compare and explain.

Rule 7: Don't expect the interviewer to tell you whether you were right or wrong.

Rule 8: Express curiosity and a willingness to learn.

Rule 9: Don't be too dogmatic: the more you know about the world, the less certain things look.

Rule 10: Don't panic if you are being asked about a topic you have never thought about: this is not a disaster, but merely a way of giving you a chance to improvise.

Or just try to remember one phrase in which a state school headmaster I knew used to sum up the interview to his pupils: "The interview explores the ability to reason and to support an argument with constructive thought – and the skill of thinking on your feet."

for a well-focused brain. If your teenager is blessed with the latter and has followed this book's advice, she stands an excellent chance. So, the thing is to be is to be optimistic and prepared. Confidence based on wise choices, well-planned school work, selective reading and an understanding of the interview process begets Oxbridge success. So does the realisation that much of this is just a game with mirrors, played by clever young people and sometimes not so smart older ones. You can join this game and win, if you understand the rules and draw on all available help. There is nothing spontaneous about the Oxbridge entrance process, and you need not comply with that absurd claim.

15

Oxbridge Medicine

Parents and students often view the medical degree courses offered by Oxbridge as the most glittering of all prizes. In this, they are both right and wrong. They are right, because Medicine is the only Oxbridge degree which almost guarantees you a job, and a well-paid, prestigious, and often highly satisfying lifetime one at that. As one young doctor I interviewed put it, it was great to be in a profession which combined science with human interaction: "You get up in the morning and you don't know what will happen. The joy of medicine is that your bleeper goes and your day changes."

However, people are wrong in that Oxbridge Medicine is not necessarily a better route to professional glory than a degree from, say, Newcastle. While Medicine involves a huge amount of academic learning, the success of a medical career depends first of all on a doctor's work record. What matters is how skilled you are in practice and how well you get on with colleagues. As a result, students rise to the top from any good medical school. The bright, enthusiastic (and privately educated) young doctor I quoted above was, in fact, rejected by Cambridge, but is, nevertheless, shooting up the career ladder. His friends, who made it into Oxbridge Medicine, have similar, but not actually better jobs.

There is, of course, something special about Oxbridge Medicine. Penicillin, the drug that continues to save millions of lives each year, was developed at Oxford in 1940 by two men, Australian medical scientist Howard Florey and a German Jewish asylum seeker, biochemist Ernst Boris Chain (although the compound had been discovered in 1928 by Alexander Fleming, who worked and trained at St. Mary's Medical School, London).

Cambridge can take credit for a more theoretical discovery. In 1953, Francis Crick and the American James Watson decoded the "double helix" structure of the DNA molecule, which carries the genetic information from old cells to new ones, in a Cambridge lab. Few individual discoveries have so quickly ushered in so many fundamental advances in so many fields, from genetics and evolutionary theory to biochemistry and medical research. Today's students attending the Oxbridge courses have yet more reasons to feel privileged. They don't just enjoy some truly brilliant staff and labs, but also have the opportunity to mix daily with contemporaries involved in quite different academic fields, which makes for a vibrant social and intellectual life. Medical students elsewhere tend to live, study and party within the far duller confines of a teaching hospital.

As a result, the competition is fierce. Oxford and Cambridge, which run similar entry systems, get five applicants for each place. (In most other subjects, the proportion of applicants to places is four or three to one.) Faced with years of bitter criticism over their selection procedures, these have been greatly restructured. No longer can a bright young chap expect to get in thanks to what older medics quaintly recall as "trial by sherry".

Medicine is, in fact, one of the very few Oxbridge subjects which has had a long, proper entrance exam, in addition to the interview, for several years. This was sat by applicants to all colleges. Each of the two universities, though, had its own exam, devised by its own medical faculty staff, and each exam was designed to test not so much an applicant's background or IQ as their aptitude for this particular course.

However, there was concern that both exams favoured public school pupils because of their broader level of knowledge and special coaching, and so both have now been scrapped. A more ability-based, pre-interview exam, the Biomedical Admissions Test (BMAT) was introduced in November 2003 for medical candidates applying to Oxford, Cambridge, University College (London) and Imperial College.

So, how do you prove that you have what it takes?

The answer lies in grasping that Medicine at Oxford and Cambridge is more theoretical than elsewhere, at the start at least. Beyond this, many aspects of the courses offered by the two universities differ, though. In order to provide a potential student with helpful details, we'll zoom in on the Oxford course below. Students considering the equally renowned Cambridge course will find some of the information relevant, especially as far as the entrance test is concerned. However, they absolutely need to also check out two Cambridge websites, www.cam.ac.uk/cambuniv/ugprospectus/applying/applying01k.html and www.cam.ac.uk/cambuniv/ugprospectus/courses/medicine4. html. (More information on the Oxford course is at www.medicine. ox.ac.uk/medsch/.)

THE OXFORD MEDICAL COURSE

While Cambridge likes to stress the patient-centred nature of its course, Oxford puts a strong emphasis on research. The Oxford course "suits the academic mind", as William James, the Dean of Admissions at its Medical Faculty, puts it. A high proportion of Oxford medical students will not just become consultants, that is medical specialists, but will combine patient care with medical research. Some will spend most of their professional lives in the computerised labs of hospitals, pharmaceutical companies or medical schools.

Tutors therefore look for the qualities that any good medical researcher needs, qualities like curiosity, persistence and an ability to accurately connect facts. A good bedside manner and a taste for the operating theatre dramas seen in medical soaps also help, of course, but are often taken for granted. This is not the place to emphasize in your personal statement that you like working with people.

Oxford also teaches medicine in the most traditional way. While some top universities move their students' knowledge forward through a problem-centred approach, for instance by taking them through all possible causes of a bad headache (Manchester, Liverpool) or by a systems-based one, for instance by teaching students "all about the lower limb" (Edinburgh), the Oxford curriculum is taught discipline by discipline. Students gradually work their way through anatomy, physiology, biochemistry etc. In their first two years they will (unlike Cambridge students) hardly see any patients. So, any reference to your enthusiasm for the theoretical sciences and not just the practice of medicine will go down well.

On the other hand, Oxford students are not expected to absorb this demanding curriculum by spending most of their time in large lecture halls or doing mainly practicals. Instead, their course is tutor-based. This means that a medical lecturer will work through the material with two students, sometimes even one to one. There is a huge reading list, but the mass of books can be absorbed because their contents is filtered through personal discussion. Tutor and student may remain together for up to three years.

All this personal attention does not just allow students to take in large amounts, it also enables them to follow their personal interests with encouragement from their tutor. There is a flipside, of course. A student really needs to be brave enough to ask questions, speculate on answers and risk being wrong.

As William James puts it: "This suits some people, but students who like to have their knowledge neatly laid out for them may not like this approach. Nor will those who like only applied science."

UNIVERSITY PLACES

For a subject which has generated so much public debate, Oxbridge medicine is surprisingly small. Oxford admits only 150 new undergraduates a year and Cambridge 280. Their postgraduate medical courses open to students with top science degrees are even smaller. Each university fills about twenty places a year.

GRADES

Top grades are essential for Oxbridge medical candidates. What this requirement means at GCSE level is mostly As and A*s. The number of GCSEs which an applicant must offer varies: privately educated pupils are expected to have close to the maximum number taken at their school, often ten or eleven, while state school pupils might be acceptable with eight.

AS-level grades too need to be high and when it comes to A-levels, candidates absolutely must have predictions of three As. There is no allowance made here for an applicant's type of school. A student from a successful comprehensive in some middle class suburb and a student from a struggling inner city one, where hard-pressed staff lack the time to coach individuals for top grades, will be judged on equal terms.

A-level subjects are not totally fixed. While one of the appplicant's three A-levels must be in Chemistry, the second one may be in any other science or maths. However, the rules vary between the two universities. Cambridge strongly prefers three science/maths A-levels and quite a few medical applicants have four. At Oxford the third A-level can be an arts one such as English or perhaps even a "soft" one like Psychology. Apparently, medical students with an English A-level get better medical degrees than students who did A-level Physics.

General Studies, as has been pointed out elsewhere, does not count as a real A-level at Oxbridge, though William James admits that it is rather helpful when it comes to answering test questions involving verbal reasoning.

In practice, a college tutor might make a promising applicant a lower grade offer in a handful of circumstances. This happens if he or she has recently changed schools or perhaps lost a parent. But there is no special allowance made for being working class. The reason that used to be given for this was that information about students' families was not available to universities anyway. Now that UCAS will at least tell universities whether an applicant's parents went to university, both Oxford and Cambridge have declared that they will not make any use of this. The reason given is that such information is uncorroborated data, i.e. unreliable.

THE ADMISSIONS TEST

The formal test for admission to the medical faculties of Oxford and Cambridge is identical, as already said. Called the Biomedical Admissions Test (BMAT), it lasts for two hours and is taken by students around six weeks before their interview at their school or some other approved centre.

Part one of the test assesses what is defined as aptitude and generic skills, that is the skills enabling a student to solve problems, understand arguments and analyse data. There is much emphasis on logic and on the ability to think in numbers: can that girl or boy handle a simple set of figures applied to a real world situation? Candidates might be given figures for incidences of multiple sclerosis and for the altitude of towns, then asked to interpret them. Questions often require you to look at graphs or test results.

(A word of advice here: when interpreting a graph, candidates should watch out for the difference between a medical cause and a correlation. A cause explains an illness, a correlation just means that the illness exists alongside another factor, causal or not. Candidates are meant to note the connection, but not jump to conclusions. For instance, Aids in the western world, largely correlates with male homosexuality. However, homosexuality does not cause Aids.)

Part two seeks out the scientific mind. While no medical knowledge is expected, candidates now need to be armoured with the background facts of GCSE science, including Physics and Maths. An interest in basic structures, such as cells, often comes in handy.

Part three is essay based, and a student trying to guess at likely topics may want to prepare for something like "Does politics determine health?" The writing tasks set are designed to explore whether the candidate understands a concept, can express herself, see both sides of an argument and offer some sort of analysis. This part of the exam is marked by the individual university, which makes it the place to hint at your aptitude for its particular course.

Sample questions and more details can be found on the exam website, listed at the end of this book.

THE MEDICAL INTERVIEW

A few weeks after the exam, applicants progress to the next stage. Once they have been put up by the college of their choice and dined in its hall or cafeteria at its expense, they sit their first interview there. This is followed by another one at a second college. The initial interview can be with any science don, but the next must be with a practising clinician (meaning a doctor who actually sees patients, rather than a medical researcher).

Interviewers now may ask what and how they like, although they have a score sheet they must fill in afterwards for the central medical faculty. The score sheet, designed to establish whether a candidate's intrinsic qualities can carry her through, is a fairly recent innovation, even more recent than the written test. It seems designed to ensure that individual tutors cannot go totally wild in their preferences for tall public school boys or sharp-witted Scottish girls.

The score sheet, like the centrally devised and marked test, also tells the outsider something important about Oxbridge: while their dons will always argue that its admissions procedures are as perfect as can be, they will somehow manage to make them just a little fairer and less idiosyncratic when there is enough outside pressure.

So, what can you expect to be asked? The warm-up question could be about anything, but quite often involves your reasons for choosing medicine. You may then be asked about your work experience. It is fairly essential for medical candidates to have worked, though it can be paid or unpaid, in a hospital or elsewhere. Any volunteer scheme involving handicapped people will go down fine. It will also count if you have cared for a relative at home. Medicine is hard work, and interviewers are looking for tough people, for "grit and determination."

Talk about how you adjusted to your work environment, and what relevant things you noticed there: the observation or non-observation of health and safety rules, pollution or shift work all have medical implications.

Much of the time allotted to each interview, though, might be spent answering specific questions. Many interviewers go for the "show and tell" type. You might be shown a simple graph or a picture of some body part and asked what this might be. The question is not designed to test whether you have done your school work (which is assumed) or whether you have read lots of extra stuff (which is helpful, but not crucial). The interviewer is not checking what you already know, but whether you can use data, make sense of information.

This means you are being invited to make an intelligent guess and to spell out clearly how you arrived at it. So, the right answer would be something like this: "This is a heart, judging by the shape and the valve, no, actually, the valve is at the bottom, so it could be a kidney. It is, isn't it?"

You might still be wrong, but you have shown that you have grasped the process of arriving at the truth.

The opposite of an intelligent guess, adopted by some panic-stricken candidates at this point, is the stupid guess. After a long silence (bad if you only have 20 minutes to impress the tutor) one desperate candidate, I was told, finally whispered: "It could be a penis." Asked to explain why, he replied crossly: "I don't know, I'm just guessing."

Was he prepared to guess again, asked the tutor. "Not much point," he snapped, clearly regretting that he had ever taken up the invitation. As you may have guessed, he was turned down.

So, the ideal medical interviewee is someone willing to think, and to think aloud. She should also be calm enough not to panic if she doesn't know something. She should be willing to try and analyse the data put in front of her, in other words, to make sense of and combine bits of data. It also helps greatly if she understands what kind of information you might get from a graph.

Much of a candidate's interview success is due to attitude. Be willing to engage with the questions put to you, even if they are about something unfamiliar. Don't go into disaster mode if you get something wrong – candidates are often accepted even if they do. Be prepared to have more than one try and, above all, don't keep mum.

Basic good manners also help, though this need not mean upper class speech. Again, don't make assumptions about Oxbridge only wanting posh students. The grander the college, the more likely it is these days to need a few working class applicants to stave off public criticism. So, don't mumble "I don't know, we didn't do that stuff at my school," if you are stuck. Instead, say "I don't know a lot about spinal vertebrae, but I'd really like to find out more, also for family reasons: my father's has a lot of problems with his spine because of his job as a warehouseman."

Allow for the fact that the interviewer herself may well have gone to a state school. Accents do fade over the years. While there is no point in worrying about your own accent, "you need to be a bit formal," as one Medicine interviewer put it. What this mainly means is wearing a jacket, using polite phrases like "would you like me to" and, of course, not smoking without first asking permission.

There are also a few human qualities that go down well. Cheerfulness is tops. Medicine will give you traumatic experiences and encounters with people who need reassurance. It also involves lots of exhausting teamwork. So, no tutor wants to take a young Victor Meldrew.

Modesty can be another useful trait. Interviewers really do hate arrogant candidates who seem to believe that they have a right to get into Oxbridge just because they are smart. Almost all candidates are.

Lastly, this is one subject in which the otherwise rather imperial demand that candidates must be able to "think on their feet" may well be justified. After all, that is what doctors faced with a new patient or a new slide of some diseased organ do every day. The fancy name for this, done on the basis of lots of knowledge, is "diagnostic skills".

HOW DOES ALL THIS PAN OUT?

Well, after their two interviews, candidates can spend the rest of the day kicking their heels, being intimidated by the seeming confidence of Oxbridge students and wondering how people living in such a beautiful place can have such atrocious dress sense.

Meanwhile, a bit of academic horse trading goes on. Each college will rank the candidates it has seen in order of perceived ability. A college with too many top ranked candidates might pass on some of them to another college less impressed with those it has seen. If that happens, the "traded" student may be called in for a further interview. Not all colleges have the same ideal candidate in mind, so quite a few of those recalled will get in nevertheless.

After that, all the selectors meet to coordinate their offers. These will be based on three equally important factors. One is a calculation based on the candidate's GCSE results: all candidates may have grade As, but what matters is how these measure up to the results generally achieved within the candidate's own school. In other words, getting three As in a school in which nobody else did gives a candidate that special edge.

The second factor are the BMAT results, which will be with the central medical facility by now. Here, no allowances are made for a candidate's school or background.

Lastly, the score sheet produced by the college as a result of the interview makes up the last third of the evaluation.

As a result, some 150 candidates will receive the offer of a place at a specific college, conditional on them getting three As at A-level. Another 16 or so will get an "open offer", which means that their college cannot yet be specified. Where they will go depends mainly on the candidates dropped because they did not get the required grades.

So, how fair is the outcome? Well, it is not as bad as the Laura Spence story suggests. In 2002, two years after the working class school girl from Whitley Bay was rejected by Oxford, the university received 51.5 per cent of its applicants from the state sector and 34 per cent from private schools (the other 13.5 per cent are foreign students etc.). Almost exactly one fifth of each group (20.8 per cent) got an offer. Since the state school group was considerably bigger, this meant that its students would make up the majority of Oxford medical students.

What about other categories, though? Well, the picture is uneven. In recent years, the Oxford medical faculty has consistently admitted a slightly higher proportion of women and of students of Asian origin than there are in the general population. It has, however, an unrepresentatively low proportion of Afro-Caribbean students and male students of working class origin. The official explanation for these last two facts is that Oxford is not a regional university. Black and working class students, I was told, generally prefer to study close to home.

There is another explanation, of course. These two groups of generally very poor young people taught in poorly equipped schools will find it hardest to obtain the qualifications required to get an interview and so will not be encouraged by their schools to apply. Also, working class boys with the right grade predictions may lack the formal manners that carry you through. The are likely to be gruff rather than polite, macho rather than carefully balanced in the way they express themselves. While these are useful qualities in their current environment, they might well shed them in a different one – university students almost invariably do. By judging them purely on what they are at this point, the Oxford medical selection system does not work for them.

The same problem, despite slightly different selection criteria, exists at Cambridge, as one story shows. A sixth form head at a London comprehensive situated between two large housing estates bitterly recalled to me how he had sent one of his very best students to a medical interview there. The teacher had spent a lot of time encouraging the boy to take this frightening step and had carefully picked a college the school had some links with. The applicant, who came from a large working class family, was rejected nevertheless. When the teacher asked for an explanation, he was told that the main problem had been "nervousness in the interview, a lack of ability to hypothesize, expand on points, a lack of verbal articulacy and of interview skills."

Working class girls generally do better in the interview, though it is not clear why. Perhaps being polite and formal comes more easily to them or perhaps the interviewers are more sympathetic towards a timid girl than a sullen boy. It is hard to tell.

DOES COACHING WORK FOR MEDICINE?

Tutors admit that quite a few of the students they see have probably been coached for the interview, but feel that it would be unfair to reject a good candidates on those grounds alone. One tutor actually suggested that such preparation did, after all, suggest a commitment to the medical profession.

Some coaching is informal. Quite a few candidates in both the state and the private sector are doctor's kids and will have had a chance to talk through likely questions at home. Alternatively, a doctor friend, relative or neighbour might be roped in.

On the formal side, many schools in the private sector also run a brief course, usually called something like "how to get into medicine", which is especially geared toward Oxbridge. In addition, private schools also run science societies which may discuss medical research or explore health related issues.

Well-off state school parents can also buy in help. As a start, some private AS level revision courses now offer interview training for a range of subjects, including medicine (by A-level revision time, it is too late for this). There are also at least two companies specifically offering Oxbridge Entrance training in science subjects, including Medicine.

Do interview training courses work? One of the medical dons I spoke to insisted that he "could not believe that the organisers of such courses could possibly deliver on their promises." Others felt certain that they would be able to spot a candidate who had been coached. They also seemed unreasonably sure that they had not encountered such a candidate yet.

At least one private company now offers a four day course for aspiring medics. Run by a company called Workshop University Conferences under the title Medlink at Nottingham University, it introduces first year A-level students to various aspects of medical practice. Here, teenagers whose parents can afford the £200 fee can treat Harvey, a state-of-the-art dummy, for a variety of conditions. They also learn about medical terms and diagnostic practices, get guidance on the university admissions process and have a mock interview. Although not especially geared towards Oxbridge, such an immersion process may help a candidate to meet the requirements set out above.

What, though, can you do to help a talented child with a genuine interest in Medicine if you cannot afford any of the above? There are, in fact, quite a few things:

1. First, get your teenager yet again in front of her computer. She needs to look at the internet archives of *The Guardian* or *The Independent* (which are free) or the more detailed online archive maintained by *The Times* (which levies a small subscription charge) under words like "public health", "cancer", "disability" or "Aids". This should throw up articles on key issues, as will a trawl through *New Scientist* or *Scientific American*. Ask her to pick out half a dozen recent pieces and read them through. What are doctors' main concerns? Which specialist deals with what medical problem and how?

2. Encourage her to think about the moral dilemmas faced by today's doctors, sometimes as the result of scientific progress. She'll find lots of articles and radio programmes dealing with those under "medical ethics".

3. Help her to make friends with medical statistics. Buy a simple statistics textbook which gives examples from real life. Your daughter need not understand everything inside (and should not panic if she doesn't), but it will help her to get used slowly and in her own home to seeing graphs etc. as information givers.

4. Persuade your daughter to borrow *Gray's Anatomy* from the library or look at the illustrations online (the text will be too hard). She may have done this in human biology before, but has probably forgotten what our various components look like.

156

Checking out enlarged online photographs of molecules or cells so she learns to identify the various types can also be of some help.

5. Find out how medics think. All sorts of medical writing can supply the reader with extremely useful insights: The *Man who Mistook his Wife for a Hat* by Oliver Sacks will serve your purposes no less well than *The Invisible Enemy: A Natural History of Viruses* by Dorothy H. Crawford.

6. Ask your GP if your daughter can shadow him. Then encourage her to take the opportunity to ask him questions, which makes the experience doubly useful. She will not just learn about the practice of medicine, but also practice talking to medics.

7. Encourage the girl to arrive at her college the night before the interview, even if you live relatively near. Medical interviews are intense and it is not a good idea to walk into yours breathlessly after getting up at five am and standing for two hours on a train. Far better to have an exploratory stroll first and meet other applicants.

These points should cover just about everything done in "entrance training courses" for potential medics, except for the treatment practice, which is less important. Applicants are not expected to have treated anyone before.

At both the beginning and the end of this process, you must also do something else. You must get across that Oxbridge, in fact, does want some candidates from a quite ordinary, non-medical background. So, your daughter has nothing to hide and should try to mention her origins. If we ever get a regulator charged with ensuring a fair distribution of university places, of course, Oxbridge might suddenly discover great promise in more young people like her.

16

Other ways of healing the sick

Medicine, especially in the era of the TV serial, offers bright young people an almost irresistible dream. The dreamer, dressed in a crisp white coat, is bending over a pale, rapidly fading patient. He then straightens up, furrows his brow and proceeds to deliver a brilliant diagnosis or to prescribe the perfect drug. The patient recovers in a jiffy and is full of gratitude. Colleagues standing near the doctor glance up at him (or her) with total admiration (or unbridled lust).

Waking up from such a dream can be tough but is often inevitable. Medical applicants, despite their sharp minds and top science A-levels, have some of the lowest UCAS success rates. Oxford admits only 14 per cent of them, Cambridge around 22 per cent. Competition means that most will not get any of their four university choices. Reaching for another, last-minute option, perhaps abroad, can be unwise. Some medical courses are not accredited in the UK, so their graduates cannot work here.

Fortunately, a sixth former determined to heal the sick has another, equally attractive option: pure science. This is because when it comes to finding out what ails people or to curing them, those who lead the field are often not doctors at all. They are scientists working in a great variety of disciplines or in cross-disciplinary ways.

By opting for a career in Chemistry, Biology or Physics, the young idealist can improve the well-being of patients all over the world. She can also earn an excellent salary, become world famous and, sometimes, even wear a white coat. Given the range of medical problems still in search of solutions, the opportunities are endless.

Despite this, a bright student's prospects of getting into one of the Oxbridge natural sciences courses are not bad at all. Oxford's Biological Sciences course admits nearly 44 per cent of all applicants. Its Chemistry course admits 47 per cent and its Biochemistry one 36 per cent. Oxford Physics admits close to 30 per cent of applicants, as does the Cambridge Natural Science course.

In view of these facts, it seems strange that relatively few students choose to apply. For a brainy sixth former wishing to both do good and to do well, one of these science options does seem an obvious choice.

CHEATING DEATH IN THE LAB

While scientists are highly respected in much of the world, their image in Britain has often been that of dangerous madmen or unworldly boffins, engaged in weird, pointless experiments. So, if you are still wondering what kind of contribution these people have made to our lives, here is a brief list.

Take our ability to explore a patient's insides without surgery. This was first made possible by Marie Curie, whose research into radioactivity led to the development of the X-ray machine. Curie, then went on to discover two medically useful new chemical elements, Polonium and Radium.

Magnetic resonance imaging (MRI) has given us a safer, more detailed way of looking inside the body, avoiding even harmful x-rays or dyes. The MRI scanner, which uses magnetism and radio waves to produce clear pictures of the human anatomy, is now a standard medical tool. It is based on research by Peter Mansfield, a physicist, and Paul Lauterbur, a chemist.

Even non-scientists have heard about the decoding of the double helix, the structure of the molecule which determines DNA. Carried out by the physicist Francis Crick and the zoologist James Watson, it has had a huge impact on medical progress. Genetic research is based on it and keeps moving forward: by revealing the structure of large complex molecules such as insulin, penicillin and vitamin B12, the crystallographer Dorothy Hodgkin made possible the development of drugs that have saved countless lives.

Aids research was much advanced by the research of Kary Mullis, a chemist and champion surfer, whose discovery of the PCR test made possible viral load counting. Chemists Sydney Brenner and Robert Horvitz, together with molecular biologist John Sulston, subsequently discovered the key genes that regulate organ development and programme cell death, which is equally crucial to the study of Aids.

By discovering RNA interference (RNAi), a naturally occurring process for switching off specific genes, mathematician Andrew Fire and Craig Mello, a biochemist, pioneered a genetic technique making possible radical new treatments for incurable disorders from blindness to heart disease and diabetes. The research findings of Paul Nurse have given doctors a way to understand, and hopefully alter, the deadly process of cell division in cancer.

You might also like to know is that the reward all those hard-working scientists reaped has not just been moral satisfaction. There is also celebrity status: each of them won a Nobel Prize for their work except for Marie Curie, who won two, one for Physics and the other for Chemistry.

Research success can have further attractive benefits. Paul Nurse, a London-born biologist who was the first person in his working class family to attend university, happily told reporters in 2001 that he had spent some of his £800,000 Nobel Prize money on a 500cc Kawasaki motorbike. As he also received a knighthood, its parking space outside his Cambridge lab is labelled Sir Paul Nurse.

CREATING A HEALTHIER EARTH

Chemists, biologists and physicists might even be able to heal our sick planet. Not only are they steadily increasing their grasp of what is causing ecological change, but they are identifying cures that can be administered with a very large spoon. Research done on ozone depletion by Nobel Prize winner Sherwood Rowland, an expert in atmospheric chemistry, led to the 1995 world ban on the use of CFCs in aerosol sprays.

Rowland is one of several hundred world experts who form part of the Intergovernmental Panel on Climate Change, the UN body which released the first comprehensive report on the problem in February 2007. Global warming, it concluded, was 90 per cent likely to be due to human activity. The consequences would be higher temperatures, a rise in sea levels, draughts, famines and more hurricanes. Having named the guilty and spelled out the world's dire prospects, the IPCC scientists will next look at options for adaptation and mitigation.

In other words, the survival of humanity (as well as that of our luxury motor cycle industry) may depend on experts like these. With an Oxbridge degree in one of the natural sciences, you could end up joining them.

17

Aftershocks

The next stage is another long wait. Only in early January will most offers and rejections arrive and your daughter needs to keep up her spirits until them. Even if she left her interview in tears (a sure sign that her interviewer was an amateur) she might well find an offer in the post.

If she does, it is time to go into top gear for A-level study. Oxbridge is not very flexible once a grade offer is made, and the admissions tutors I spoke to could only recall two recent case in which a candidate had been accepted although he had not come up to the offer level: the first was a girl who had fallen seriously ill. The second candidate had been evicted from the hostel in which he lived, and the grades accepted were ABB rather than AAB.

So, it is time for the study plan, revision course, and a (partial) withdrawal from the endless social whirl that is teenage life. It is also time to withdraw from paid work. If you are a totally penniless, self-supporting A-level student, Oxbridge might be able to help. There is a handful of small study grants for disadvantaged candidates, which the college bursar can tell you about. Cambridge Special Access offers things like accommodation assistance in very exceptional cases.

Let us next assume that the bright girl actually got in. What this means is that you can look forward to several months of mutual incomprehension. Dropping in after her first term, she will confuse you by talking about mysterious things like formal hall, mods and prelims, and you will shock her by failing to understand the basics of existentialist philosophy. Her school friends will wonder who gave her the haircut from hell. When she tries to talk about her new life, her brother is likely to tell the poor girl that her accent stinks and her sister might accuse her of being stuck up.

Unlike students at many other universities, she will rarely come home at weekends. Oxbridge workloads and college social life do not allow for it. Those who see their parents every Sunday are perceived as odd.

After the first giddy year, though, an Oxbridge student and her family usually rediscover their common humanity, or at least a shared liking for Becks. By now, the dizzy girl might have learnt to appreciate your cooking and the fact that money does not grow on trees. She will also have become bilingual: she might still talk posh for a day or so, but will then switch out of it. Knowing that she managed to cope with an initially terrifying study schedule will have calmed her. She'll be smug but sympathetic. She might even go bowling with the younger kids. Holidays will no longer feel like a battle zone. This is the moment for you to rejoice in your Oxbridge work, and for her to help repaint the flat.

AMONG ALIENS

The bad news is that even if your teenager has got in, the Oxbridge dream can still go wrong. What if your visiting daughter confesses that she has not really unpacked anything more than her teddy bear after three weeks of Oxbridge life, because she does not feel she fits in? She hates the whole place, made a terrible mistake and is planning to drop out as soon as she can find someone who will promise to feed the tame rat which the poor lonely little soul had adopted.

That Valium suddenly seems a good idea, after all. What are you supposed to do? Offer to drive up so she can collect her stuff ? Or should you just tell her that the feeling will pass and that she ought to pull herself together?

The answer is that it would be a good idea to first know more. The first sight of student life anywhere can be exhilarating for some and terrifying for others, and student life at Oxbridge comes with added medieval pomp. Most students adjust fast, often by doing all the things you warned them against. This may not happen if they encounter situations which they had not expected to find and are not equipped to handle alone. A student in this predicament might become depressed, feel unable to study or decide to drop out. Some Oxbridge students in every year do. (Mercifully, student suicides are rare; they also occur mainly at the final degree stage.)

Given these frightening possibilities, you should try and get your daughter to explain what exactly bothers her. Sometimes the mere act of pouring out all her small initial failures or disappointments will make everything all right.

Chances are, your fears will prove unjustified. The problem is, more often than not, a disappointing grade, a tutor who speaks too fast or the discovery that nobody else in her year likes Jamie Teakstone. The best thing is to let her go on uninterruptedly about those, even if that means having your roast burn to cinders. After three to four hours of woes, she might suddenly jump up, grab her backpack and run for the next bus back because she has just remembered that there is a college entz (club night) at ten thirty.

The girl has just been letting off steam, which is normal behaviour among students. So, don't rush in with advice, or agree that going to Oxbridge was perhaps a mistake for someone from a background like hers.

Still there are areas of Oxbridge life that can give rise to real grievances, and students and their parents need to know about them.

18

Women's troubles

"When I walk home through the quad at 2 a.m. and see the moon rise above the college battlements I can't believe how lucky I am, and I really hate the idea that just two years from now I got to leave again," one girl from a South London housing estate last year wrote to a cousin she was encouraging to apply to Oxford. She is not alone. Female students of all backgrounds often fall in love at first sight with their beautiful old university.

This love has not always been reciprocated. For the first six hundred years of Oxford and Cambridge, women were banned from both universities. Their sheer presence was deemed unacceptable. College fellows (researchers and lecturers) were not allowed to marry until the end of the 19th century, and while a man could do so once he had reached the status of professor, many had lost interest by that stage, wrote Vera Britten in her history The Women at Oxford.

Women's attempts to gain at least partial access to higher learning were greeted with contempt. Even liberal figures like John Ruskin, who served as Oxford Professor of Art, declared in 1871: "I cannot let the bonnets in, on any conditions, this term. The three public lectures will chiefly be on angles, degrees of colour-prisms (without any prunes) and other such things, of no use to the female mind and they would occupy the seats in mere disappointed puzzlement."

After the first female students were admitted to Oxford in 1879, the Canon of Christ Church, Professor Edward Pusey, described women's colleges as "one of the greatest misfortunes that have happened even in our own time in Oxford".

In order to save male students from distraction, female students could not initially attend lectures or enter any of the men's junior common rooms in which much of the university's intellectual life took place.

Even when the lecture halls were opened to women, it was not in order to enable them to qualify. They were still denied access to the all-important degree at the end of their course. Without this document, of course, the few dozen exceptionally bright and determined women who had been accepted could contribute to society only as volunteers. Eleanor Rathbone became an outstanding social reformer, while Gertrude Bell joined her ambassador uncle as an unpaid assistant and went on to create the new state of Iraq out of various tribal territories.

Another graduate, Margery Fry, fought to improve the conditions for prisoners in British gaols, organised war relief for Europe during WW1, founded the National Council for the Abolition of the Death Penalty and became a governor of the BBC.

Those who needed the official qualification in order to get paid work had a very long wait. Oxford only started to issue degrees to its women graduates in 1920, Cambridge in 1947.

Women students remained outsiders for decades. They were banished to colleges far from the main university facilities, which initially lacked all basic amenities, from bathrooms to libraries. They were also condemned to an almost prison-like existence. Female students were not allowed out, even to the shops, without being chaperoned by "a respectable, elderly woman". During lectures, the chaperone would sit in the back of the hall knitting until she could take her charge home again.

The female principals who ran the women's colleges tried hard to gain acceptance by being as unfeminine as possible in their meetings with male academic colleagues. "Not a word was wasted, not a charm nor a wile exercised," a biographer approvingly wrote of Emily Penrose, the first principal of the Oxford women's college, Somerville.

Students too were expected to conform to almost unearthly standards of perfection. Elizabeth Wordsworth, who founded Lady Margaret Hall, suggested that it should be named after Lady Margaret Beaufort, the mother of Henry VII: "She was a gentlewoman, a scholar, and a saint, and after having been three times married she took a vow of celibacy. What more could be expected of a woman?"

None of this was enough to change male students' preference for someone who could shoot grouse. Public misogyny was rampant. In 1926, the majority of Oxford Union members voted in favour of a resolution which stated: "The women's colleges should be levelled to the ground."

Widely reported, the resolution caused some embarrassment to Oxford in the outside world. The university's male students were perceived as having gone too far, as being out of touch with the modern world.

Things improved gradually for women students after that, though not to everybody's satisfaction. "The presence of women at Oxford was now a deterrent for friendships between men," the head of one of the town's men's colleges recalled peevishly in his 1940s memoirs. Lest this deterrent should completely scupper the chances of the lonely male don, the number of women students at Oxford and Cambridge was formally restricted to one sixth of all students until 1957.

MODERN TIMES

But all that is history now. Oxbridge is about learning and this could not be restricted to academic fields. The universities gradually came to agree with the anonymous don who had warned in the Oxford Magazine: "The young men and young women are not going to spend their lives here, and we make it difficult for them to learn a very important part of human behaviour, how to conduct oneself in relation the opposite sex. We isolate the problem, give it more thought than it is worth, enact regulations which, if they are effective, postpone till a later age adjustments which have to be made some time and somehow. The world is not a world of chaperones, of perfect vigilance . . ."

Equal opportunities legislation did the rest to turn both Oxford and Cambridge into something other than the rowdy boys' towns of yore. Today, numbers are equal, and all colleges and facilities are open to both women and men. Even more importantly, it's fun to be a young woman at Oxbridge, as all the female students I spoke to made absolutely clear.

For a start, living in a smallish town dominated by students can make young women feel very safe. Although neither Cambridge nor Oxford are crime-free, many praised the physical mobility they enjoyed by being able to cycle or walk almost everywhere, day and night. "I really love working my way through a pile of books until I have totally grasped something, and here I can stay in the library all night and walk home at 3 a.m.," one girl said enthusiastically.

There are other advantages, especially for those who have other plans for 3 a.m. The academic atmosphere, plus the presence of so many bright young male students can create new rules of attraction. Elsewhere, talking to a really clever girl can make quite a few men nervous, but at Oxbridge female brains qualify as a definite turn-on.

And, when it comes to careers, not just paid but highly paid employment today beckons after graduation. Oxbridge women do notably better than women from other universities, just like Oxbridge men do.

SIX FOOT IRRITATIONS

This is not to say that Oxbridge is a gender-equal utopia. While most academics are very careful to observe equality legislation and some can seem positively delighted at the progress of an especially bright female student, this is not a universal rule. Some very elderly dons can be awkward or subtly dismissive when forced to tutor a girl. After all, these strange creatures have been wandering among the college walls for a mere thirty years.

Even male fellow students can be irritating. Girls from single sex grammar schools, which are very brainy places, often complain that far less bright boys will hog the conversation in a tutorial, seminar or burger bar. As a result, getting into Oxbridge can be the beginning of a new kind of battle if you are a girl.

Oxford's 2002–3 Student Union Vice President (Women), Melanie Marshall, points out that there are considerable inequalities when it comes to university and college spending on sport. Women's sports are invariably under-funded. Far more money goes on facilities for cricket and rowing than on those for aerobics or yoga. There is also an assumption that what women do in sport is less important; the men's boat race and its outcome are reported in the national press. The women's boat race, an equally annual event, rarely ever gets a mention in the college rag.

The imbalance, Melanie explains, is a leftover from the university's men-only days, and it helps to make male students feel a sense of ownership of the place. This sounds terribly abstract until you look around and see a few young men happily throw about a ball on a manicured college lawn, while two or three girls stand around awkwardly as if someone still needs to hand them a script.

When asked to recall a case of individual discrimination, though, Melanie couldn't come up with one, however hard she tried. What there is of gender injustice is clearly not grave enough to leave any indelible trauma. We parted following her promise that she would consult her archives, in case they contained any striking cases, and that was the last I heard.

THE BRAIN RACE

Academic inequality is a different matter. In 2002, 26.2 per cent of men, but only 16.6 per cent of women studying at Cambridge got

Firsts in their final exams. The gap is similar each year, but rather puzzling. After all, female pupils do as well, or slightly better than male ones in each year's A-levels. One key factor pointed to has been the level of encouragement received from a student's academic supervisor. This, apparently, is more easily given to young men whose aggressive "intellectual muscle flexing" is often taken as a sign of excellence.

What actual discrimination there is at Oxbridge mainly affects female staff. Career prospects for women are limited at the two universities. At both Oxford and Cambridge, women in 2002 constituted about 20 per cent of academic staff, mostly in the lower ranks. By 2007 that figure had risen to just 23 per cent, despite and active women's academic network and the introduction of career development support. Less than 10 per cent of Oxford's professors are female.

This has financial, as well status consequences. In 2006, the pay gap between full time male and female academics was 16.5 per cent at Oxford and 19.7 per cent at Cambridge. While women academics earn less everywhere, such gaps are among the highest in the country. At Bolton University the pay differential is 1.5 per cent.

Women have been more successful at gaining top administration posts. Cambridge has had a female Vice Chancellor, Professor Alison Richard, since 2003 and three of the university's five Pro-Vice Chancellors (deputies) are female. At Oxford the figure for this group is four out of twelve. Oxford by 2007 also had seven female college heads, but this leaves nearly thirty colleges headed by men.

Generally, most female academics still work in the current or former women's colleges, especially in St. Hilda's at Oxford and Newnham and New Hall at Cambridge. Oxbridge is an ambitious world in which men are often that little bit more ambitious, but at least if there are only women to fill the jobs, women get them.

Even the honorary jobs held by students, much contested because they will look good on future job applications, fall to the more pushy, namely men. Take the role of the president of the junior common room (the college union). Despite there being as many female as male students at Oxford, only six of 36 such positions went to women in 2002. Somerville, one of the old Oxford women's colleges which admitted men in 1995, has not had a single woman in the post since.

This matters because female staff might pick students by more women-friendly criteria. Interviewed about sexism at Cambridge a few years ago, the feminist writer and English don Germaine Greer complained that whenever a women's college had taken on male staff, they had shown a worrying interview preference for admitting "fluffy blondes", rather than earnest and sometimes plainer girls with an obvious academic bent.

Equally, female academics can be more sympathetic to women-centred projects. A female student who proposes to do her degree research on, say, maternal needs in public housing, is likely to elicit more support from a female don than from her male equivalent.

WOMEN'S WORLDS

As a result of such differences, current students, old girls and the female staff at the remaining women's colleges have made sure to protect their single-sex status whenever a change was put to the vote. After all, they can offer a roll call of successful women.

St. Hilda's College, Oxford, which educated prize-winning scientist Susan Greenfield, former Tory Education Secretary Gillian Shephard, poet Wendy Cope and broadcaster Joan Bakewell, decided in 2003 against going co-ed. The defenders of the status quo argued that not only are the opportunities there better for women than in mixed-sex colleges (there are no all-male ones anymore), but that the atmosphere is better. Many female graduates describe it as more collaborative, supportive and conducive to lasting friendships.

So, would your daughter be best off in a place like that? Well, it depends. Those with academic ambitions should know that women at mixed colleges get more Firsts than those at women's colleges. There are several reasons for this. Women's library facilities may have caught up since their foundation stage, but the most high-flying academics tend to be attached to mixed colleges. Also, the old Catch 22 problem remains: as fewer of the women's college staff are eminent enough to be involved in setting the exams, fewer of their students get the best possible exam preparation.

In addition, the students who attend the women's colleges are no longer mainly the bookish, hardworking spinsters of yore. The outcome is that exam results are middling at best. St. Hilda's languishes towards the bottom of the Norrington table, the informal ranking of Oxford colleges by degree results.

There is also the general atmosphere. It is not totally female anymore: male friends come to visit and one women's college, Newnham, now has male lecturers too. The odd boyfriend from another college even stays the night. It is hard to imagine now that all girls from this college had to be tutored in pairs until well into the 20th century, as a female student could not possibly be left alone with a male tutor.

Contemporary female concerns are of a different kind. The Cambridge women's officer proudly talks of the improvements she has made in contraceptive facilities. Female pressure also resulted in the introduction of a university night bus, funded by bankers Goldman Sachs, which takes female students safely home to their colleges after clubbing in town. After a long debate, it was decided that male ones could hop on too.

On the other hand, tutorials and seminars in Newnham, New Hall and St. Hilda's remain women-only. For girls educated at a mixed comprehensive (as are most state school pupils) this can be a hell of a shock. Student life, after all, is not just about doing work. They are young women and most of them fully expect to have torrid love affairs with young men at their own level during their student years.

This can still happen, you might want to reassure your girl: lectures, university societies, voluntary work and (ahem) pub crawls bring the sexes together, but finding a boyfriend could be harder work for the girl who does not knock them out at first sight. She might not relish sitting in the JCR or college bar surrounded mainly (or, depending on the day, only) by other girls. Cycling through the pouring rain into the distant town centre to lectures, the superior main library and one of the livelier pubs does make you envy those more conveniently housed.

So, why do a small majority vote to keep things as they are every time? The main reason, I was repeatedly told, was ambition. You do get to try your hand at more things than you would otherwise. Want to be captain of the rugby team? Edit the college paper? Be president of the JCR? At a women's college, no bossy, overconfident public school boy will snatch these things from you. Even a small, speccy girl might get her chance.

Students also have fewer temptations to just skive off and do nothing. There is some excellent teaching, notably in Newnham. Girls from very religious or traditionalist backgrounds also find the environment more congenial or at least their parents think they should.

For many female students the women's colleges remain, initially at least, a poor second choice. One of the few criticism I heard from the otherwise terribly positive Student Access volunteers about the entrance system was that it advised girls from "non-traditional backgrounds" to not specify their college choice. Far too often, they said, this resulted in them being shunted off into a women's college. Was it so bad then? I asked. "No, of course not," was the invariable reply. "They are quite pretty places, less draughty than some of the older mixed and formerly all-male ones. Seminars can be great too. But it's harder to have real fun there." It is arguments like those, I suspect, which made St. Hilda's students recently decide to go co-ed in 2010, after all.

So, if your daughter is at one of the few remaining women's college, expect a few complaints, perhaps slightly more than you would get if she was at a mixed one. However, don't accept that this is a good reason for leaving. Inequalities exist at other universities and students at any Oxbridge women's college make great friends, complete interesting projects, obtain Firsts and end up in fabulous jobs.

And, as mentioned before, no student is obliged to drink her nightly glass of Hooch or Perrier in her own college. One girl from a northern grammar school consigned to a women's college spent all her evenings at the bar of the mixed one attended by her older brother. Not surprisingly perhaps, she is now living with his closest university friend. Whether you regard this as a happy ending depends, I suspect, on whether you are a parent or a teenager.

19

Race

The publicity material sent out by Oxford and Cambridge shows young people of all different skin colours studying and hanging out together. The pictures are real enough and so, by all accounts, is the happy student experience. Such jolly images, though, can leave an ethnic minority teenager unprepared for what can be a fairly tough start.

Oxford and Cambridge are among the whitest universities in the country, by far the whitest in Britain's multicultural south. This means that a student who has so far been part of an often large ethnic minority group will take time to adjust. Living among people who don't look like you, don't speak like you or don't eat Ackee can be amazingly stressful, no matter how much you were looking forward to leaving home.

What can make this situation worse are the attitudes of others. The days in which blatant, in-your-face racism was tolerated in Britain are long over. It is hard to imagine now that in the 1960s it was possible for pubs to display signs saying "no Blacks, no Irish", or that some grammar schools would not admit Asian students. Such acts are illegal now and public attitudes have changed well beyond the law.

Ethnic minority students, though, can still feel left out even if there is no conscious intention to do so. Sometimes, this is just an assumption that anyone who is not white must be profoundly different. As Pria, a Muslim Liverpudlian of Pakistani origin told me with a shrug: "The fact that you are wearing a headscarf does not mean you don't want to be asked along when the rest of the girls go shoe shopping."

Chima, an extremely bright and outgoing black first year student from East London, loves her Cambridge course but says with slight exasperation: "It's not that anyone has ever been hostile, just that it is always me who has to start the conversation . . . And not wanting to step on anyone's toes can make people edge around meaning."

Chima was not imagining her problem. Since Oxbridge students tend to come from middle class schools, whether state or private, some have never talked to a Black person before. "We do have one Black chap on my course, but he rather keeps to himself," a first year from a rural boy's public school told me in reply to a question, then went on slightly nervously: "S'ppose one should make more of an effort, but I'm just not sure what kind of things he'd be into."

At other times, the assumptions made can be deeply offensive. Jad, a well-dressed Black student, was quietly sitting in his JCR, when a passing female college worker threw him a suspicious glance, before inquiring politely: "Are you lost, dear?"

A black civil servant recalls once being mistaken for a cleaner by another student during her first week in college. Apologising that he had only just got up, he beckoned her in so she could get started on his room.

A seemingly funny remark may also sting. The white student who takes his black fellow tutee to a club, but then quips: "I thought you people had dancing in your blood," is not just being silly. He is generalising and so might well believe other lies about Blacks.

For some reason, asking someone "do you cheer for the West Indies, then?" is still regarded an OK question over a post-game drink in a few colleges.

Ethnic minority students also often feel irritated by hostile remarks on immigration and asylum. After all, many of their parents arrived in Britain by this painful route as, of course, did the people who founded such very British institutions as Marks and Spencer, ITV, the Glyndebourne Opera Festival and the RSPCA.

As a result, your son may return from college in the first weeks tense and unsure. Black male students, in particular, can react badly to their first encounter with Oxbridge life. They may feel they are not being treated with respect and almost every year a few of them drop out.

If your son is actually considering this, it will not help to remind him of the long-term payoff in terms of opportunities and careers (which can be impossible to focus on if nobody at his college has yet invited him for coffee). Nor will it do much good to say that Black students have reported very similar experiences at Britain's other top universities, so a switch will not necessarily make the problem go away. The best thing to do, probably, is to ask the lad to defer judgment a little longer, at least until the end of his first year.

At this point, having struggled to get into Oxbridge and then to fit into life there, everything often suddenly falls into place, at least for those Black students willing to persist in their initiatives.

Chima, who had struggled in her first term to even keep a student conversation going, six months later had a rich social life involving students of every colour and background. She was vice president of the Cambridge University English Society, social secretary of her college badminton club, a theatre critic for her college magazine and active in the Target Schools campaign seeking to encourage more Black applicants. Despite her earlier experiences, she had no doubts at all that going to Oxbridge had, for her at least, been the right choice.

This is not to say that ethnic minority students should passively accept racist behaviour. All universities, including Oxford and Cambridge, now have strong anti-racism policies and will act on reports of racist incidents. The problem can be, of course, that a student, may not feel that her experience was bad enough to mention. A study by the Cambridge student union, CUSU, suggested that one off the cuff comment in the college bar may be enough to cause tremendous upset but not seen as worth reporting. Besides, how do you react to something that was probably not meant to be a snub?

One way of reacting is by getting support from within your own group, and far more of this is now available than there was even five years ago. Sometimes, this just means a club in which you can meet other ethnic minority students from different colleges. This is often supplemented by events designed to spread information about your minority group.

At Cambridge, for instance, the Caribbean Association seeks to bridge the gap through cook-outs, lectures and what they claim are the best parties in the university. Others, like the Hindu society, organize regular talks but also, as the culmination of their annual events a widely popular, colourful Diwali ball.

Some societies are more overtly political. Oxford Black and Asian Caucus (BAC), which was revived in 2003, targets racism, which it regards as a real problem, through events like Black History Week and showings of black films. In this way it aims to "promote equality and celebrate diversity, helping to make the university a tolerant and supportive place for its dynamic student community".

CUSU puts much of its efforts into campaigning for the same aim, but also insists that the atmosphere in its colleges and faculties is broadly anti-racist. Most incidents reported to its officials involve racial taunting on the football pitch. This is not exactly a practice confined to Oxbridge, but most students find it deeply objectionable and their union is determined to stamp it out.

All these bodies, to which has to be added GEEMA (Group to Encourage Ethnic Minority Applications), seek to emphasize the positive about their culture and about the university's efforts, so much so that, as one white anti-racist student put it to me, you sometimes wish they would just draw up a checklist of the things they absolutely hate!

These societies often meet more urgent needs. According to one activist, the benefits of membership are that "it gives a sense of security, it motivates you to discuss things and to deal with it. It gives you mutual support and counseling... We are in a white institution, we have to encourage each other to be proud. We are role models."

One such role model is Pav Akhtar, the president of Cambridge University's Student Union in 2001–2, who is an ethnic minority student. Asked to comment about the situation, he has said that he is optimistic about the future: "I didn't think that it was a place for me, a lower class Asian northerner, but the university has accommodated me... It's by coming here that we will change things here and change perceptions."

OFFICIAL LINES

The social experience of ethnic minority students at Oxbridge is not something the university as a whole used to take much interest in. It was implicitly, and sometimes openly assumed that these people had no right to fuss; they were expected to be just grateful for the opportunities offered to them.

Many present day academics feel very differently and will go to great length to make an individual black student feel at ease. However, when you bring up the subject of race with certain Oxbridge dons, these rugged individualists mysteriously produce an almost identical phrase: "Actually, we have a slight overrepresentation of Asian students in certain courses. Some people, you know, have complained about this." A look at the available statistics for Cambridge really does not justify such complacency. Students of Indian origin, who apply in their hundreds, indeed have a reasonable success rate. Around a fifth of them, or 21 per cent, were admitted in 2005. The success rate of Chinese students in the same year stood at 28 per cent.

However, these are young people from established communities and many of their Oxbridge students, when you meet them, turn out to be privately educated. Quite a few of the others too have been raised in families running small or medium size businesses.

According to a 2001 study, Asians from Bangladesh, a very poor community, had only a 13 per cent success rate.

The picture turns really grim when it comes to blacks. Not all that many Afro-Caribbean students apply, but their success rate is abysmal. In 2001, two(!) out of 23 applicants got in, or 8 per cent.

The obvious reason, and that invariably given by dons, is schooling. Afro-Caribbeans tend to live in the most deprived areas and consequently go to the worst schools. As a result, they may lack the knowledge base required to get in. There is also a cultural factor. Black students often talk in a very direct way and can come across as dogmatic or abrasive.

To see whether the key factors are really just culture and schooling, though, it is worth looking at another statistic from that Cambridge list, that for Black African applicants. This includes students of all classes and income groups with parents (or grand-parents) from all over the world. Teachers I spoke to felt that most were probably Nigerian and from comfortably off and educated homes. So, how well did this group do? The answer is, not much better than Afro-Caribbeans. In 2001, only 12 per cent (eight out of 67) were accepted by Cambridge.

The percentage of white applicants accepted by Cambridge, incidentally then was 35 per cent.

When asked for an explanation, dons often point to subject choice. Black African parents strongly encourage their children to apply for Medicine, Economics and Law, the courses most difficult to gain admission to. However, black applicants to other courses do not seem to do very much better.

At Oxford, the situation is fairly similar. In 2001, for example, 38.7 per cent of white students who applied for undergraduate places were successful; 100 black students applied, just 1.3 of the total, and only 18 got in.

Admissions figures have not exactly shot up since. In 2005, the success rate of black students at Cambridge had risen to 17 per cent but fallen to 13.5 per cent at Oxford. This has to be measured against a rate of 28 per cent for white applicants.

TEA FOR TWO

There is, of course, an additional explanation, which has its root in the informal, unwritten structure of the entrance process. Until recently, a high proportion of interviews would take place between two people, the admissions tutor and the applicant. Some admissions tutors may be just a little more gruff, a little less welcoming to an ethnic minority candidate than they would be to a white one. This need not even be a conscious process, but can still lower the quality of a candidate's performance. I certainly found that those accepted are less likely to have had a cold, hostile reception.

The new practice of having almost all interviews conducted by two admissions tutors could have a positive impact on this problem, but there are other ones. Interviewers might also react to the candidate's use of "Black" English, or to his refusal to engage in a mannered but very rapid response dialogue, preferring to instead slowly ponder over an unfamiliar question. As the American psychologist Alexenia Y. Baldwin puts it in her study *The Gifted and Talented: development perspectives,* gifted black teenagers do not necessarily "present the classical intelligence or achievement profile that is equated with giftedness."

None of the above, of course, proves that the races are treated unequally at Oxbridge. However, unless the figures improve soon, there might be a strong argument for inviting observers from the Commission for Racial Equality to sit in on a few interviews.

A CASE FOR SCRUTINY

Some sixth form teachers would certainly like to see more scrutiny. As one of them put it, the very whiteness of Oxbridge already discourages applications. The better and more confident black students are in their abilities, the more they insist that they will only consider a university which appreciates minority groups. Teachers often try to counteract this Catch-22 factor by promoting Oxbridge as a top student's natural home, but this does no good if their students then fail to get in.

Chris Bland (not his real name), a Maths teacher, told me how he had, a couple of years ago, sent two of his students for an Oxbridge interview. One, a boy with a white and an Asian parent, was a sound mathematician, good rather than brilliant. The other, an Afro-Caribbean boy, was considered by the school to be absolutely outstanding. Guess who was accepted? The black student's Maths teacher, although prone to cynicism after years of sending out Oxbridge candidates, was still livid at the outcome.

This is not to say that such discrimination happens every year – it does not need to. Faced with students hesitant to go where so few academics seem to want them, and with universities unable to appreciate more than a handful of their students, teachers of black pupils sometimes decide to err on the side of caution. Why expose an already doubting student to the prospect of rejection?

Oxbridge staff are horrified if you suggest that anyone teaching at their university might be racist, but the problem remains. Someone does need to explain how the average don finds it so much easier to see intellectual promise in a polite, blond home counties chap or a delicate, soft-spoken Indian girl than in a hulking Afro-Caribbean boy.

By accepting that talent can be found where genteel white manners are not, the best American universities educate huge numbers of brilliant Black students. In Britain too attitudes are changing. Inner city teachers were full of praise for the ability of top universities like Imperial College London, UCL and Manchester to identify top potential in all sorts of different applicants.

The academic powerhouse of Oxbridge, though, trusts to instinct, which means that Black students, especially, can spend their first months feeling odd, home-sick and cross.

COPING STRATEGIES

Many black students at Oxbridge are actively trying to improve the situation. Having concluded that their key problem is gross underrepresentation, they put a lot of effort into Access projects aimed at communities and schools with large black populations.

Asian students, who are only slightly underrepresented, can face a different problem, rooted in British youth culture. This is that the two key student leisure pursuits, in Oxbridge and elsewhere, are drink and sex. For Muslims, the fact that they reject alcohol can be a serious barrier to the initial bonding process. Sipping your coke while others are on their fifth, hilariously funny pint of Grolsh can make you feel an outsider, as well as terribly bored. For Asian girls, Muslim or not, the more casual approach to sex taken by their white fellow students can be quite shocking.

Abstinence can certainly slow down integration, giving rise to comments like "he doesn't pull" or "she's a bit of a prude." Luckily, this stage tends to be short. Even in the face of great cultural differences, shared tutorials and the shared worries about seminar tasks or impossible deadlines create real bonds. Future doctors working long hours in the lab rapidly conclude that they have far more in common with one another than with any of their fellow students outside Medicine, perceived as idle slobs.

And there are other ways of meeting people. One young doctor from a Punjabi family I interviewed recalled that she really enjoyed hanging out with the Christian Union students at her university, who shared her moral stance. A Bengal-born London girl, now a young executive, had a wonderful three years as an active member of the Pakistani Society, the Islamic Society, the Iranian Society and the Oxford Union, all without ever touching a drop of alcohol or uncovering her knees. Two of the male Arab students I spoke to admitted somewhat shamefacedly that they did drink in their first month, "because it helps to get to know people". Once they had bought the required number of rounds, though, both confidently reverted to tonic water. Those awkward first term nights in the pub had brought them into contact with a range of people they could pick their friends from, and those they picked had interests that could be pursued sober. An Egyptian-born writer, now approaching forty, recalls that he enthusiastically took up football and rowing, but avoided rugby "which was for drunks". Coming from a political family, he spent the rest of his free time arguing about Palestinian rights with fellow students. One of the lifelong friends he made in the course of this is now a London newspaper editor, the other a (Jewish) professor of Politics. If you are confident in your own culture, you can clearly get away without drinking.

To sum up, an ethnic minority student seeking a happy social life often needs to do three things. One is to be aware that the dominant culture among Oxbridge students is anti-racist, another is to take lots of initiatives, and the third is to be reasonably flexible. As one female Indian undergraduate said to me: "We girls get on fine but quite a few Asian men wander around all on their own. And when I ask such a chap whether he has joined any societies or mixed much with people from other colleges, the answer is always no. 'You know, how busy us science students are,' one young man said to me. That's quite true, but most of the white students still belonged to something like the boat club or the film society. You can be too cautious, I think."

A DEGREE OF DIFFERENCE

It would be tempting to stop on this positive note, if there were not another, rather crucial fact worth being aware of. This is the degree results.

A "significant" number of black students are underperforming at Cambridge, according to a four-year study commissioned by the university. Published in February 2003, the study results showed that far fewer black students scored Firsts and many more got third class degrees than their white peers.

While 21 per cent of white students got firsts and only 2.4 per cent Thirds, the proportion of blacks who left the university with a top class degree was just 3.1 per cent, while 15.6 per cent got Thirds.

Students from Indian families got the highest proportion of Firsts – 23.7 per cent – compared with 17.9 per cent of students from Chinese families.

How to explain that disparity? Some of it may be due to the schools which students come from. The "better" the school, the better prepared students will be for Oxbridge in terms of working habits and background knowledge. The main answer, though, probably lies somewhere between the Oxbridge teaching structure and its exam system.

To get a First, a student needs active, sympathetic support from his personal tutor and seminar tutor. Those who do well have often also built up a close rapport with other teaching staff. This creates a circle of people around them which they can ask for help with problems, and who will point them in the direction of suitable reading. Perhaps some of the Oxbridge teaching staff are not quite supportive enough of their black students.

There certainly seems to be a clearer case for greater monitoring, and a compulsory staff training course in racism awareness. These are now routinely run for public sector employees elsewhere. In the course of writing this book, I asked most academics I met whether they had had any form of racism awareness training. I might as well have asked for their favourite sexual position. No reply was ever forthcoming.

Still, Oxbridge is forever changing, also when it comes to race. Some colleges have already started to provide general "equal opportunities" training for their dons. The problem is that participation is difficult to enforce across both universities, because of the colleges' self-governing nature.

IS IT WORTH THE HASSLE?

Ethnic minority students who had come for the academic buzz of Oxbridge, for a carefully picked course or for contact with a special academic expert, certainly tend to think so. So did students who were keen to get practical experience in fields like drama, public speaking or journalism. The semiprofessional Oxbridge societies offering such experiences not only welcomed them but often encouraged them to take up official posts.

Nor does this mean that you have to pay with loneliness for these benefits. All the ethnic minority students I spoke to had made close friends from different backgrounds at Oxbridge, if sometimes after a very hairy start. Quite a few did not feel totally integrated until the beginning of their second year, unlike most white students, but the college system usually worked its magic in the end. Black and Asian students, if they stay the course, tend to leave Oxbridge not less embedded in the Oxbridge network than the rest.

Oxbridge also remains the place for moving you beyond your own world on the careers ladder. Black Oxbridge graduates, especially, seem to go on to top jobs in the higher civil service, the arts, media and politics more easily than other educated members of their communities.

Academic prospects are a different matter. Should your gifted son stay if he cannot be sure to get a First from Oxford or Cambridge? Well, he should certainly be given a fair chance to. It is important to remember, though, that in the end most students at both universities get Seconds, not Firsts, and that still makes a graduate extremely employable in most fields. In fact, some employers prefer Oxbridge Seconds.

What if they do worse in the exam stakes? Well, Zadie Smith, whose first novel, White Teeth, won just about every literary prize in Britain, got a Third in her Cambridge part-one exams. Her old college, King's, now lists her on its alumni page as one of two prominent contemporary British writers. The other writer listed in its official publicity material is one of its 1960s graduates, Salman Rushdie.

20

Working class heroes

There have always been some working class students at Oxbridge. Hand-picked for truly exceptional ability by the local parson or schoolteacher, sponsored by a gentleman through grammar school and encouraged to sit for the pitifully few full university scholarship places, the son of a skilled, respectable working man occasionally managed to get in. In a good decade, there could even be two such students. Careful not to presume and grateful beyond belief, these young men posed no challenge to Oxbridge.

Tension only arose when workers' aspirations increased. The introduction of free, compulsory schooling in 1870 had created a hunger for more education. Demand for the right to study at university also came from those with political ambitions. Working men now had the vote, and the Labour Party was concerned that its leaders should be men with the best possible education; so should the teachers who would raise up the working class and the trade unionists negotiating with employers.

In 1897, the TUC resolved "that the workers... should not be satisfied until the highest educational advantages which the country affords are within reach of all." This was followed by more concrete demands for access to "the deep draughts of knowledge" which only Britain's two oldest universities, so it was felt, could provide.

Cambridge offered a handful of places, but what many talented workers sought was the opportunity to study history, politics and economics at Oxford. This remained out of their reach, both because they lacked the right schooling and because they could not pay.

"We want Oxford to open wide her doors to the best of our people and take them in," declared J.M. MacTavish, a Labour member of the Portsmouth Town Council, in 1907. If the university only realised what enthusiasm there was amongst ordinary people for this education, it "would sell its plate" to help fund it, he argued, adding that such access would benefit both sides. If workers were admitted, "a true view of social questions would be taught...

182

Although we are supposed to have no recorded history, without us all history was and is impossible."

CLOSED GATES

Gradually, the tone became less conciliatory. When told that Oxford could not accommodate working class students, campaigners angrily asked whether it was the true function of a university "to train the nation's best men, or to sell its gifts to the rich?"

There was some minority support for this stand within Oxford. A handful of dons already travelled for miles once a week to teach extension classes to men who had just completed a ten hour working day. Some of these academics had no doubt that their best pupils ought to be continuing their education at the university. Charles Gore, later Bishop of Birmingham, stated in the 1908 Toynbee Report that he hoped for "a great displacement of rich or well-to-do young men who wanted to have a good time, by serious students who would come from all classes but in large measure from among the workers".

Still, when a few of the 29 Labour MPs who had been elected to Parliament in 1906 suggested that Oxford should admit at least a tiny number of outstanding working men who had prepared for this with infinite patience at the night schools of the Workers Educational Association, the response was hysterical.

Writing in the Fortnightly Review, F.C.S. Schiller, a Philosophy don at Corpus Christi College, Oxford, warned that "the workers know what they want, and what they want is destructive of progress in knowledge... What they want is an education for their purposes, an education specifically adjusted to their needs, to wit, a study of economics, politics and history... Of course, the spokesmen of the workers fail to understand the aesthetic function of Oxford... the athletic aspect of the university is equally unintelligible to them... Work people cannot understand that men whose chief interest seems to be 'play' should be allowed to remain at a University... a demand for social equality is included in their demand for 'equality of opportunity and it would almost seem that they were snobs enough to find a chance of slapping a Lord on the back in their cups one of the indispensable attractions of College life."

In any case, the reputable don argued, all clever men already had access to Oxbridge. For this reason "it is becoming more and more difficult to believe that there exists untapped reservoirs of intellectual ability among the workers. This is not to say, of course that there is no practical ability among them..."

Where that ability should take itself Schiller had no doubt: "It ought to be much easier for the new universities to satisfy the legitimate educational aspirations of the 'workers' and so to save the lily-likeness of Oxford from the hands of the uprooter."

And thus Oxford was again "saved" from the workers. Only after WW1 were the entry requirements marginally eased. This was too late for many aspiring students, but talent still won out in a few cases. One of the trainees in a 1908 extension class taught by a sympathetic Balliol don was A.P. Wadsworth, who went on to edit *The Manchester Guardian* (now known simply as *The Guardian*) without the benefits of an Oxbridge degree.

PICK A NUMBER

It is the folk memory of that ugly debate which has dogged working class entrance to Oxbridge. Young people from working class homes remain deeply uncertain about whether they can get in and fit in. "It's not for the likes of us," is a common view. Having arranged for the year's best student to attend a day school at Cambridge, a teacher at an inner city sixth form college found himself faced with a cross, miserable lad who kept asking: "What's the point of it? Must I go?"

The point, of course, is that working class pupils do get in. In the course of researching this book, I have talked to one Oxbridge student who was the daughter of a care worker and another who was the son of a cook. I have met young Oxbridge graduates whose fathers were lorry drivers or plumbers and an Oxbridge-educated professor whose father was a tailor. Most found their university life a positive experience and a great help with their careers. "It's wonderful that even someone like me can hope to get a job in the city," a girl whose father was a print-worker told me with shining eyes. Those 19th century campaigners for working class access would turn in their graves at the thought of "their" graduates becoming investment analysts but, heck, times do change.

The question remains how much else has changed. Just how rare a bird must a working class student expect to be once he has unpacked his CDs and bought his cap and gown? The answer matters not just because is suggests how fair the entrance process really is. It also determines how comfortable such students will be at Oxbridge. Oxbridge dons can be remarkably vague about student proportions, as was exposed by a very public spat between Margaret Hodge, the Lifelong Learning and Education Minister, and the University of Cambridge on 4th February 2003. After Hodge had remarked during a visit that the university ought to do much more to attract youngsters from working class backgrounds, the university's vice chancellor, Sir Alec Broers, responded by issuing a strong statement. "It is simply not true that only 'rich kids' are accepted into Cambridge. Last year, 23 per cent of home students at Cambridge did not pay any tuition fees and were therefore eligible for the full student loans and for the bursaries offered by Cambridge."

The middle class parents of Cambridge students may have nodded assent. Not so people who understand the difference between money and class. Many a self-employed business person's accountant can produce a perfectly legal income-expenditure balance which results in a taxable income of £17,000 or less. This defines the bread winner as disadvantaged in the university's eyes and qualifies his children for considerable financial help. On the other hand, a working class couple raising two children while doing low-paid PAYE jobs might be earning just a little above that figure. This means they'll have to cover most education expenses. Even if their children go to university at all, they'll probably live at home, not pay rent to a college.

So, the beneficiaries of the funding system are, in practice, often the self-employed or divorced middle class mothers. It's a great help for sure, but not a way of improving the class balance.

Talking about 23 per cent, therefore, merely muddies the water.

DO THEY REALLY EXIST?

Most dons agree that a wider range of backgrounds in the student population would be nice, but they usually refuse to define the issue any further. They certainly don't like to use the "c" word – class. Academics involved in Access projects often proved to be the ones most adamant that there is no longer any such thing as the British working class, though there were, of course, deprived people.

Student Access campaigners employed in university-sponsored projects take a similar line. When I asked one of these how to contact working class undergraduates so I could find out how they felt about being at Oxbridge, the response was a long silence. I might as well have asked the poor girl what sanitary towels she used. When she finally spoke, her embarrassment was so profound I could almost watch her blush over the phone: "We can't actually... you see, we don't define it like this... how would one measure it really... it is really an outdated definition."

185

Did she not know which students were working class, I asked, trying to relax her. "Well, not really . . . you know, it's not that, though," came the nervous reply.

What was it then? "It's just that it would be wrong to single out people as working class, you know, we never ask them anyway, so nobody knows."

Surely, the students themselves would know whether they are working class, and they might want to talk about it," I snapped, getting exasperated.

"Perhaps," was the reply. "But you can't be sure, and I don't really want to go down that route. I'm afraid I cannot help you." Was she unique? Clearly not: another Access campaigner I contacted insisted that even to mention the term working class in her Access group circular would be insulting.

So, what term did Student Access use? The answer, here too, was that vague and all embracing one, "non-traditional", which covered several other areas quite apart from class.

It took a great deal of persistence to get beyond that point and a special appeal to the university's press officer but, a clutch of emails later, I was told that a face-saving category had been found. Although nobody would tell me what it was, students started to email me. This was my chance to add to the sample I had contacted by other means.

The wait proved thoroughly worthwhile. I met yet more outstanding young people who had no regrets about their university choice, but also no doubt about their identity. They were, despite a range of accents that ranged from Estuary to mildly posh, all working class, and proud of it.

One of the most interesting things that emerged from this research was that even their interviewers had not necessarily known this fact. Universities might theoretically strive for "wider participation", but practically they operated in a void. Although UCAS recorded the social class of every applicant's parents, it did not pass that information to the university. Unless mentioned by the school, admissions tutors could only guess at this key fact. It was a bit like trying to hit a target with a sack over your head, and while doubting that the target was actually there.

BEING AN "ONLY"

Still, 10 per cent is a substantial figure, a sizeable chunk of any small town's population, and it was puzzling why working class Freshers were so often uncomfortable at Oxbridge. Surely, their accents would be everywhere, even if they themselves could not be picked out; thanks to youth culture, all classes dress much the same. However, those students I managed to meet who were of clear working class origin, which meant they had strong local accents, fathers who were truck drivers and mothers who did piece work on their sewing machine, were adamant that they were unique.

All recalled how they had looked around for "people like me" at their colleges and on their university course, only to find that there weren't any. Lizzie, a third year student in a small college which had 300 students and a reputation as sympathetic to state school pupils, was adamant that she was the only "real" working class person there. Nobody else came from a housing estate and everybody else had parents who were much more educated than hers.

If Lizzie was right, and given that she had by then spent almost three years in the place I have no reason to believe she was not, then this would make her one in 300, or well below one per cent. Quite a different proportion.

So, where does the official figure of 9 or 10 per cent comes from? Detailed research I undertook led to a unexpected discovery. Its sole source is the UCAS form, in which all applicants under 21 are asked to put in the occupation of the highest earner in their household – the very information not passed on to admissions tutors.

Using this figure can lead to considerable inaccuracies, as a friendly UCAS statistician explained to me. The first of these is due to the fact that 19 per cent of student applicants (almost one in five) leave this section blank. Others give an occupation that cannot later be classified.

A specific job title too is not enough to ensure a correct statistical outcome. An engineer, for instance, can be either a skilled worker or a middle class graduate.

Even if accurately defined, one parent's occupation is not enough to define a family's class. The "highest earner" in today's Britain may well be married to a low-earning middle class partner, an electrician to a teacher, or a carpenter to a writer.

To complicate matters further, there is no category called "working class". Instead. UCAS divides householders into eight categories. In place of the three old categories of "skilled manual," "partly skilled" and "unskilled", there are now four at the bottom of the list, called "lower supervisory," "technical occupations," "semiroutine" and "routine". It is from these data that the Higher

Education Funding Council (HEFC) deduces the number of working class students at Oxbridge.

In other words, your teenage Fresher may well be in more of a minority than he expected to be, and as a result feel out of sorts. So, don't just tell the poor lad he should count himself lucky for getting in. Show some sympathy. He is in an unexpectedly alien environment and this can spell trouble.

SPECIAL HURDLES

Vaguely recalling that Oxbridge used not to want working class students and definitely finding himself in a minority, the lost lad may respond by withdrawing – mentally at first. Why bother to speak up? Student like him, he may have concluded, are expected to lie low, put up with what they are offered and hat-check their culture at the college gates. Such beliefs can affect not just his social life but also his studies.

What can make this worse is the likely discovery that his course is not pitched at comprehensive school level, and even less so at the level of even the brightest students from disadvantaged schools. Some of this can just be a matter of cultural references. The frequent use of classical imagery in science, as well as arts courses, often stumps those who grew up without any mention of Greek gods. Luckily, this is an obstacle fairly easily overcome. One Hackney student finally ended three months of unhappy puzzlement over references to Zeus by buying an encyclopaedia of classical myths.

The generous use of Latin proverbs by dons may also grate. So can being unable to understand the inscription on one's own college gate. Although no comprehensive student can read Latin, those with educated parents sometimes manage to puzzle out what is meant and, if they can't, seem remarkably unbothered. A working class student often worries far more and needs to understand, as they do, that his education is not threatened by this.

Another handicap can be not knowing that academic help is often available as long as you ask. Paul, a working class student keen to do a course option involving European History in his second year abandoned the idea when he realised that this required a knowledge of German. A middle class student fancying the same course just discussed the problem with her supervisor, who revealed that the girl could acquire the basics of the missing language at the university language lab. There was even the possibility of a vacation grant that would enable her to get some practical language experience.

Other solutions can sometimes be found if a poor student faces what may seem like an insolvable problem. June, a very able English student, found it impossible to study in the holidays, as her family lived in one of Britain's urban war zones. When she explained to her tutor that "it's a bit difficult to read Paradise Lost when people are committing GBH outside," he suggested she should stay in college next time. Told that she could not possibly afford the £8 per night it charged outside term, he just nodded.

A week later, June's tutor mentioned that some funds might be available. When she pressed him for details at the next tutorial, he told her where to go. In the end, June got a hardship grant and spent most of the next holiday in college.

So, much can be done to smooth a working class student's study problems, but that student really needs to be clear about her needs and quite persistent. The more eminent her tutor, the more vague he might be about the basic facilities available. Requests may have to be put to other dons, or the bursar. Another useful starting point can be the college JCR. In fact, Oxbridge is so well equipped that almost any course-related request can usually be met, at least if put forward well in advance.

THE MANY AND THE FEW

With only (perhaps) 10 per cent of new undergraduates being working class, social life for them can still be tough, at least at the beginning. Several students I met revealed that they had hated Fresher's week, because they felt everybody talked so much posher than they did and seemed so much more confident. While public school pupils all seemed to know one another and even many middle class kids from comprehensives formed little groups, a working class student from a struggling school had usually arrived alone.

Even the getting to know you chitchat in class can make a poorer working class student feel different from the norm. One girl said that what she found hardest at first were those endless questions about "what did you do in your gap year?" Another added that she just wished people wouldn't talk so much about their foreign holidays. Her family did not travel abroad and before coming to Oxbridge she had never even been outside London.

Having less experience of academic work can cause insecurity too. Dave, a shop worker's son, accepted by Cambridge for his outstanding potential, remembered that when he was given four books to read for his first Geography essay, the task was so terrifying he could hardly open them. There had not been any books in his home and he was unused to writing long essays or to reading outside the syllabus. He was convinced that all the privately educated students were far cleverer than him. Only after the first term did he accept that he might be any good.

By the time I met Dave, he had become a quite outstanding student, but he still worked extremely hard, sometimes to the extent of making himself ill. He admitted that he was worried that he might not impress otherwise. He knew several other working class students who behaved in the same way. Most of the time, he said, "they all think they are impostors."

This is not to say that Dave has any regrets. As he put it: "Studying elsewhere is probably less stressed, there is more balance in one's life. Cambridge is very competitive. But then other universities would not have challenged me so much. It is harder to excel elsewhere. Here there is so much opportunity and such good expert supervision which develops you. I know that if I can cope with demands here, I can cope with anything."

There is no doubt that many of the working class students were not just bright, but far brighter and more resourceful than others at Oxbridge. One girl worked out all there was to know about the Oxbridge application process herself, after her teacher warned her that it might be too complicated. Another responded to the problem of being asked at her interview about knowledge she did not have by firing back lots of intelligent questions. Her interviewers were suitably impressed.

THE HOME FRONT

Yet another disadvantage working class students can face is their family's attitude. One girl I spoke to had been warned by her mother not to tell any other relatives that she was sitting for Oxbridge, in case she was mocked.

Often, even a well-meaning working class family was unable to offer support to a student coming home after a stressful term. This was the case even if there were no external problems, such as crime. Parents and sibling might find it hard to talk to her and tend to watch for any signs of "uppertiness". On visits, the student might be expected to constantly play down her "other life", except when put in front of relatives to show off. Ruth, a SPS student with particular interest in sociology, commented that working class families often seemed unaware that a young person who moves away from home will change, wherever she might go, and might indeed develop opinions and ideas different from their own. As a result, the student's new identity is sometimes taken as a personal insult. The result can be serious family fall outs. This is a price not exacted from more middle class students.

Still, none of the students wished they had made a different choice. June remarked how wonderful it was to live without the TV blazing away, to discuss issues and develop theories, all things she had never done at home. At Oxbridge, she said with a smile, nobody gets angry if they disagree.

The main problem, though, was living in quite such a middle class set-up, in which your behaviour and speech patterns always stuck out. Unlike ethnic minority students, white working class boys, in particular, seemed initially stunned by this. They had had some concerns, but nothing in their lives had prepared them for being outsiders. On the other hand, many did, thanks to time and obvious effort, completely blend it.

Those white working class students I spoke to certainly still loved Oxbridge, usually for its intellectual buzz and the opportunities it had given them, rather than for its social customs. All of them also wished that there would be more people like them, so they could feel more at home.

WHO'S A POSH KID, THEN?
Having said this, it is important to realise that the gap is not always as big as it may seem. Those who come across as "posh" on first sight are often, as the student gradually discovers, young people from all sorts of unrich homes who went to Britain's handful of remaining grammar schools. This group makes up almost 17 per cent of state school students. Many of the privately educated students at Oxbridge are not even the sons of gentlemen farmers anymore. They are more likely to have fathers who are lawyers, shopkeepers or managers and mothers who work in an office just to pay the school fees. Quite a few Oxbridge parents are said to be self-employed builders.

These people are not sending their bright kids to public school so that they can look down on others, but in order to ensure that they are taught for longer hours, by more qualified teachers and with more attention to their ability, in short, to give them the kind of education which is free and taken for granted in much of Europe.

THE ETONIANS

There are, of course, some very posh students at Oxbridge. There was one question to which all working class students I eventually met responded in exactly the same way. Asked what they found strangest at Oxbridge, the answer was invariably: the Etonians. There seemed to be a huge number of them about, roaming the place in tightly knit, well-spoken groups, utterly at ease there from day one.

This was slightly puzzling since there are, in fact, relatively few Etonians at Oxbridge today. Britain's most exclusive boarding school, whose intake, in any given year, includes one third landed gentry and at least a dozen boys with aristocratic titles, sends most of its trust-funded pupils to slightly less demanding places. The most popular destinations are Durham, Bristol, Exeter or a nearby agricultural college. Still, Eton is a big school with a big scholarship form and at any moment there can indeed be over 200 Etonians at Oxbridge. All of them too seem to know one another or at least someone's younger brother. Most of them are found at Christ Church, Oxford, the college which the school has centuries-old links with, so you can, as said earlier, always avoid it.

On the other hand, why should you? Eton does not actually produce monsters of snobbery, but polite, charming young men who wear their privilege lightly. Despite what you have seen in the movies, they don't ever line up to bray at northern lads for wearing elasticated bow ties. They are all male and, when sober, sweetly polite with the female sex, which they have before mainly known as matron. When drunk, they go in for strange tribal sing-songs, and tend to monopolise the universities wine societies, where they can be rather less charming to outsiders. As the wine societies are almost the only university societies that charge, knowing this can save you lots of money.

However, nearly half of the Oxbridge British student intake does come from various private schools, and it eventually dawned on me that state school students tended to use "Etonian" as a generic term for any male students from a private school. This view can be daunting, as well as misleading. What Oxbridge has, in fact, is a quickly formed fraternity or sorority of people who have never met, but play squash and know what Rugby or Teddy's are (they're boarding schools). Most also live in the same part of the home counties or green belt areas around London.

Once at Oxbridge, all these students indeed stand out by the relaxed way in which they move around their strange new home.

There are good reasons for this. The oak beams, stained glass windows and coats of arms on the wall of the college dining hall will be familiar to them from their school, even if that establishment was only launched after the Beatles' first LP. Their teachers too are likely to have worn black gowns over their M & S suits, at least at formal occasions. The Latin names of various obscure Oxbridge practices and sites are no mystery to those who survived a decade of compulsory Classics.

Most importantly, perhaps, pupils from the private sector do not arrive at Oxbridge alone. Even the smallest rural establishment which will take anyone who pays expects to send a bunch of pupils to Oxbridge a year. What parent would pay some £10,000 per year without at least the distant prospect of a place? The handful of schools that pick (and expel) pupils on the basis of academic achievement alone might each send up to 40 students each autumn. This begets the little groups of first years with the plummy voices.

But do they want to stay among themselves? Well, initially they do, I suspect. In a new place, it is reassuring to be among friends, and so you find clusters of new students swapping fond memories of their housemaster, Mr. Chips, in some distant corner of an Oxbridge playing field. If you went to a comprehensive, this can make you feel excluded, but I wouldn't jump to conclusions yet. Usually, it's nothing more than a bit of childish nostalgia and the boys will soon drift back into grown-up life.

Asked whether they think it is best to stay among one's own kind, the numerous private schools students I have met over the years certainly responded with an emphatic no. They are at university to meet exciting new people, and some would go as far as drop their h's to that end. There is even a better reason that few will admit to: private schools tend to be single sex, so getting to university is at least partly about escaping this hellish state.

DIFFERENT COPING STRATEGIES

Still, being working class at Oxbridge can often be harder than expected at the earlier stages, and there are problems which do not go away. Having less spending money than others is one of those. When you first arrive, it can often seem as if all the interesting people go out for a restaurant dinner every night, rather than eat in college. Fortunately, this is not actually true.

Drink is a more serious issue. Binge drinking is now so deeply rooted in student culture that it threatens to not just destroy a

193

whole generation's livers, but also all efforts towards integration. Student leaders who are serious about Access must, I feel, confront the reality that if the normal student is spending every night at the bar, then many poorer, working class student will invariably be excluded. So, of course, will all Muslim students. Could this be the moment for a bit of creative lifestyle change?

Meanwhile, working class students need to be prepared for the fact that Oxbridge is a very middle class world, albeit not one necessarily hostile to outsiders. Many of those I spoke to were quite thrown at first by the extent to which they stuck out. Each one also recalled, without prompting, one thoughtless, hurtful remark. When you are 18 and new to a place, being referred to in jest as "our Prole" can really upset you. Of course it's a joke and you should joke back, but that does take confidence.

The most common advice working class students gave was to relax: everybody experiences a bad response once, so there is no point in letting this confirm your insecurity. You are in the modern world, among fellow students. It is crucial to realize that you are not constantly being snubbed. Don't let anyone intimidate you, but don't be too easily slighted.

You also need to reach out. As Ruth, the SPS student I met, put it: "Working class students sometimes don't understand that the way of mixing at Oxbridge is not necessarily by finding similar people, but by doing similar things. They wait for someone congenial to turn up in their year or course, rather than join societies to develop joint interests."

Some students adjust by completely losing their working class manners and accent. "You'd never know he was working class," one girl said of a passing young man with flowing locks, dressed in pure Brideshead. Others play the wide boy for all it's worth, even claiming to be related to the Krays. A few spend far more money than they can afford and have to take a college job to pay back their debts. Others again just look ahead and seize the opportunities with both hands. Some, to their own surprise, simply enjoy the terrific features of the place.

It is easier to do the last thing if your parents told you that everybody is an equally worthy human being, and if you are blessed with a sharp wit. It would be even easier if more middle class people taught the young that good manners are not really about gripping a wine glass with three fingers at the stem; they are about making the person opposite you feel at ease. The truth, though, is that in the end both sides adapt a little. Middle class students learn to play darts, working class ones become experts on vintage dry sherry. The bad old days when Oxbridge was a lily that needed protection from the workers are over. If you can persuade yourself that you deserve to be there, you should have three or four great student years.

21

What if he didn't get in?

However, talented your teenager, and however good the preparations he made, the fact remains that more people apply for Oxbridge than get in. There are between three and five applicant for every place. Readers can massively improve the odds by following the advice in this book, but in the end candidates and their parents must also accept that there is an element of luck involved. Young people of equal ability, suitability and amiability compete for the same places every year. It is, therefore, possible that the lad will suffer the disappointment of not getting an offer, or of not getting the grades required to take up the offer made.

Being told that the university you chose has not chosen you can come as a nasty shock, even to those who thought they had allowed for it. So, if you don't want your son's self-esteem to be damaged, don't wait until the rejection letter is in his clenched fist. Instead, think ahead and positively consider other options when you are first looking at university prospectuses, or when he tells you about his teachers' recommendations.

This means that you should say good, constructive things about the second and (if possible) third place he is thinking of applying to. You do not need to be a university expert for this. Just point out that the course in University B looks interesting, the staff friendly and young. Talk with genuine warmth about the location of University C even if your own memories of the bleak East Anglian landscape or crowded central London make your heart sink.

None of this makes you a hypocrite. Students can be deliriously happy in a concrete jungle, as long as it offers them good teaching and a lively campus. Encourage the lad to find out more and perhaps visit the place. Encourage him also to check where his own role models have studied; it may well not be Oxbridge.

What you want is for your son to feel that all the choices he has made are good ones, that he can look forward to his university education, whatever happens. True, Oxbridge particularly suits some students, being more theoretical and more intense than other places. It is also so much better funded. If the lad goes elsewhere, though, he will reap other benefits, not least the skills to survive in the real world and he'll learn about much the same academic subjects.

Again, you need not feel that you are dishonest by telling him this. Britain's world class experts studied at all sorts of universities and many still lecture there. Top careers are made by people who have graduated from all sorts of degree courses or none at all. A great university experience is determined not just by the status of the institution: it can come from the friendships formed and the infectious enthusiasm of one single staff member, plus the kind of bands which the student union gets in for gigs. And this experience, in turn, generates the kind of self-confidence that bolsters careers.

So, do make your son feel from the start that he has a range of attractive options ahead of him. Don't be afraid that unless you turn his getting into Oxbridge into a life or death matter he will rush off to Skate City or the pub, rather than cram for his exams. Firstly, this is not true and, secondly, such brinkmanship will not do him any good. By now he will know from his teachers, his environment and everything said at home that he needs to work to the max. Those with a clutch of strong university choices do so in better spirits and with a lighter heart.

If you follow this advice, the lad will still have something to look forward to, should the Oxbridge offer not materialise. Being rejected always hurts. Without other attractive prospects, your son may well feel cast out into limbo, or appalled at the prospect of studying at a place he has taken absolutely no interest in or treated with scorn.

Nor is being positive about other options merely a fall-back position, as you might think. It is also a great way of enabling your son to impress his first choice. Oxbridge, like the perfect lover, comes to him who is cool – not desperate.

HANDLING THE BAD NEWS

Faced with a glum boy who picked up the courage to apply to Oxbridge or a tear-stained girl who fell in love with the medieval quads on her school's Outreach visit, the temptation is nevertheless to curse that stupid, snobbish place. Or you might want to mumble something about playing the game being more important than winning.

My advice is to do neither. All is not lost yet. If there is real talent here and not just parental pushiness, and if your teenager remains determined, there is always the option of reapplying in the next academic year. The cobblestones of Oxbridge are trodden by a surprising number of students who did just that. However, the steps a student must take depend on the precise situation.

WHAT IF SHE DIDN'T GET AN OFFER?

Let's say your daughter was expected to get above-average grades relevant to the degree subject she had hoped to do at Cambridge. However, as a result of her interview and/or exam not going as well as expected, or of some other mysterious factor, perhaps a tepid reference from her school, she was not offered a place.

If she does not want to go to another university instead, she will have no choice but to wait. Her first wait will have to be for her A-level results. If these are in the top range, meaning three or more As, Oxbridge is still an option the following year. Anastasia Fedotova, a Manchester pupil rejected in 2001 by Brasenose College, Oxford, although she was sitting six A-levels, dealt with this by taking a year out. After receiving her exam results, which were six A-grades, five of them in the sciences, she then applied to Trinity College, Cambridge, and went on to happily read Maths there.

But where should your daughter try next? Theoretically, students can just reapply to another college in the same university, but the dirt among the private Oxbridge tutors is that your chances in these circumstances are vastly better if you try "the other place" instead. In other words, if your daughter was turned down by Cambridge, she should try Oxford next. Apparently, there is a mild form of one-upmanship in taking a good candidate rejected by the competition.

WHAT IF SHE DIDN'T GET THE RIGHT GRADES?

This is quite a different situation. Grades well below those specified in the Oxbridge offer obviously mean that another university offer should be accepted. However, if your daughter missed the required grades by a hare's breath, you needn't give up.

You must accept that there is no prospect of the college reconsidering its specifications, unless there are documented reasons for the girl's poor showing. A serious illness suffered during the exam period and backed by a doctor's certificate will be taken into consideration. A bog standard, self-treated, runny nose will not.

If your daughter's results were due to a clear factor such as emigration or bereavement it may very occasionally pay off to resit. But if it is just that one of her grades was a B, rather than the required A, the girl might be wiser to obtain further qualifications for the desired course instead. This could mean taking a third science A-level (Cambridge is less keen on applicants with a mix of arts and science subjects than Oxford) or a course-related AEA. What might also be worthwhile is learning an extra language or, in the case of Law applicants, working for a solicitor.

The girl may also want to pick a different college to apply to, which can be at the same university. All Oxbridge colleges accept the occasional retry student, but your daughter's chances are better if she now lowers her expectations a little. The top colleges, generally those in the centre of town, will be less interested than those at the outskirts.

No less importantly, this may be the time to consider another, perhaps slightly less competitive Oxbridge course. Determined students now tend to shift from English Lit. to Modern Languages, or from Medicine to Chemistry. It is too late to make the more drastic switch from arts to sciences or the other way round.

Before considering such a route, though, look carefully at all the facts. First, be sure that your daughter is capable of getting the right grades. Look at the precise marks she obtained in every part of the A-level exam, which are detailed in the certificate. B-grades and A-grades may seem close, but if the document shows that the girl only just scraped her three B's, despite good teaching at a school which regularly sends other pupils to Oxbridge, then you should probably encourage her to take up her second offer. Cambridge is unlikely to consider an Oxford reject with middling grades and the prospect of much the same.

PREPARING FOR THE RESIT

Even if your son's grade results were a narrow miss, you need to make very sure he really wants to time-travel back to the classroom. Students usually prepare for resits at a local authority (or private) sixth form college, a place without pack drill or uniforms, but we are still talking about 30 hours of schooling per week, plus homework. Much of the work will not be exactly new to the resit student, even though the syllabus changes slightly every year.

Oxbridge is now an option again, and if your son knuckles down to the work, this is the time to cook him his favourite meal or go fishing with him. You can also help him achieve his goal by insisting he takes a part-time job. Carefully chosen, such a job might give him an extra edge in the Oxbridge race; it might also, of course, help pay the supermarket bill.

Don't be put off by claims that he can't possibly find the time: even resit students have evenings, weekends and summer holidays; ample time to practice your foreign languages in some tourist hotel, or to scrub hospital corridors in preparation for Medicine. Such activities show that you are a determined, eager young person and might even give you something to talk about at your interview. What a student hoping for a second Oxbridge chance must do alongside all this, though, is work out where else he and his vast DVD collection could be happy. With the number of Oxbridge applicants steadily growing, second-timers do not stand quite as good an admission chance as they did a decade ago.

LAST CHANCE SALOON

Even those who've failed to get into an Oxbridge undergraduate course at all, and this includes some of the brightest and most successful people I know, need not completely give up. If your son does brilliantly in his degree course at another good university there is always the option of doing a higher degree. He might even want to read for a third qualification, the doctorate (known as a PhD or DPhil.), at Oxbridge.

This is not a second-rate choice. The Russell Group universities, and especially Imperial College, London, and the London School of Economics, rank right up there with Oxford and Cambridge in the academic world. Other universities may have less famous staff, but their approach may be more modern or more down to earth, and this can make their lecturers the academic stars of the future. Also, some students feel more inspired by younger staff, and these are less common at Oxbridge.

If you want to continue an academic career started elsewhere at Oxbridge, all you need is a First and a good recommendation. You will not be looked down upon. After all, many of the great discoveries that constitute the glory of Oxford and Cambridge were made by people who had studied first at less fussy, more accessible universities.

For a student in need of a reassuring example (beyond that of the outsiders who developed Penicillin at Oxford) there is always Professor Bob Edwards of Cambridge. Edwards who, together with the late Patrick Steptoe, invented the fertility treatment which has so far created a million test tube babies, initially studied at Edinburgh.

IF ONLY

It may be too late for this but you should be aware of another, somewhat devious route into Oxbridge. The advice given to pupils at more than one private tutorial college has been to concentrate on getting into the course in which there was least competition from outstanding applicants, no matter what course the candidate actually wanted to do. This could mean, for instance, applying for Materials Science, even if you were really an engineer at heart. A week or so after starting his course, so the student is advised, all he needs to do is to confide in his supervisor that he feels he has made a terrible mistake. Materials Science, however worthy a calling, does not suit him. Would it therefore be possible for him to change to his true passion, Engineering?

He is likely to discover that a college can be remarkably flexible once it has accepted a student. While there are no guarantees, and while switching is most easily accepted between different language courses, the request will be considered. Assuming the waverer has the relevant A-levels, he might even be found a place on the coveted course.

There are, however, three points to remember if your son might wish to adopt this underhand, but not unknown, strategy. One is that the change of mind really has to take place within the first two weeks of starting the course. The second is that the student might find it rather hard to keep up academically with those who managed to get in the conventional way. Thirdly, and most crucially, it is pointless to try this as a bypass road into Medicine. It never works.

22
Best in show

What I have tried to show in the preceding chapters is that Oxbridge students come in all shapes and sizes. It's a miracle some of them don't bang their heads on those low medieval doorways. There is one group, though, which does have an amazing success rate. What I discovered after interviewing dozens of state school students who had gone to Oxbridge was that the majority had one key trait in common. This had nothing to do with their individual character or type of ability. Instead, what linked them was their parents' workplace. To stand a fair chance of getting into Oxbridge from a private school all you need is a parent who can pay (or a scholarship). To get in from elsewhere, a pupil needs a parent who is employed by a school.

To some people this will seem an obvious matter. After all, a teacher is likely to know which areas of the syllabus his son needs to cover to get good grades and will be able to help with homework and projects. That sort of parent will also stress the value of studying, although the poor little swot forced to stay at home and study non-stop by his ogre of a teacher–parent is a figure of the past.

Many of the successful Oxbridge entrants I talked to, whether they were white, Asian or Black, had a strong school connection. The majority of those had mothers trained as schoolteachers. A few had fathers who taught at university, but had started their careers in schools. This factor was so common that after interviewing my first three dozen Oxbridge students (past and present) I had to resist the temptation of asking "What does your mother teach?" rather than "What does your mother do?"

But beyond this common feature my interviewees varied tremendously. Some were chatty, others quiet. Some had the kind of curiosity that even an Oxbridge course could not satisfy, while others seemed very focused. Some had well-off middle class fathers and their mothers taught only a few hours a week. Others were raised by a single parent, who barely managed to pay the mortgage with the help of her full-time classroom job.

The story, though, does not end here. Lots of these parents taught at primary schools. This meant they were not equipped to explain the A-level syllabus or help with school work. Nor were they in touch with Oxbridge requirements.

Quite a few parents, moreover, did not teach at all. The mother of a young Oxbridge-educated doctor had given up teaching years before her daughter's birth and had, in any case, only ever taught in Pakistan. Another girl, one of very few "real" working class students, had a mother who had been a school dinner lady. Yet another student's mother was a special needs assistant at a junior school. These mothers were in no position to tutor anybody, yet their bright children still made it into Oxbridge.

By the time the proportion of interviewees with school connection had reached around two thirds of my largely random sample, this became deeply puzzling.

BEING SUSSED

By refining my questions, gradually I discovered that there were important contributions even a non-teacher parent working at a school could make. Often this had to do with realising that not all schools were equally good. Even the dinner lady, it turned out, had heard enough staff room talk to move her daughter out of a poorly performing school and into a more highly rated sixth form college.

Such parents were also often remarkably clued up about the different career paths pupils could take, or the timetable involved. Words like resit did not flummox them. If the school had certain problems, they would hear about it. They had a positive attitude to teachers, but were not overawed by them.

One former student, the daughter of a school caretaker, recalled that she had received a sympathetic but not actually helpful response from her class teacher when she mentioned an Oxbridge course. Her father, who worked at a different school, advised her to consult another teacher before giving up; and this swung it for her. As she put it to me, her father, although not an educated man, was "very sussed" about anything to do with school.

"LIKE A CONVERSATION WITH A TEACHER"

Perhaps the main clue lies in the phrase used by one highly successful Oxbridge graduate, now a research scientist with a big pharmaceutical firm. I had expected the London-born daughter of a South

Indian junior school teacher to describe her interview as a highly intimidating experience. After all, many others had done.

Instead the young woman thought for a moment, then smiled. "My interview was alright," she said. "It was like a conversation with a teacher." In other words, neither the setup nor the adults asking tough questions had felt alien enough to scare her.

The result is, if my impressions are correct, that teachers' children constitute a staggering proportion of Oxbridge students, far beyond their proportion in the general population.

FINDING OUT MORE

So what is wrong about this? Given that these students seemed as talented, varied and likeable a group as one could wish for, it took me a little while to pinpoint the cause of my unease about my – however provisional – findings. The problem is, in fact, pretty obvious. If the Oxbridge Entrance process is working best for one specific group, students whose parents have school-related jobs, then "widening participation" has some way to go.

It is, of course, possible that my findings were a fluke; that actually the majority of state school students at Oxbridge do not share this common trait. Even the fact that many students themselves had noticed the high proportion of teacher's kids in their year or college may still be an accident.

It would take a much larger and more scientifically structured survey (ideally one based on the entire student population) to reach any definite conclusion. I would, however, be very surprised if I was wrong. There is certainly an argument for Oxbridge commissioning such research. While the bright young people I met clearly deserved their university places, we need to understand why students from their backgrounds, more easily than others, negotiate the Oxbridge maze.

My suspicion is that ability is not always enough. Even the brightest students need in-crowd knowledge to succeed in a system not primarily based on scientific testing but on un-standardised verbal interviews. Meanwhile, I suspect that the range of backgrounds within the Oxbridge student body is somewhat narrower than the statistics suggest and the bright "non-traditional" student who gets in is quite often the daughter of a teacher and an engineer.

BE A COPYCAT

But what, you may ask, does this rather provisional insight do for the student whose mother or father is a bus conductor, cellist or IT manager? The answer is quite a lot: it enables them to improve their Oxbridge chances by copying the strategies that work for teachers' kids.

The most obvious strategy is that of studying hard but in a well-focused way; but there are other, less obvious ones. Among these is keeping up with a school's changing reputation. The retirement of a good headteacher can send a school into tail spin, while its upgrading to specialist status can dramatically improve results. As parents are unlikely to find out about these consequences from the staff, their local paper can be a great source of information.

What also matters is being aware that information about university entrance, and Oxbridge entrance in particular, can be spread out among a number of people in a school. So, if you cannot work out the course requirements, or don't understand the vocabulary, ask around. If you are a pupil, this can mean consulting not just your subject teacher or careers advisor, but also perhaps your head of department. Write out a list of things you want to know and take it with you, in case you get nervous.

If you are a parent, don't be shy about asking "stupid" questions at parents' meetings, or to make a special appointment with one of your teenager's teachers to clarify a point. Not only do entry rules periodically change, but this really is a specialized field. Even the scraps of information you picked up could be out of date. Many parents, for instance, still assume that to get into Oxbridge a pupil needs to stay an extra term at school.

On the other hand, it is important not to be overawed by a teacher's opinion. This is especially true if it conflicts with a student's own. If your dream is to study Chinese (as part of Oriental Studies) but your teacher feels you ought to do a degree in Geography, you need to ask why. If it is because she thinks more highly of her own subject, you might want to stick to your guns assuming you are doing the right A-levels.

Don't assume that teachers are infallible when it comes to picking Oxbridge candidates. If your son wants to apply, has very good GCSEs and is blessed with some of the key qualities outlined earlier, do encourage him to go ahead, even if his teacher is not so sure. Unfortunately, a few teachers identify only the well-behaved, mature pupil as an Oxbridge candidate. You may, therefore, have to consult other staff, or just trust you own instincts before both of you decide. A renowned science writer I know recalled with a chuckle that he had (successfully) applied to Oxbridge against all his teachers' advice.

Teachers have a lot of knowledge at their fingertips and the best interest of their pupils at heart, so take advantage of this, just like their own children do. However, not all of them have the time to keep up with Oxbridge rules, especially the unwritten ones. Fortunately, reading this book gives you the best of both worlds.

23

Nailing down the Oxbridge dream

The road to Oxbridge, as you will have concluded by now, is more open than most people believe and can sometimes be opened up further. However, it is equally true that access remains far from equal. So, how can real progress be made? The good news is that further change is not directly up to you, the parent or potential Oxbridge student. You just need to play the ball where it lies. The bad news is that action needs to be taken by two monoliths, Oxbridge and the Government.

Having said this, it is worth pointing out that there is periodic progress anyway, though not always as a result of deliberate action. When the makers of the Harry Potter films decided to shoot part of the first sequel in Oxford, they had no idea of what they were doing for British education. Visiting pupils, who would once have been intimidated by its venerable sites, now squealed with delight as they recognised the Hogwarts library (the Bodleian) and Hogwarts hall (the dining room of Christ Church). The university town with its crenellated walls and medieval towers had suddenly become a familiar, inviting place. Applications followed.

Other changes, previously unthinkable, suddenly become possible if enough fuss is made. An example of this is the saga of the Oxford medical entry procedure, centred on an exam set by the university's own medical staff. It was this exam which had resulted in the rejection of Laura Spence in January 2000. Known to work best for articulate middle class entrants who already knew a great deal about medicine, it was crammed for at almost every private school in small groups.

Despite this well known fact, Oxbridge academics defended the outcome to the hilt. They were backed up by the President of the Oxford Student Union, Will Straw, who wrote in The Guardian as late as 4th July 2003, "there was no prejudice in the procedure... Spence had applied for a particularly difficult course with very few spaces. Tutors at Magdalen College had interviewed over 40 applicants for five places all with similarly outstanding predicted A-level grades. According to the college principal, Anthony Smith, she had come tenth..."

While Straw still blithely argued that there was nothing wrong with the procedure, Oxford had already ditched it in embarrassment. As already mentioned, medical candidates aiming for Oxford, Cambridge and University College London were by November 2003 sitting a completely different exam, devised by experts in ability testing, rather than by medics. The new exam is still combined with a college interview, but the procedure is designed to ensure that cramming and cultural factors play less of a role in medical selection.

Oxbridge, as said before, is ever changing, and those too eager to defend current practices can end up with egg on their face.

IS THE WHOLE ENTRANCE PROCESS GOING TO IMPROVE?
Despite the examples given above, I would not bet my child's higher education savings on this. A series of 2003 Government announcements of plans for intervention ended with the hasty retreat described in Chapter One and, at Oxford at least, the new University Chancellor, Chris Patten, is taking a robustly anti-interventionist line.

In an interview with *The Times* immediately after his March 2003 appointment, Patten argued that if too few state school and especially working class students are entering Oxbridge, the blame lies with the schools' "spectacular failure in the past 30 years to raise standards... It is outrageous for politicians to blame universities over access." In his investiture speech on 25th June 2003, Patten spelt out his stand further: "It is insulting to the able, and damaging to the universities that seek to educate them, to make the issue of access a crowbar for social engineers rather than a challenge for educationalists, and it is downright vulgar to allow it to become a populist political slogan."

While many dons (and parents) might agree that teaching standards have fallen and that basic skills are sometimes absent, the problem with this position is that it implies Oxbridge has a "right" to teach only pupils who have already been taught very well. This, in turn, implies that what it is really looking for is not talent but a candidate who has already been taken through much of their first year university course at school as pupils from the best private school indeed are.

What this approach disregards, say its critics, especially among teachers, is that the state school standard happens to be the national norm. Even the top national universities, therefore, should really teach upwards from it. After all, the education that state school pupils receive is meant to equip them for university and so it does. Those who get in cope. More than that, quite a few excel, even at Oxbridge.

This is not to say that there are no problems. It would clearly be desirable for state school entrants to know rather more grammar or more science. However, eighteen year olds are still capable of learning anything, and in amazingly short time. It is hard to see why a week's transition course, for instance, could not be offered either just before university entrance or in the first Christmas holidays. Devised to bridge the most damaging gaps, it could also point students towards further reading. Such a course could even be devised in website form. Alternatively, a few transitional texts could at least be included in students' pre-Oxbridge reading lists. Encouragingly, some of this already happens in Maths and a couple of other subjects.

Still, dons to whom I have put these bridging proposals have, on the whole, been less than enthusiastic. "Surely, we cannot now also be expected to teach remedial courses," one scientist remarked, his facial expression implying that I might as well have suggested a spot of child abuse. Others politely said that if the Government really wanted to safe-guard their world-famous research standards, a smaller teaching burden, rather than an even bigger one, would be very nice, thank you.

While it is hard not to sympathise with the latter point, too many bright state school students have not been taught up to Oxbridge entrance standard, and it is hard to see how student proportions can change if the private sector, or rather the top of the private sector, continues to set the pace.

A FEW MODEST PROPOSALS

All this suggests that at least part of official Oxbridge might be happy to passively wait until state education improves, thereby punishing at least some bright pupils for their local authority's failures. As mentioned earlier in this book, the situation at both Oxford and Cambridge is, in fact, slightly better. Many dons seek to bring in able student from a wider range than before and try to modify their entrance procedures accordingly. New standardized, subject-specific entrance tests have been introduced in Maths, History and

English at Oxford. Cambridge has experimented with a broader aptitude test, the TST, though fears that cramming can distort the result means it is only used by some colleges. Admissions tutors now often trust more in a student 's carefully dissected GCSE and AS-level marks.

Change, in fact, has become a feature of the entrance process. University admissions departments have revised some unhelpful entrance procedures and are reconsidering others. Colleges now share information about candidates and quite a few dons are improving their interview techniques to reassure non-traditional students.

The Department of Higher and Further Education has sunk money into a myriad of new initiatives, aimed at students, teachers, parents and universities.

Unfortunately, this is not the same as having an effective strategy. Even worse, there are no generally agreed targets. It seems, therefore, important to list some specific measures which could at least create a more level playing field, preferably before the Harry Potter craze fades. Below are the most urgent ones.

WHAT THE GOVERNMENT SHOULD DO:

1. Reform access
The most urgent thing the Government must do, without doubt, is to end the funding of Access type projects in their current form. Not only has Access swallowed millions of pounds in funding over the last five years without perceptibly changing student proportions at Oxbridge; it is also in danger of setting teachers, parents and pupils at different types of state schools against one another.

Access funding, as described earlier in this book, is based on the assumption that the under-representation of state school pupils at Oxbridge is primarily due to low self-esteem. By telling them to visit the two universities and to apply, the problem is expected to go away. Unfortunately, application does not equal acceptance. Those active in Access have no real influence on acceptance policies, and so the balance has essentially remained unchanged.

In the meantime, Access policies are having another, rather unpleasant effect. As much of the funding depends on inventing new types of projects, efforts are increasingly fragmented. There are now Access projects directed at mining areas and rural schools, at further education colleges and at schools which have never sent a pupil to Oxbridge, at ethnic minorities and children in low income groups. Oxbridge sends out videos and email messages. Young people all over the country are told that if they work hard and attend an Oxbridge event, they stand a fair chance of getting in.

Given that the part of the cake allocated to the state school sector has remained the same size, though, this inevitably multiplies disappointment and not just among pupils. To illustrate what this means, let me give an example from a very mixed area of London.

The story starts at a comprehensive, renowned for the quality of its teaching and its excellent Ofsted reports. It is also part of a sixth form consortium which achieves some of the inner city's best state school exam result. Proud of its orderly atmosphere, anti-bullying policy and highly qualified teachers, the school attracts a wide range of pupils. Some, including children from ethnic minorities and asylum seekers, came from the poor neighbouring housing estates. Many others come from the opposite end of the spectrum; they are the children of doctors, lawyers, university lecturers, journalists and civil servants.

In this top-university orientated school, pupils are helped to prepare by teachers who regularly attended Oxbridge staff seminars and are encouraged to participate in every sort of Access project. Usually, out of a sixth form of some 370 pupils, five to eight succeeded in getting in.

In 2002, the school confidently sent off twelve of its pupils to be interviewed. The results were unexpected. Only one pupil, a middle class boy whom the school had not actually picked as a high flyer, received an offer. As the head of sixth form put it: "There is not really much point in our overworked staff putting weeks of effort into encouraging, persuading and preparing pupils for Oxbridge, just to see a single one getting in. All Access has done to build up our kids' expectations, only to dash them again."

Meanwhile, a few miles away in the same area, the staff of the area's largest sixth form college were equally bewildered. The college, whose devoted, well qualified teachers have changed lives, had thought that their pupils were just what Oxbridge wanted now. Most of them were, after all, working class, or from particularly disadvantaged ethnic minorities.

Not that the teachers had ever relied on such assumptions. Over the years, they had instead built up links with a total of six colleges, two in Oxford and four in Cambridge. They also ran enrichment activities which gave pupils experience in journalism, photography and poetry. The college had invested time and expertise in Oxbridge preparation, and this seemed to pay off. Out of a sixth form of 280 pupils, it would annually send up to a dozen interviewees. Between three and five of these would be offered a place. The grades stipulated in the offers remained inappropriately high, but two to three pupils a year were getting in.

When the replies to the 2002 applications dropped through the doors in January 2003, though, the news was really bad. Not one college pupil had even received an offer. Some of the teachers' comments were not printable, but a veteran Maths teacher expressed what many others clearly felt: "It's back to the same old thing. The ones we send are really exceptional, but Oxbridge won't see that."

The college teacher also got on the phone to colleagues in order to find out where "their" Oxbridge places had gone. A chat with a friend teaching in a well-known private school situated between the college and the area's comprehensive revealed that they had not gone there. The private school, which has a sixth form of 90 pupils and prides itself on accepting pupils of widely varying abilities, had received the same number of offers as usual – fourteen(!).

It was a teacher whose sister taught in a small town with a high unemployment rate who finally came up with an answer. For the first time ever, her school had received an offer from Oxbridge. So had another school in the same town, targeted by Access under the "Widening Participation" scheme.

In other words, Access had "worked", but not as most people naively thought it was meant to. Faced with an unprecedented number of "good" state school candidates, an outcome Oxbridge had mysteriously not foreseen, it had decided to redistribute its places within the state school group.

The college teacher, who has an English degree from a good university, found no difficulty in expressing how he felt. "Perhaps they should rename 'Widening Participation' something more appropriate. How about 'Thinning the Soup?'" he said.

On the parents days of some urban comprehensives, the talk can be uglier than that. "Just as our school got itself sorted out, they take it all away and give it to the kids of people who don't even pay taxes," said the mother of a girl put on her school's gifted and talented list, but rejected by Oxbridge.

Unless Access has been created to sow despondency and discord, the Government really needs to restructure it now. Money needs to go to projects which raise acceptance prospects, rather than aspirations.

Perhaps a few seminars for admissions tutors on the way to communicate with inner city pupils would be a start. Or perhaps all funding for Access projects should initially come from Oxbridge itself, which would be repaid by the Government if a project resulted in an acceptance rate of, let's say, 30 per cent.

2. Balance the scales

There is, of course, an alternative. The Government could simply set a quota for state school students. What this would mean in practice is that the Secretary of State for Education would decide what proportion of state school pupil (and perhaps also of working class pupils) should be accepted by Oxbridge. Given that state school students currently constitute just over half of its undergraduates, but around 90 per cent of the total school population, the proportion fixed would, presumably, be higher than it is now.

This is not a suggestion that has gone down well at Oxbridge. Jane Minto, the director of the Oxford admissions office, spoke for many of its academics when she told journalists on 6th March 2003: "We don't subscribe to quotas at Oxford... Students should be selected purely on academic merit." At Cambridge, her counter-part Susan Stobbs took a similar line.

This would be a convincing argument if only it did not leave the listener with a nagging question. How come academic merit manifests itself in quite such a static way among Oxbridge applicants, and among them alone? Surely, different young people from different schools should produce different proportional intakes? Alas, it doesn't and none of my academic interviewees was prepared to comment on this staggering coincidence. In fact, cooperation often dried up at this point.

Nevertheless, the matter remains puzzling for those who understand the rules of mathematical probability, which I am sure includes many Oxbridge academics. It is as if a roulette wheel, once spun, would always land on one of the same narrow range of numbers between 49 and 58. Magic, or what? Please don't try this at your nearest casino.

The reality, of course, is different. There is a quota already. In fact, there are several. Most Oxbridge colleges seem to divide the university places they can offer almost 50/50 between state school and private school pupils, no matter how many applications they receive from each group. On the other hand, some faculties, notably Oxford medicine, accept the same proportion of candidates from each group, usually 20 per cent. Since the state school group is larger, this results in rather more of its pupils getting in.

A few colleges specifically aim for a much higher state school intake, something between 60 and 75 per cent, and reach their precise target every year.

In the end, though, all these decisions are coordinated at Oxford and Cambridge during post-interview meetings of admissions tutors and other university staff. The result is an overall result for each university which is roughly 55 per cent of state school students and 45 per cent private students, year after year after year...

There is what some people may regard as a benevolent explanation for this process. Several dons I spoke to hinted that they made allowances for state school candidates. If they were to go purely by evidence of ability alone, so they suggested, their proportion would be even lower than it is now. Instead, the number of state school candidates accepted was regularly rounded upwards, up to a point.

There are two not so small problems with this explanation. One, as already suggested, is the implicit assumption that state school candidates are not only less intelligent than private school ones, but also that all of them are less intelligent year after year. The other problem is that this intellectual difference is assumed to exist despite the fact that both types of candidates obtain very similar A-level grades. It is, of course, possible that the interview, which has at its centre a certain type of highly educated middle class discourse, does not work as well for applicants from other backgrounds, as suggested earlier on, and this would be a strong argument for its abolition.

On the other hand, the whole differential ability claim can just be dismissed as nonsense. Wadham College, which has the second highest state school intake in Oxford, has consistently been in the top half of the Norrington table: in fact, it came second out of 29 colleges in 2003. Clearly, state school pupils can do as well as the rest if given the chance.

It certainly seems hard to think of a convincing argument against a new, more representative quota. The only real question is how high it should be. One suggestion I heard often was that since the Government funds 70 per cent of Oxbridge university expenditure, the figure of students accepted from the public education sector should be identical. This would leave the private sector, which educates 8 per cent of pupils, with 30 per cent, still a high proportion but one that acknowledges that it does educate many talented young people, often as sixth form scholars.

3. Make schools more equal

One major obstacle to a more representative Oxbridge intake remains the inequality among state schools themselves. Rather than creating ever-new categories of secondaries, the government must now close the gap among the existing ones. A sixth former doing science A-levels should be taught by someone who has a degree in Chemistry, Physics or Maths, irrespective of whether she is attending a state grammar, specialist school, city academy or bog-standard comprehensive. The current situation, in which a third of all of Physics teachers in state secondary schools (and 70 per cent of all those teaching Physics) are unqualified in the subject, is a real outrage.

So are Britain's class sizes, which are the largest in the developed world. How can a pupil taught in a state sixth form of twenty-eight possibly compete with someone from a private A-level class of twelve? While government funding for education has been sharply raised, much of the record education budget of £36bn. announced in 2006 was earmarked for capital expenditure; it will pay for the construction or refurbishment of some 12,000 schools. It might be nice for every school to have a shiny new steel-and-glass atrium, but having a large, fully qualified teaching staff is more urgent.

Nor should the location of a school make a difference. Merely living in a British city can condemn you to an inferior education. London's state schools hardly feature among the country's top 500. In Birmingham and Liverpool things are even worse. Given that our famous cities attract the most motivated, able people, the fact that their children achieve educationally less than those in small farming towns should not be blamed on the parents. True, some urban areas are struggling with the loss of manufacturing jobs, but this is surely yet another argument for sending in more, better qualified teachers.

The current situation does tempt at least some Oxbridge admissions tutors to pick their state school students from a small range of academically strong schools in cosy suburbs. A league table obtained by *The Times* in 2007 under freedom of information laws revealed that 20 per cent of secondaries were providing all the Oxbridge entrants from the state sector. It also showed that most successful applicants come from state grammar schools or sixth-form colleges.

While Oxbridge really should not get away with making its dons' lives quite so easy, government does have a duty to prepare our brightest students for the most appropriate universities.

215

4. Modernise

Lastly, the Government must take the lead in defining what the Oxbridge debate fiercely fought already within Government departments, in the media and among parents is really about.

Those who wish to preserve the Oxbridge entrance structure largely unchanged define this, in the words of Anthony Smith, the President of Magdalen College, Oxford, as "a matter of autonomy". The two universities, from this angle, must be allowed to stick with their current system if they so wish. Nobody else is allowed to impose anything on them because they are autonomous bodies in law.

The problem with this argument is that the autonomy enjoyed by all British universities is essentially designed to cover what they teach and nobody is suggesting that this should change. Admissions is a different matter. Legislation, or the threat of it, gradually compelled the universities over the last 130 years to accept Jews and Catholics, Dissenters and women. A-levels too became a universal entrance requirement only because Government wished it, although the pupils of Britain's seven top public schools (Eton, Harrow, Westminster, Rugby, Winchester, Charterhouse and Shrewsbury) were exempted until the mid 1960s.

Usually, such changes are imposed by means of the carrot and the stick. Government, or the Department of Education, states what it would like, and Oxbridge refuses until threatened with sharp cuts in funding. At this point, internal reform kicks in. There is no reason why the same should not happen now, though there are few signs that the current Labour Government has any desire to wave a stick.

Another way of defining the Oxbridge debate was offered by the President of the National Students Union, Mandy Telford, when she stated that the universities needed to reform their entrance process for the sake of opportunity. In a modern society, she argued, a small group of society should not be allowed a disproportionate hold over this.

In the end, though, it would be easiest if the Government looked at Oxbridge entrance in terms of simple justice. If this is indeed the best place to develop certain types of knowledge and to acquire certain skills, then those who can be scientifically shown to be most suited for this endeavour should be allowed in.

This might, of course, require the introduction of universal tests, already pioneered by a few faculties, but need not change much else.

College places could be allocated on the basis of results, and if colleges wished to preserve their individual characteristics, this would be fine, as long as the nature of those characteristics was spelt out.

In other words, Oxbridge could remain the impressive, unusual place it always was, but also embody more of the values of our age.

WHAT OXBRIDGE SHOULD DO:

1. Reconsider the interview

The change that would have the greatest impact would be for dons to acknowledge that the interview, which is central to the admissions procedure, is not an effective ability test. This is not to question the good intentions of those administering it. Contrary to the widespread impression that dons just seek to pick out posh students, Oxbridge is almost obsessed with finding the most able ones.

One elderly science don, determined to get more gifted working class students into his renowned college, confidently told me that he had solved the problem. "The way is to dive straight into the subject questions at the interview, if you want to get the measure of their abilities. Being talked to about this and that for the first few minutes only confuses them," he told me in a firm voice clearly used to imparting universal wisdom.

For a moment I wondered if as if I should also ask him to tell me also the secret of composing music or of writing a great novel. Clearly a man so certain about his expertise in a field not his own could provide the answer to everything. He had certainly created a new scientific truth: all working class candidates were alike and those who didn't sparkle in response to his majestic, well-spoken approach were just not bright.

The scientist was not alone. Other tutors seemed equally certain that they had found the philosopher's stone, albeit a different one. A mathematician sought to relax all male candidates by discussing sport. One engineering don seemed certain that only through disorientating a candidate completely by remaining silent could he identify brains, while another relied on discussing a subject miles from the one which a student had applied for. A historian would confess, after defending the interview process, that she spent a lot of her time thinking up ways of further perfecting it, of making it even more fair.

Listening to this as I was doing my initial research in 2001–2, I sometimes felt as if I was in the presence of a very bright young child who knew nothing of the real world. After all, the question of how to identify gifted candidates, a relatively new concern for Oxbridge, has been professionally pondered for decades. The people who administer detailed scientific tests in order to pinpoint abilities are called educational psychologists. Their research has given us ways of spotting talent irrespective of class and methods which reduce cultural bias. They have worked out which background data can be relevant and how to weigh the results accordingly. These experts produce journal pieces and books which, as their authors tend to be non-Oxbridge, never seemed to impact on the two universities.

However, new selection practices are now emerging. Oxford and Cambridge are putting applicants for their Law and Medicine courses through the same, externally devised ability tests as other top universities. Between them, they have also introduced detailed written tests of their own for nearly a dozen other courses.

That they embarked on much of this shortly after the Government-commissioned Schwartz report criticized the university entrance process (and just as the first edition of this book appeared) was pure coincidence – perhaps.

At the same time, the precise role of the tests has been left open. Neither Oxford nor Cambridge will say how much even a top result in the BMAT, LNAT, TST or the Oxford exam in History, English and Maths actually counts for. Teachers have been shocked to discover that a 90 per cent test score may not compensate for a stumbling interview performance by a nervous inner city student. Verbal performance has apparently remained decisive.

The problem is that good talk is based on comprehension. University speak is normally learned at university; you cannot pick it up by walking into a don's room. Some interviewers are able to conduct an intellectual cross-examination in colloquial English, but others have communicated in upper middle class, academic language all their lives and are unable to change. So, student unfamiliar with elaborate wording or vague, open-ended questions may not come across well.

Test were seemingly introduced to resolve this, but if they are merely an add-on which does not determine outcomes, there is little point to them. True, testing for brains has not yet been perfected and some dons warn that intensive training may produce misleadingly good test results. Nevertheless, experts can usually refine the questions to minimize this. Written tests are at least familiar to most students, unlike the interview, and so should be given more weight. As the warden of New College Oxford, Alan Ryan, has pointed out, they also more accurately reflect academic reality: "What students do at university is write."

2. Join the youth club

The recent, official renunciation of extra-curricular activities as a selection factor will improve many students' admissions prospects. A sign of the commitment to widening participation by Oxbridge, it also reflects the changing social origins of its dons. Around half of them now come from state schools and so know more than their predecessors about how ordinary people live. They are aware that most families don't go to church, that teenagers often hate school sports and that modern music lovers tend to indulge this passion by listening to a CD.

We can glimpse just how resourceful many past state school candidates really were from the fact that they managed to assemble that old, slightly sad parcel of spare time activities. Not only was it a century removed from today's youth culture, but it was also so much easier to fill if you had cash.

Moreover, what sixth formers do determines how they speak and what they understand. This means not just that interview questions should not be worded in ways that are hopelessly incomprehensible to them. It also means that bright students who use every-day or youth culture language ought not be lightly dismissed as un-academic. As long as they have a library card, they too might be "interesting young people".

It might even be useful for dons to know more about applicants' general background. The Universities and Colleges Admissions Service (UCAS) has been trying to help: from 2008, it will tell universities whether either of an applicant's parents is a university graduate. There is no longer any need to blindly guess about this pivotal fact. Knowing it could enable Oxbridge to make allowances for educational disadvantage, even in the case of students not poor enough to qualify for special support.

Sadly, both Oxford and Cambridge have announced that they will disregard this information as "uncorroborated data". Some admissions tutors openly say that they fear applicants might lie. A more constructive approach seems essential if the Oxbridge intake balance is to change.

Failing that, there may be a clamour for a more structured solution. Since the introduction of tuition fees, students look at educational provisions with a rather critical eye. They see themselves as consumers and want to know precisely how things work. What might satisfy them are universal entrance exams, a solution already quietly discussed and favoured by a few dons.

Meanwhile, though, it would be nice if the existing entrance criteria were applied with more care. Before insisting, yet again, that "we're just not getting the applicants" as almost every admissions tutor I spoke to did, it may be an idea for Oxbridge to look at the characteristics of those it rejects. Returning from an Oxbridge day school to his inner city comprehensive, one frustrated teacher summed up his feelings to me: "Now that we've learnt all we can about the admissions process, maybe their admissions tutors should get some training. We need to train Oxbridge; our students cannot conform to their criteria, but they are bright young people and will achieve."

Anyone doubting his words only needs to look at the final twist in the Laura Spence saga. The working class school girl who was rejected by Oxford in 2000 went on to excel in the Harvard entrance test, winning not just a place but a £37,000 scholarship. At Harvard, Laura became one of only five women named "All-Ivy" for her academic achievements. Returning to Britain with a top Biochemistry degree, she then applied to the tiny, hugely contested Cambridge postgraduate medical course. She got in, you will be glad to hear. Still, there must be a faster, easier way of proving your worth.

3. Learn to love teachers

One of the most important things which a university that wants to be sent lots of good, enthusiastic candidates does is to cultivate their teachers. This is a relationship that Oxbridge has yet to build, at least with regard to state school teachers. Quite a few Oxbridge dons seem to regard them as unreliable suppliers of goods: they don't answer Access circulars, I was told; they don't send enough candidates or send the wrong ones. There was a distinct sense of impatience, almost a feeling that the teachers were not really doing their job.

The most serious crime, and indeed one I often heard state school teachers accused of, was anti-elitism. Pushed a little further, some dons spelt out to me what they meant. "There's a lot of left-wingers, of course, among the teaching profession. People thinking that Oxbridge is a posh place, so one mustn't encourage pupils to go there," I was told by an elderly male don, educated at a famous school, in the quiet, confidential tone used by gentlemen to imply that one's butler may have been at the gin.

In the course of writing this book, I went to great lengths to examine this assertion. That there are many left-wingers among state school teachers is undoubtedly true. The kind of people who opt to develop the potential of children whose family has never earned more than the minimum wage tend not to be on the right in their political sympathies. Neither are those who see potential in a scruffy boy with battered trainers.

But does this mean left-wing teachers are against Oxbridge? To find out, I deliberately arranged in-depth interviews about Oxbridge entrance with sixth form and careers teachers I knew not just to be vaguely on the left, but politically committed. Some were active in leftwing branches of the Labour Party. Several were Trotskyites, members of Britain's Socialist Workers Party. Others defined themselves as Communists.

They had a lot in common. All were fully clued up about the technical requirements for Oxbridge entry. Most had read the piles of special bumph emanating from there, on top of other university entrance publications. Some had been on college visits; others were booked on yet another Oxbridge teachers day. This required massive form-filling and a rearrangement of the school's timetable, because their kind of schools was always short-staffed. They would have to take home papers for marking to compensate for the time lost. All had sent pupils up for interviews after preparing them to the best of their abilities. By January 2003, almost all of them also had failed to get even a single Oxbridge offer for a pupil. You might have expected them to proclaim that, as enemies of the people, the two universities should be burnt down, or at least picketed. Instead, the teachers were downcast as well as fearful that I might identify them or their schools.

"It's not an effective use of my time if nobody gets into Oxbridge, yet I don't send a student who I don't think is really good," one teacher in a battered leather jacket sighed. A colleague wearing a Stop-the-War badge nodded, adding with quiet understatement: "We despair a little after having spent so much time and effort on Oxbridge, yet middle class applicants still do much better."

These teachers were, nevertheless, prepared to soldier on. Next year things might improve, was the hope if the Government intervened. What set them apart from others was not any hostility to Oxbridge, though they were scathing about its selection criteria.

These were not people who thought of the two universities as precious national heritage institutions with mysterious, unfathomable ways, unlike quite a few other teachers I had met. Oxbridge, to them, was just top of the Russell Group, to whose universities they directed their very best pupils.

But that's left-wing teachers. What my research suggested is that Oxbridge is doing no better with teachers holding more mainstream political views or none at all. These are people who unreservedly admire the two universities, yet would wistfully say: "We thought we had built a relationship with Oxbridge." Usually, this meant with one of the universities and two or three of its colleges. These teachers had talked to dons, trying to explain their students' backgrounds and strengths. They'd had tea, dinner at high table, promises of consideration.

The problem, so they told me, is that most of this relationship does not bear fruit, at least not on an annual basis. A college which used to take two or three students out of a sixth form of almost 400 kids suddenly stops doing so. Another college keeps taking one student every other year, but the applicant mustn't be too black, it seems, whatever his other qualities. Or there is a sudden, unexplained, several year long gap.

Somehow, an Oxbridge college's relationship with a private school never breaks down. The school may only have a sixth form of 80, and may admit students on the strength of parental paying ability, not student's talent, but it will be going steady with the college.

The state school, on the other hand, can have quite a different experience. It may only find itself taken out for a whirl ever so often if the Government has recently made a fuss; if priorities have not shifted to another part of the state sector, say rural comprehensives; if it is compatible with the quota which is blatantly there but never admitted to. The state school is like the girl you can take for granted, the girl who will put out even if you won't elevate her to girlfriend status or show her respect. No wonder state school teachers feel hurt.

To make things harder still, all those teachers were, by choice, working in large urban schools, and this created constant dilemmas. As one sixth form head put it: "You know, it can take up to 20 hours to prepare a kid for Oxbridge, but we do it. Sometimes it's really hard to decide. I had a student living on a really bad estate. He was not a genius, but still a capable kid with a potential for higher education. I could either spend lots of time getting him into some former Poly in another town, away from his criminal environment. Or I could concentrate on getting a kid from a safer, more stable home background into Oxbridge. What would you have done?"

In the event, the committed professional did a bit of both. Unless such efforts are regularly rewarded at the Oxbridge end, it would hard to blame him if he slackened.

4. Stop the nostalgia

When discussing the unrepresentative student proportions at Oxbridge, dons almost invariably launch into a nostalgic account of how much better things were when the grammar school system was still in force all over Britain.

Despite the heartfelt emotion, the statement is factual nonsense. There never was any golden age in which Oxbridge threw open its gates to those outside its traditional catchment area. In 1955, the number of students who had fathers in manual work was 9 per cent in Cambridge (the same as in 2002) and 13 per cent in Oxford (compared to 10 per cent in 2002). In 1963, the heyday of the grammar schools, 25 per cent of students at Cambridge and 39 per cent at Oxford came from state schools (compared to roughly 55 per cent in 2002).

In fact, the pre-comprehensive school figures are even worse than they look, because the proportion of manual workers among the public was far higher than today. Also, the number of children at private schools was half what it is now. Meanwhile, the vast majority of children were attending secondary moderns, schools that led nowhere in educational terms. Still, the nostalgia persists because among those bright youngsters fortunate enough to then enter Oxbridge were many of today's dons. Ultimately, there is something cranky about the way in which today's top educators go on about a system that was abolished 30 years ago. It is as if they feel no duty to relate to current reality, which is that most children in Britain are schooled in comprehensives.

There is indeed a great deal wrong with comprehensives: they are shamefully under-funded and short of teachers and equipment. They also often cater poorly for both slow and fast learners. There could even be a strong argument for educating very able children separately from a certain age, if there was a way of identifying ability irrespective of class – not something the old grammar schools did well. Such a change would certainly be welcomed by the parents of such children. Among those, I am sure, would be thousands of middle class couples crippled by school fees. Meanwhile, though, the comprehensives are our main national secondary schools, and therefore the nation's top universities really must pick more of their bright students. That many dons would genuinely like to do so I have no doubt. That they often don't because they've failed to grasp just how bright and resourceful a state school applicant needs to be in order to merely get interviewed is equally true. Fortunately, the detailed preparation offered to pupils by this book should make the two universities' selection job much easier.

24

At the gates

If you have been able to put your video games, or the housekeeping, or your employer's demands on standby for long enough to read through this book, then your family dream of Oxbridge has become an actual possibility. You now know the real rules of the entrance process, a prerequisite for effectively competing in this snakes and ladders game. Knowledge, in turn, tends to raise a person's confidence, and confidence is another ingredient of Oxbridge success.

You will also be able to distinguish between the two universities' present reality and their past. No longer are talented young people automatically excluded just because they didn't go to public school, or don't have middle class parents, or are not white. Nor need such students expect three years of humiliation if they do get in. True, all those things were a feature of Oxbridge history for hundreds of years, but so were outside lavatories. Government reforms, internal restructuring and new types of schools have changed Oxbridge so much it would be unrecognisable to those fighting over its "lily-whiteness".

This is not to say that today's entrance rules are equally fair to all bright students, and this book has no magic formula to offer which would alter this. What it can do, primarily, is to provide you with the tools to achieve the best possible outcome. It can also point out which aspects require further change.

Many self-help books give the impression that everything desirable will come to those ready to take a few easy steps. "Everyone can be a millionaire," "Think yourself thin," or "Be the person you want to be" are the mantras of their optimistic authors.

Unfortunately, the real world can be less flexible than these books imply. Powerful forces may thwart even the most determined. There are still Oxbridge rules which prevent some of the best students from getting in. Hardly ever talked about, they remain in place alongside all those friendly invitations, worthy proclamations and jolly Access booklets produced with the taxpayer's help.

Some of the obstacles created by these rules are unintentional, I am sure. Others are based on surprisingly sloppy thinking by academics paid to do rather better than that. Lastly, there are a few obstacles whose continued existence can only be due to a determination to keep student proportions roughly as they are, often by people who have invested much money to gain a lifelong advantage for their family or group.

On the other hand, my research showed that not all dons are happy with the present situation. Younger, state-educated ones would like to see the Oxbridge intake reflect the modern world. Quite a few older academics feel that, in the age of the human genome, Oxbridge will miss out on its intellectual lead if too many fine minds are snapped up by Imperial College, the LSE, UMIST or Harvard. Lastly, the fear of Government sanctions in the form of lower per capita allowances concentrates many a don's mind.

Student intake proportions, though, will not change because of some academics' good will. Nor can a young person's talent alone turn an obstacle course into a level playing field. This would require either more ability-test based entrance rules by Oxbridge or a new, quota-based higher education policy by the Government or both. The new aptitude exams added in certain subjects are a big step forward, but not necessarily one that will solve the problem.

More changes are needed and none of these will come about simply because they would make life fairer for bright students. They depend on strong, long-term pressure from several directions. If you're a potential candidate, a parent or a teacher at a school whose best pupils fail to get in, this can be done in the standard ways: badger the media, the Government, public bodies like your union and your MP. State school pupils who made it through Oxbridge might also consider forming a lobby group.

Meanwhile, though, you must be willing to take the emotional risk of applying or to encourage your teenager to apply. If he is bright and hard-working, if she is focused and original, the process, despite its flaws, could well result in success.

All this is hard work, and some of you may be tempted to give up on Oxbridge instead. Together with many of its devoted students and graduates, I would advise you to persist because the rewards are so great. Oxbridge is that rare, amazing thing in today's Britain, a well-funded, high-level, stunningly beautiful public education facility. It is already enjoyed by thousands of state school students every year, and if public opinion can be hitched to individual effort, might yet welcome more.

Contact list

UNIVERSITY OF CAMBRIDGE

Cambridge Admissions Office

Tel. 01223 333 308
Email: admissions@cam.ac.uk
Website: www.cam.ac.uk/admissions/undergraduate/
General website: www.cam.ac.uk

Cambridge University Students Union

Email: info@cusu.ac.uk
Website: www.cusu.cam.ac.uk

UNIVERSITY OF OXFORD

Oxford Colleges Admissions Office

Tel. 01865 288 000
Email: undergraduate.admissions@admin.ox.ac.uk
Website: www.admissions.ox.ac.uk
General website: www.ox.ac.uk

Oxford University Students Union

Email: info@ousu.org
Website: www.ousu.org

UCAS

Tel. 0870 1122211 (human response)
Email: enquiries@ucas.ac.uk (automated response)
Website: www.ucas.com

TARGET SCHOOLS INITIATIVES CAMBRIDGE

Website: www.cusu.cam.ac.uk/campaigns/target/

TARGET SCHOOLS INITIATIVES OXFORD
Website: www.targetschools.com

WIDENING PARTICIPATION TEAM CAMBRIDGE
Email: access@cao.cam.ac.uk

CAMBRIDGE GROUP TO ENCOURAGE ETHNIC MINORITY APPLICATIONS (GEEMA)
Email: geema@cao.cam.ac.uk

ACCESS SCHEME OXFORD
Website: www.oxford-access.org

OXFORD SCHOOLS LIAISON & EDUCATION EVENTS
Email: paul.teulon@admin.ox.ac.uk

CAMBRIDGE OPEN DAYS
Website: www.cam.ac.uk/opendays/

OXFORD OPEN DAYS
Website: www.admissions.ox.ac.uk/opendays/

NATIONAL ACADEMY FOR GIFTED AND TALENTED YOUTH (NAGTY)
Tel. 024 7657 4213
Website: www.nagty.ac.uk
Email: gifted@warwick.ac.uk

SUTTON TRUST
Tel. 020 8788 3223
Website: www.suttontrust.com

AIM HIGHER
Tel. 0800 587 8500
Website: www.aimhigher.ac.uk